Copyright © 2020 by Brad P. Finkbeiner

ALL RIGHTS RESERVED. No part of this book may be reproduced or transmitted in any form by any means, electronic or mechanical, including photocopying or recording, or by an information storage or retrieval system, except as may be expressly permitted in writing from the author. Requests for permission should be addressed to the author.

First Edition

Table of Contents

Unit I: Introduction to Argument

1.	Facts, Propositions, and Truth	4
2.	Cultural Confusions about Truth	13
3.	Cultural Confusions about Belief	19
4.	Plato on Chaining Down True Beliefs with Arguments	32
5.	The Nature of Argument	36
6.	Perceiving Arguments	41
7.	Diagramming Arguments	46
8.	Character in Argument	51
9.	Sophistry (i) Its Origins and Nature	55
10.	Sophistry (ii) *Ad Hominem* Fallacies	58
11.	Sophistry (iii) *Ad Populum* Fallacies	62
12.	Sophistry (iv) Fallacies of Distraction	65
13.	The Three Tests for Evaluating Arguments	68

Unit II: The Semantic Side of Argument

14.	The Power of Words: Lessons from *1984*	71
15.	Words, Thoughts, and Things	76
16.	The Meanings of "Meaning" (1)	80
17.	The Meanings of "Meaning" (2)	86
18.	The Problem of Ambiguity	90
19.	Denotative Definitions	98
20.	Rules for Testing Definitions (1) Equivalence	103
21.	Rules for Testing Definitions (2) Informative and Positive	107
22.	Rules for Testing Definitions (3) Essence and Accidence	113
23.	Excursus: Aristotle's Method of Specific Difference	116
24.	Rules for Testing Definitions (4) Clarity and Brevity	126
25.	Rules for Testing Definition (5) Equity	134
26.	Biconditional Definitions	139

Unit III: The Inferential Side of Argument

27. Deduction and Induction	144
28. Soundness and Cogency	150

PART 1: NECESSARY INFERENCE

Section 1: Categorical Reasoning

29. Introduction to Categorical Inference	156
30. Immediate Inference (1) Compatibility	159
31. Immediate Inference (2) Equivalence	164
32. Mediate Inference (i.e., Syllogisms)	167
33. Proving Invalidity by Counter Examples	170
34. Distribution of Terms	172
35. Rules for Testing Syllogisms	174
36. Non-Standard Syllogisms (1) Enthymemes	179
37. Non-Standard Syllogisms (2) Sorites	181
38. Non-Standard Syllogisms (3) Natural Language	183

Section 2: Propositional Reasoning

39. Introduction to Propositional Inference	188
40. Inferences Using Sufficient Conditionals	191
41. Inferences Using Necessary Conditionals	196
42. Inferences Using Biconditionals	200
43. Non-Standard Formulations of Conditionals	203
44. Disjunctive Inferences	206
45. Complex Arguments	209
46. The Process of Elimination	210
47. The Dilemma	213

PART 2: PROBABLE INFERENCE

48. Introduction to General Induction	218
49. The Uniformity of Nature	223
50. Making Generalizations	228
51. Applying Generalizations	234
52. Introduction to Analogical Arguments	239
53. Evaluating Analogical Arguments	244
54. Causal Arguments	251

Unit IV: The Evidential Side of Argument
(forthcoming in second volume)

```
                              Argument

   1              2                   3                    4
Introduction   Semantic          Inferential           Evidential
                Side                Side                  Side

                                PART 1       PART 2
   Meaning     Definition      Deduction    Induction

                                                        Generalizations
                                                       (Making\Applying)
               Denotative    A] Categorical  B] Propositional

                                                          Analogical
                                                          Inference
               Connotative     Syllogisms    Sufficient
                                            Conditionals
                                                            Causal
                                                          Inference
               Biconditional
                                Enthyemes    Necessary
                                            Conditionals

                                  Sorites   Bicondiitionals


                                            Disjunctives
```

(1)
Semantic
Question

What do
the terms
mean?

ARGUMENT
TRIANGLE

(2)   (3)
Inferential   Evidential
Question   Question

Does the   Are the
conclusion   premises
follow?   true?

1) Facts, Propositions, and Truth

Imagine overhearing a man and woman discussing the topic of abortion. The man argues that abortion is wrong, since the unborn baby is an innocent human being. The woman angrily replies,

> "Who are you to form an opinion on this topic? You cannot become pregnant or share in the experience of women. It might be your truth, but it is not my truth. If a woman feels peace in her heart about aborting her fetus, then her decision is right for her. Stop imposing your beliefs on us. That is so arrogant and judgmental!"[1]

Clearly the woman disagrees with the man. But is there anything in her reply that *addresses* his *claims*? If the woman is correct to oppose him, we should expect her to explain (1) why the unborn baby is *not a human*, or (2) why the unborn baby is *not an innocent* human, or (3) why it is *not wrong* to kill an innocent human. And yet, nothing that she says touches any of these points.

Instead, her comments are all about the people debating abortion, not about abortion itself. Half of her response is about the *man*—about his gender, his experiences, his beliefs, his motives, his attitude, and his character. The remainder are about *women*—about their experiences, their feelings, their decisions, and so on. What's really striking, here, is that none of her comments are about the status of unborn babies or the morality of aborting them. And yet, isn't that what the debate *should* be about? Shouldn't the focus be on the *truth* (or falsehood) of what people believe, rather than on the *people* who happen to believe such things?

The woman's style of reasoning is all too common in today's culture. Some historians refer to it as a "postmodern" mindset, or (more pointedly) as a "post-truth" mindset. Whatever we choose to call it, one thing is for sure: it's a relatively *recent* mindset. People living before the mid-twentieth century would have been mystified by the woman's comments. Her claims would have struck them as confused at best, if not altogether bizarre. While past generations might have suspected her of being intoxicated, many today find her reply perfectly reasonable. Like her, they have learned to *subjectivize truth*. The meaning of this phrase will become clear in the pages ahead. (See esp. p.19 onward for details.) In the following

---

[1] This fictitious exchange represents the way that many people today reason. Perhaps you have heard some or all these replies, or others very much like them. I've crammed them together for illustrative purposes.

three lessons you will learn some of the key ideas needed for understanding it. (For a visual summary, see p.31.)

Two meanings of "Fact": The word "fact" has two related but distinct meanings. As one author writes, "In normal linguistic usage, the meaning of 'fact' is ambiguous. It can refer to a *statement* that expresses the fact, and it can also refer to the *state of affairs* referred to by such a statement" (emphasis added).[2] Let's make this explicit:

Meaning 1 of 'Fact' = an actual state of affairs.[3]
Meaning 2 of 'Fact' = a statement that there is an actual state of affairs.

To understand this distinction, consider the following sentence:

"It is a fact that a woman's unborn baby is a human being."

In this sentence, the word 'fact' refers to a state of affairs, namely, to the actual status, nature, or identity of an unborn child. The preborn child is not a reptile; he or she is a human being; that is what the unborn baby *really is*; this is a "fact" in the sense of *the way things are*. But notice that we are communicating this fact by means of a statement, which is here italicized:

"It is a fact that *a woman's unborn baby is a human being.*"

It is *because* unborn children *really are* human beings that we use the statement to communicate this state of affairs. Note well that the statement does not *make* the state of affairs what it is; it only *mirrors* the state of affairs. Therefore, the state of affairs ("fact" in sense 1) is *more basic* or *foundational* than the statement ("fact" in sense 2).

This is why, in this book, we will generally use the word "fact" to mean a state of affairs, not a statement. We will define "fact" to mean *that which is real*, in contrast to what is unreal. A fact is *a reality*.

Types of facts (or states of affairs): This broad definition of 'fact' leaves open the question of what kinds of facts there are for us to discover. Some people define 'fact' very narrowly, to include only those things that are *material* (having

---

[2] A.F. Chalmers, in *What Is This Thing Called Science?* (3rd ed., p.10)
[3] By saying "actual state of affairs," we mean to contrast this with imaginary states of affairs like Middle Earth or the Land of Oz.

mass, size, and shape) or *sensible* (touchable, observable, audible). These are philosophically biased definitions of 'fact.' They exclude the possibility of there being immaterial and nonsensible facts. Our broader definition, on the other hand, allows for many different types of states of affairs that are obviously (or arguably) real, such as:

- *Psychological* facts—e.g., consciousness, beliefs, memories, desires, feelings, motives;

- *Moral* facts—e.g., the duty to keep promises, the right to life, the virtue of courage;

- *Theological* facts—e.g., God's omniscience or providence or miraculous acts;

- *Logical* facts—e.g., the law of non-contradiction or the validity of modus ponens ($p \rightarrow q; p \therefore q$);

- *Universal* facts—e.g., the force of gravity operating everywhere and always, in contrast to particular facts, such as this apple falling here and now;

- *Mathematical* facts—e.g., sets, theorems ($a^2 + b^2 = c^2$), sums ($2 + 2 = 4$);

- *Scientific* facts—e.g., the speed of light, carbon decay rates, electromagnetism, conservation of energy, the fine-tuning of the Universe for life;

- *Relational* facts—e.g., being the sister or mother of someone, standing above or below something, or being older or younger than another.

As this partial list shows, not all facts have the same nature. It is hard to exaggerate the importance of this point. Many debates revolve around the very definition of "fact." This is especially apparent in debates over worldviews. For example, there are two related philosophies, *materialism* and *empiricism*, which bias people's understanding of what constitutes a fact. Materialism is a thesis about the nature of *reality*, and empiricism is a thesis about the nature of *knowledge*. In their strongest or purist forms, materialism states that only material things are real (it equates reality with matter), and empiricism states that only sensible things are knowable (it equates knowledge with sensation). Children who grow up under the influence of these philosophies—like those in Marxist countries or those in the secular West—are conditioned to define "facts" in terms of what is material and sensible. (For a humorous portrayal of an educator who thinks this way, you may enjoy reading about Thomas Gradgrind, a character in Charles Dicken's *Hard*

Times, who Dickens mockingly calls "A man of realities. A man of fact and calculations.")

How might this notion of fact affect one's reasoning? Suppose two people are debating the existence of God. One of them is a materialist, who argues as follows:

> *Claim 1*: A rational person believes only in facts.
> *Claim 2*: All facts are material.
> *Claim 3*: God is not material.
> Therefore, God is not a fact.
> Therefore, no rational person believes in God.

Claim 3 is true by definition and claim 1 is at least plausible. What about claim 2? That's not at all obvious. To the contrary, some people think it's obviously false. But materialists certainly *believe* it is correct. And if they are right, it follows that our beliefs about morality and religion, for example, are not even factual. And if that is true, there is no point in debating them.[4]

We will address this and related questions in Unit 4, where we discuss the nature of evidence, knowledge, and worldview. For now, the point is simply to note that one's definition of "fact" can bias the way we reason.

Propositions (or statements): A proposition is a *declaration of fact*: it is an assertion that something is or is not the case. For example:

- "Clouds are composed of water."
- "Murder is a crime."
- "Caesar was not a tyrant."
- "Three added to three equals six."
- "Marxism resulted in the deaths of millions of people."
- "Sasquatches live in Washington State."

We are using the word "proposition" as roughly synonymous with what we earlier called a "statement."[5] Grammatically speaking, a proposition is an *indicative sentence* (also called a declarative sentence). The word "indicative" comes from the Latin *indicare*, which means 'to point out' or 'to show.' We can think of an indicative

---

[4] Materialists and empiricists often argue that moral and religious beliefs are nothing more than feelings or personal preferences. What is ironic, though, is that neither beliefs nor feelings are literally *sensible* or obviously material. So materialists and empiricists cannot consistently refer to beliefs and feelings, including their beliefs and feelings about materialism or empiricism!

[5] By the end of this lesson, it will be clear that "fact" in sense 2 above (i.e., "fact" as a *statement*) really means a *truth*. In this text we will distinguish between facts and truths.

sentence as an instrument for pointing out facts. The sentence "Earth is spherical" is a linguistic tool for informing people about the fact of Earth's shape.

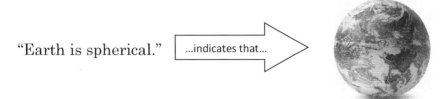

Philosophically speaking, a proposition is the *meaning* of an indicative sentence. To understand the difference, how many propositions do you notice below?

1. Snow is white. (English)
2. Schnee ist weiss. (German)
3. Nix est alba. (Latin)
4. Nieve es blanca. (Spanish)

The answer is either four or one, depending on whether we're thinking of a proposition grammatically or philosophically. There are four different propositions in the grammatical sense, but there is only one proposition in the philosophical sense. The four different indicative sentences have the same meaning. We can think of the four sentences as physical vehicles, and the proposition (in the philosophical sense) as the non-physical thought delivered by means of those vehicles. The one message "Will you marry me?" can be sent by electronic email, or a telegraph, or sign language, or Morse Code, or even skywriting. The different physical media convey the same information. This is what makes it possible for a translator to find a sentence in German ("Schnee ist weiss") that carries the *same meaning* as the English sentence "Snow is white." The non-physical proposition is *what* we communicate, and the physical sentence is *how* we communicate it.

In its philosophical sense, the proposition is not identical to either the visible sentence (as physical ink on paper) or the audible utterance (as physical sound waves) used to express the proposition. If this seems bizarre, just imagine seeing a foreign script like Japanese. You assume it means something, but you have no idea of what it means. You *see* the markings with your eyes, but your mind does not grasp its *meaning*. This proves that the meaning as such is *not* a *physical, sensible* thing, but rather an *abstract, intelligible* thing, an idea understood by the mind.

As an aside, it's worth noting that materialists and empiricists have a notoriously difficult time trying to explain the *fact* of propositional meaning. Does propositional meaning exist? Is it real? Of course it is! But is it *material*? Is it *sensible*? Historically, most philosophers have said no, and this is one of many reasons for rejecting materialism and empiricism.

The distinction between facts (i.e., states of affairs) and declarations of fact (i.e., statements): You may have wondered why we used the statement "Sasquatches live in Washington State" as an example of a declaration of fact. Well, it is one thing to *declare* a fact and another thing for there to *be* a fact. For any declaration of fact (or statement), there may or may not be a fact (or state of affairs) corresponding to the declaration. We must therefore guard against a potential confusion, which can be exposed by contrasting these propositions:

"Earth is spherical."
"Earth is flat."

Since a proposition is a declaration of fact, does this imply that both propositions are declaring *facts*? Surely not. Earth is spherical, not flat. This means that the phrase "declaration of fact" is ambiguous. We can make the ambiguity clear by using emphasis in the following phrases:

"A declaration of *fact*"
"A *declaration* of fact"

The first suggests that there is a fact corresponding to every proposition. The second does not necessarily suggest that: maybe there is, maybe isn't. From this point onward, we will use the term "proposition" to mean only a *declaration* of fact, not necessarily a declaration of *fact*. This goes back to the difference between "statements" and "states of affairs." Statements can be mistaken, but states of affairs cannot. As a state of affairs, an aircraft in the sky is *real*. But statements about this state of affairs ("That is a UFO") can be incorrect.

Recall that an indicative sentence functions to point out facts. This implies that there is a possibility for success or failure in our use of indicative sentences. Suppose my seven-year-old daughter does not know that Earth is the third planet from the Sun. I inform her of this fact by means of the sentence, "Earth is the third planet from the Sun." Now suppose that her teacher (in a moment of forgetfulness or confusion) says to her, "Earth is the fourth planet from the Sun." Clearly the teacher is also intending to convey a fact. The difference, of course, is that while there is a fact corresponding to my sentence, there is not a fact corresponding to her sentence. The difference between us is not in our intentions (since we both meant to represent reality) nor in our mode of speech (since we both used indicative sentences). The difference is that only one of our two sentences successfully indicated (or pointed out) a fact.

We must therefore distinguish how an indicative sentence is *supposed* to function (to declare a fact) and *whether* it functions *successfully* (whether there really is such a fact). Using an indicative sentence is like shooting an arrow. The "target" is to point out a fact. Whether we actually hit the target depends on whether the world is as the sentence purports it to be. This leads us to the concept of truth.

Truth: A proposition portrays the world as being a particular way (e.g., "Earth is spherical" or "Jesus rose from the dead"). It therefore follows that either:

> (1) the world *is* as the proposition portrays it to be, in which case the proposition is "true," or
>
> (2) the world is *not* as the proposition portrays it to be, in which case the proposition is "false."

In other words, a statement will correspond with the facts (actual states of affairs) or it will not. If it does, the statement is true; if it does not, it is false.

The proposition "Jesus rose from the dead" declares a historic event. This event either occurred or it did not occur. If it occurred, the proposition is true. If it did not occur, the proposition is false. In the words of the previous section, if a sentence successfully points out a fact, it is true. If it fails to point out a fact, it is false. In Aristotle's terms, a proposition is true if it "says of what is, that it is, and of what is not, that it is not." If things are as the proposition asserts them to be, the proposition is true. If things are not as the proposition asserts them to be, the proposition is false. In sum, a declaration of fact is *true* if and only if there is a fact that corresponds to it.

Though there are other senses of "true" or "truth" (as when Jesus calls himself "The truth," or as when one says, "That was spoken like a true American"), we are concerned with what is called "propositional truth."[6]

---

[6] Sometimes we speak of things being true or false. We say that a particular thing is true if it represents a class:
  -He is a true southerner (not a poser)
  -He is a true disciple of Christ (not a nominal one)
  -This is a true dollar (not a counterfeit)
  -This is true gold (not "fool's gold")
We recognize there are certain kinds of things in the world and that they are what they are. There are southerners, disciples of Christ, dollar bills, gold, and so on. Whenever we encounter a genuine member of a category, we say it is a "true" instance of that category. Such a thing is said to be "true" because it is the sort of thing it appears to be; it is genuine, authentic, the "real deal." Likewise, there are other things that look and act like the previous things, and which cause us to confuse them for those things. We say they are "false" because they do not truly represent the category of thing to

Regarding propositional truth, the word "truth" signifies the *property of a proposition*. For it is the *proposition* "Earth is spherical" that *is true*.

Truth as "correspondence to reality": Propositional truth consists in the correspondence of a proposition (what is said) to reality (the way things are). As the illustration shows, the truth of the proposition "There are cookies in the jar" is in its correspondence to the fact, or state of affairs, of there being cookies in the jar. Philosophers call this "the correspondence theory of truth." From this point onward, we will define truth as *propositions that correspond to reality*.

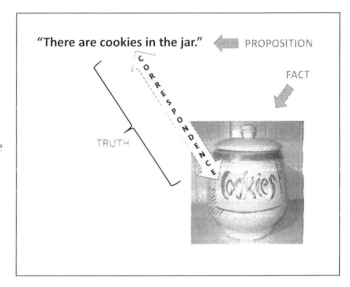

Propositions have "truth-value." Since a proposition declares that something is the case, a proposition must be either true or not true (i.e., false). A sentence's status of being either true or false is called its "truth-value." Positive truth-value is the status of being true. Negative truth-value is the status of being false. (Note that the phrase "*has* truth-*value*" does not mean "*is true*.").

Finally, since only indicative sentences assert or deny something, it follows that only indicative sentences have truth-value. The following non-propositional expressions do not have truth-value.

- "Planet"
- "Is Pluto a planet?"
- "Stop calling Pluto a 'planet'!"
- "Boo!" (to the new, non-planetary status of Pluto)

Consider each one in turn. First, there is nothing true or false about the *word* "planet"; nor is there truth-value in the mere *idea* signified by that word; neither one *asserts* anything. Secondly, there is nothing true or false about the *question* of whether Pluto is a planet. Suppose someone asked you, "Is Pluto is a planet?" It would not make sense to reply, "You are incorrect." Thirdly, a command itself (as a command) cannot be false. We might say that the command is unjust or unreasonable, but this is not disagreeing with the truth of the command itself, since

---

which they apparently belong; they appear to be the sort of thing they are not; they are fakes, frauds, posers, or mere imitations.

it has no truth-value. We are only disagreeing with the justness of the command, or with the assumption that the command should be obeyed. Finally, when someone shouts "Boo!," they are only revealing their preferences, like two men quarreling about whether ketchup tastes better than BBQ sauce.

"Fact" and "truth" are not identical concepts. Though people often use them interchangeably, the words "fact" and "truth" should be distinguished. The Earth's being the third planet from the Sun is a fact. The proposition asserting this fact ("Earth is the third planet from the Sun") is true.

Facts are "truth-*makers*" (they cause propositions to be true); propositions are "truth-*bearers*" (they are true). Truths do not make facts. Facts make truth. Aristotle puts it this way:

> "The fact of the being of a man carries with it the truth of the proposition that 'he is,' and the implication is reciprocal: for if a man is, the proposition wherein we allege that 'he is' is true, and conversely, if the proposition wherein we allege that 'he is' is true, then he is. The true proposition, however, is in no way the cause of the being of the man, but the fact of the man's being does seem somehow to be the cause of the truth of the proposition, for the truth or falsity of the proposition depends on the fact of the man's being or not being" (emphasis added).[12]

The truth of the proposition results from the reality of what the proposition is about. The truth of the proposition "Caesar crossed the Rubicon" is grounded in the fact that such a man crossed such a river. It is not because the proposition "Caesar crossed the Rubicon" is true that Caesar actually crossed the Rubicon; rather, the proposition is true because the said man crossed the said river. Likewise, for any proposition, its truth will depend on whether things are as it purports them to be. If things are that way, the proposition is true, not because it *asserts* that they are that way, but because they *are in fact* that way. In sum, the truth of a proposition does not make reality; reality makes the truth of a proposition.

2) Cultural Confusions about Truth

In this lesson we will try to clarify and defend the concept of truth in the face of popular confusions, which are often expressed in the form of slogans.

"There is no truth." Suppose a skeptic asserts that "There is no truth." Presumably, he's asserting this proposition because he believes it, which is to say, he thinks it's *true* that "There is no truth." But he cannot think that *that* is true unless he thinks it's *false* that "There is *no* truth." The skeptic is running up against the fact that the statement "There is no truth" is self-refuting: it must be false for us to think of it as true!

"Truth is a meaningless idea." Some might suggest that "truth" is a word without any clear meaning. But again, why would one assert this unless one thinks it is true? But if one thinks *that*, mustn't one have at least some idea of what "truth" *means*? If one literally has no idea of what people mean by "truth," one has no idea of what one is talking about when one says that truth has no meaning.

The skeptic faces a dilemma: He is either trying to express a truth when he says that "Truth is a meaningless idea," or he is not. If he is, then he refutes himself. If he is not, then we can ignore him.

All people have some concept of truth. Though the English invented the word "truth," as a physical symbol, they did not invent the *concept* of truth. Hundreds of languages have their own symbol for it (in Korean it's 진실). When Pontius Pilate asked Jesus, "What is truth?" (John 18), he was not implying that truth is meaningless. He was wondering where truth resides or how it can be found. That's the real question. Jesus claimed to have the answer, "I am."

"Truth changes": Take the statement "The United States is a Christian country." Is this true or false? Some might say that it is both. The U.S. was a Christian country but now it's not. Has truth itself changed? No. It all depends on which period in history we are thinking about when we assert that the U.S. is a Christian country. It was true in (say) 1810, but now (in the 2000s) it's false. The sentence "The United States is a Christian country" does not, by itself, specify a period of time. This forces us to read different periods into the statement, which means that we are dealing with *different propositions*, e.g.,

[i] The United States (of 1810) is a Christian country.
[ii] The United States (of 2002) is a Christian country.

Let's suppose [i] is true, and that [ii] is false. Does this mean that the truth of [i] changed into the falsity of [ii]? No. They are different propositions since they are about different historical periods. Notice that the truth of [i] was true in 1810 and that it *remains* true today; that is, it remains true that the United States was a Christian country *in 1810*. The historical realities or states of affairs have changed, but propositional truths about them do not change.

"There are degrees of truth." Now suppose someone objects that the U.S. in 1810 was filled with people who were not genuine Christians; there were many cultural Christians along with Unitarians and Deists. Therefore, to some degree it was a Christian country and to some degree it was not.[7] This does not mean that truth itself comes in degrees. We need to define what we mean by "Christian country." We could make it mean any number of things. For example, it might mean that at least 75% are genuinely Christian (i.e., bearing fruit), or nominally Christian (i.e., self-identifying), or culturally Christian (i.e., conditioned by the Christian worldview). Depending on how we define it, we'll find that our proposition "The United States is a Christian country" is true or false.

To take a different case, suppose one says that it is true that "The apple is red." Someone else might reply, "No, since there are *degrees* of redness, including reddish-*orange*, it is both truth and false that the apple is red." This is a confused reply. All we need to do is specify different shades (Red #1, Red #2, Red #3, etc.) and then state which shade of red is in view. Here too we have one sentence ("The apple is red") that can be used to express different propositions:

"The apple is red (in sense #1)" <True, perhaps
"The apple is red (in sense #2)" <False, perhaps

A proposition is not "sort of true" and "sort of false," or "mostly true" or "mostly false." Once we fix the exact meaning, it is wholly true or wholly false.

"Truth is relative." Imagine sitting still on your sofa in your living room. Are you stationary? Yes and no. Relative to your house, you are stationary. And yet, the Earth is rotating on its axis, which means that you are moving at thousands of miles per hour. (It's actually more complicated than that. The Earth orbits the Sun, and our solar system moves within the Milky Way, which is moving within a larger

---

[7] Others might object that the adjective "Christian" cannot apply to a *country*, on the grounds that countries are geo-political entities (i.e., they have political borders and civil governments), and that such things cannot be "Christianized."

galactic cluster.) Does this mean truth is relative? No. It only means that we must identify the exact proposition being asserted.

"I am sitting still relative to the house" ← True
"I am sitting still relative to the Sun" ← False

In Islamic cultures, showing the soles of your shoes in public is offensive, though it is not offensive in America. In light of this, one might be tempted to think that the following sentence expresses a "relative truth."

[1] Showing the soles of one's shoes in public is offensive.

It initially seems right to say that this is true for some but not for others. But let's think it through a bit more. Is it saying that it is always and everywhere offensive? If so, then [1] is (only) false. Or is it saying that it's only offensive in some places or at some periods in history? If so, then [1] is (only) true. So why does the sentence seem like a relative truth? We are reading into it. We are bringing our background knowledge about American and Islamic countries to our interpretation of the sentence, so as to make the one sentence mean two different things at one time:

[2] Showing the soles of one's shoes in public is offensive *in Islamic countries*.
[3] Showing the soles of one's shoes in public is offensive *in America*.

But notice that neither [2] nor [3] is what [1] *says*. By splitting [1] into these two different meanings, we are still left with only truth or falsehood: [2] is true and [3] is false. In sum, when proponents of "relative truth" put forth statements like [1] above, we should ask them to clarify their statement. It should then become clear that the statement is not a "relative truth," except in one of the harmless senses already noted.

"My truth" and "Your truth"; or "What is true for you is not true for me": These are deeply muddled expressions. Take the phrase "true for me." Depending on what is meant, this could be logical or illogical.

Let's start with a logical use of the phrase. Suppose Gregg's stomach hurts and that Sally's stomach does not hurt. If Gregg uses the sentence "My stomach hurts," it would be true for him but not for Sally. In this sense, Gregg could say, "It would be true for me to use the sentence 'My stomach hurts,' but it would not be true for you (Sally) to do so." Notice that (once again) we simply specified the proposition.

Let's now consider an illogical use of the phrase "true for me but not for you." Take the proposition, "Abraham Lincoln was assassinated." How could this be true for *Henry* but not true for *Hilda*? Lincoln was assassinated or he wasn't. What could Hilda possibly mean in saying, "Lincoln's assassination is your truth, Henry, but it is not my truth"? If Lincoln was assassinated, the proposition "Lincoln was assassinated" is true *for everyone*.

It may be that Hilda does not *believe* that Lincoln was assassinated, but this is a different issue. Hilda's belief is not "her truth"; it is only *her belief*. And her belief is either true or false, depending on what actually happened to Lincoln. Hilda's beliefs do not create or destroy past events. So rather than say "his truth" and "her truth," we should say "his belief" and "her belief." We could then say, "It is true that Henry believes Abraham Lincoln was assassinated, but it is not true that Hilda believes it." Notice, however, that this is not a claim about Abraham Lincoln anymore; it is only a claim about the beliefs of Henry and Hilda. (We'll address these matters further in the next lesson on the nature of belief.)

"There are no absolute truths": Here again, the answer is Yes and No, depending on what we mean. Is "Vegetables are healthy" an absolute truth? If it means that vegetables benefit everyone who eats them, then it might be false. What if Bobby has a rare vegetable allergy? We could then say that proposition "Vegetables are healthy" is true for most people but false for Bobby. More accurately stated, the proposition "Vegetables are healthy" is a general truth. General truths, such as "Boys like sports," stand in contrast to universal truths, such as "Boys are male."

Universal Truths	General Truths
Triangles have three sides.	Convicted criminals are guilty of crimes.
Ants are insects.	Pastors preach from the Bible.
Water is hydrogen and oxygen.	Maryland winters bring snowfall.
Men cannot hold their breath for an hour.	Canadians enjoy ice hockey.

As the names themselves indicate, "universal truths" are truths about all members of a class, and "general truths" are truths about most members of a class. Universal truths have implied "All's" and "No's." General truths have implied "Most's" in front of them. But notice that none of the statements in the box have quantifiers. There are no "All's" or "Most's" or "No's." This is because, in everyday discourse, we assume our listeners have enough common sense to interpret our claims rightly. Ordinarily we do not feel the need to say that "All water droplets consist of hydrogen and oxygen," or that "Most convicted criminals are guilty of crimes."

The distinction between general truths and universal truths can be a bit troublesome at times. My students are required to argue a thesis each year. Some try proving universal truths (e.g., "All cases of doctor-assisted suicide are murder") and some try proving only general truths (e.g., "The death penalty deters men from murder"). The latter type of thesis tends to confuse or frustrate students. They are bothered by the suspicion that "exceptions to the rule" refute the rule. Suppose a student finds evidence that the death penalty deters most people, but not all people, from murdering. Would the exceptions undermine the thesis? Not if the thesis is meant only as a general truth rather than a universal truth.

What exactly is confusing these students? I think they are reasoning this way: "In order for my thesis to be true, it must be *absolutely* true; but an absolute truth admits of no exceptions." To clear away their confusion, we must show them that the word "absolute" can mean one of two things:

(1) *Universally* true, such that there are no exceptions, or

(2) *Objectively* true, such that the proposition is true regardless of what people think or feel about it.

The proposition "Dogs catch Frisbees" is not universally true (since some dogs do not catch frisbees), but it is objectively true (since the dogs who do catch frisbees really do catch them). Even general truths are "absolute" truths if we mean *objective* truths (e.g., it is absolutely true that most boys like sports). The phrase "absolute truth" is therefore ambiguous.

If we only mean to state a universal truth (All x's are y's), we should probably say "universal" rather than "absolute." If we want to say that truth is objective rather than subjective, we should use the word "objective," not "absolute." The only time we should use the phrase "absolute truth" is when contrasting it with "relative truth." But by this point you should understand that "relative truth" is ultimately a misnomer. A proposition is either true or false. In that regard, the notion of "absolute truth" is sort of redundant, like "circular globe" or "wet water."

Though meaning is fluid, truth is not. Suppose we are asked whether men are different from women. We cannot answer with a simple "Yes" or "No." With regard to intelligence, the answer is No. With regard to anatomy, the answer is Yes. This is called making a "sense distinction." We are saying "in one sense, yes" and "in another sense, no." By saying "Yes and No" or "It depends on what you mean," we are not relativists about *truth* per se. But we *are* relativists (if you want to say that) about the *meaning* of people's sentences.

Is the United States a Christian nation? Yes and No. It all depends on what we mean. In one sense, yes, it was founded and formed by Puritans in the 17th century, and their descendants continued to think of their society in Christian terms well into the 18th century. In another sense, no: later generations drifted away from these original beliefs, practices, and institutions, and adopted an openly secular plan of life.

Or again, if someone asks whether Earth is "big," we can answer with Yes and No, "relative to" one's standard of comparison. But we are not implying that *truth* itself is relative. We are dealing with different propositions:

> "Earth is big *relative to the moon*."
> "Earth is not big *relative to Jupiter*."

We could go on and on with examples of sense-distinctions. The point is this: once we fix the meaning of a proposition in a definite way, that proposition is either true or false. End of story.

3) Cultural Confusions about Belief

De gustibus non est disputandum: While sitting in a restaurant, you overhear two men in a heated "debate." One of them insists that steak is delicious. The other says that steak is disgusting. This appears to be a genuine disagreement. The men are ascribing what appear to be incompatible qualities (deliciousness and disgustingness) to the same subject (steak). In reality, though, when one of them (Joe) says that "steak is delicious," his statement really means, "I like steak." When the other (Bill) says that steak is disgusting, his statement means "I dislike steak." When translated logically, their apparent debate reduces to this:

"I, Joe, like steak!" "I, Bill, do not like steak!"

Notice what these revised statements are *about*. As the arrows show, the first is about Joe (not about steak) and the second is about Bill (not about steak). It's now apparent that these men are *not talking about the same subject*. Though it initially seems that they are talking about steak, they are really talking about *themselves*, about their different felt reactions to the taste of steak. Their statements are what we call "autobiographical."

This means that the two men are not even *disagreeing* with each other. It's no different than Joe saying "*I* am wearing blue" and Bill saying "*I* am not wearing blue." There is no logical opposition between these statements, since they are not about the same subject.

In a genuine debate, one person must deny the *same claim* that the other affirms. Suppose that after their meal, Joe says to Bill, "We've waited ten minutes for the check." Bill replies, "No, we've not waited *that* long." Here we have a genuine disagreement. Bill is denying what Joe is affirming.

> *Joe*: "We've waited for ten minutes."
> *Bill*: We've waited less than ten minutes."

This disagreement is possible because they are now talking about the same thing, namely, about the amount of time they have been waiting for the waiter. We can visualize the two examples as follows:

CLASH

"We've waited ten minutes." → 💥 ← "We've not waited ten minutes."

NO CLASH

"I, Joe, like steak. ⟶

⟵ I, Bill, dislike steak."

As debaters often say, in the second example Joe and Bill are like ships passing in the night: they are not clashing or bumping into each other at all.

The moral of the story, here, is that personal tastes are not the sort of thing we *can* debate. Nor, then, *should* we try to debate them. As the ancient Romans said, *De gustibus non est disputandum*. ("Tastes are not to be disputed.")

"That's just your personal opinion": Now imagine that, instead of a restaurant, you find yourself in a university classroom. Your history professor asserts that Jesus is a mythical figure. A fellow student expresses disagreement with the professor. The student provides reasons for believing that Jesus rose from the dead. In no mood to argue, however, the professor retorts, "Well, that is just your personal opinion."

You would be an instant billionaire if you had a dollar for every time an American said this. The slogan "That is just your personal opinion" comes in many different varieties:

- That is merely what you believe.
- That is what you think.
- You're entitled to your opinion.
- Not everyone believes what you believe.

Why is it that, in the face of disagreement, so many people use these slogans? What do they mean? What are they supposed to accomplish?

One explanation is that, given the emphasis on "you" and "your," the point of the slogans is to say that the belief in question is held by only one person, in which case the belief is surely suspect. But this can't be right. In addition to being logically mistaken,[8] this is not realistic. There are millions of people who believe that Jesus rose from the dead, or who believe that abortion is murder, and yet opponents still respond to Christians by saying, "Well, that is just your personal opinion."

A second and more likely explanation is that people are using these slogans to mean that these *sorts* of beliefs are in the same category as *tastes*. If one cannot and should not dispute tastes, one cannot and should not dispute these sorts of beliefs. In fact, plenty of Americans speak *as if* the debate about Jesus is like a difference in taste. When it comes to "religious" beliefs, they say, such beliefs are matters of "personal preference." Many say the same thing about moral beliefs. If Joe and Bill disagreed over abortion, this would be no different than their "disagreement" over steak. No one seriously tries correcting another's tastes, since there is no right or wrong preference when it comes to food (as long as we are considering taste rather than health). There is nothing to correct. One person gets pleasure from one thing and another from another thing. If religion and morality are matters of taste, perhaps we should accept our differences in these areas just as we accept our different tastes in food.

This might be the message behind this bumper sticker.[9] It suggests that no one can (or should) correct others for their moral or religious beliefs. We must learn to accept one another's "tastes" (or "feelings") in religion and morality. These are only differences of personal preference. In fact, for many people, the expressions "personal preference" and "personal opinion" are perfectly synonymous.

A third explanation (which ties in with the second) is that these slogans are *calculated to shut down debate*. The slogan "That's just your opinion" is a conversation stopper. If opinion is merely taste, and if taste is not to be disputed, then classifying someone's belief as a taste or preference makes that belief non-discussable. Notice, by the way, that the person who uses the slogan no longer needs to *argue for* his own side of the debate. Suppose that Sam denies the resurrection and supports abortion, but that he knows of *no good reasons* for either belief. (In other words, he would be badly beaten in a debate.) This wouldn't matter

---

[8] I am probably the only person in the world who believes that there are three scratch marks on the desk in my study. Does that make my belief false or suspicious?
[9] Here we have a symbolic representation of philosophies and religions. The T represents Christianity; the O is a modern peace symbol; the L is a Native American peace pipe; the E is a symbol for gender equality; the R is a Native American fertility deity; the A is the Jewish Star of David; the N is the symbol of the Baha'i religion; the C is the symbol of Islam; and the E is the symbol of Science (Einstein's $E=mc^2$).

as long as Sam can persuade others that his unbelief is also a matter of taste. For it would then follow that he need not rationally defend himself. Sam is off the hook.

A fourth[10] explanation (which flows from the previous two) is that these slogans are meant to keep religious beliefs (and certain moral beliefs) *out of the public square*. If beliefs about Jesus and abortion are merely personal preferences, they should also be kept "private." This is the point of those who say, "Keep your religious opinions *to yourself*." This is an essentially secular viewpoint. It's the logic behind the related slogan that "Christians should not *impose their beliefs on others*." Again, this assumes that such beliefs are personal preferences. It's as if Christians are trying to get Americans to prefer red over blue.

So, what do we say to all of this? Are "moral" and "religious" beliefs merely tastes or personal preferences, which (as such) are not even debatable?[11] To answer this, we need to take up the next major concept in our study—the nature of *belief*.

"BELIEVE!" As you're probably aware, this slogan is on billboards, bumper stickers, and plaques in people's homes. It takes the form of a command or an exhortation. It's also nonsense. For we immediately ask ourselves, "Believe *what*?" The command "Believe!" requires a *proposition* to believe *in*. The slogan only makes sense when we supply a proposition, such as "Believe that *you are awesome*" or "Believe that *you can change the world!*" or "Believe that *you can fulfill your dreams!*" Without a proposition to believe in, the slogan tells us virtually nothing. It could just as well mean, "Believe that *you are no-good-for-nothing!*" That's not quite as inspirational, though.

Definition of "belief". To "believe" is to *assent to a proposition*. To "assent" is to *agree* with a proposition. To agree with a proposition is to think that it *is true* or *likely* to be true. Assent has been called a "mental nod."

Like propositions, beliefs are either true or false. Since a proposition is true or false, it follows that a belief must be true or false. If one assents to a true proposition, one's assent is correct. If one assents to a false proposition, one's assent is incorrect.

Whether we believe or disbelieve a proposition implies nothing about its truth-value. Believing a proposition does not make it true. Disbelieving

---

[10] For a fifth but very different explanation of "That is just your personal belief," see lesson 4 for the concept of "*un*provable" beliefs.
[11] I put these words in scare quotes to remind us that people who use them often have no clear idea of what they mean or how they differ from *non*-moral or *non*-religious beliefs.

a proposition does not make it false. If Jesus did *not* rise from the dead, but I assent to the proposition "Jesus rose," my believing it does not change the fact that he did not rise. Rather, I have mistakenly assented to a false proposition. Likewise, if Jesus *did* rise from the dead, but I assent to the proposition "Jesus did not rise," I have mistakenly assented to a false proposition. In either case, my believing has no influence on the facts or on the truth-value of the proposition. The only thing that makes the belief true (or false) is whether the alleged fact is a fact.

The Apostle Paul was alive to this distinction in his teaching about the Gospel. He defines the gospel as a set of propositions about which one could (in principle) be right or wrong.

> [3] For what I received I passed on to you as of first importance: that Christ died for our sins according to the Scriptures, [4] that he was buried, that he was raised on the third day according to the Scriptures, [5] and that he appeared to Cephas, and then to the Twelve. [6] After that, he appeared to more than five hundred of the brothers and sisters at the same time, most of whom are still living, though some have fallen asleep. [7] Then he appeared to James, then to all the apostles, [8] and last of all he appeared to me also, as to one abnormally born" (1 Cor. 15:1-7).

These propositions are either true or false, regardless of whether we believe them. Paul notes that if we believe them though they are false, we are to be "pitied" (15:14-18). By the same token, however, if we disbelieve them though they are true, we are to be pitied even more!

The fallacy of "If you believe it, it is true for you" & "If I don't believe it, it is not true for me": To see why this is absurd, suppose that believing a proposition made it true and that disbelieving it made it false. This would imply, first of all, that *whatever* one believes would be true. If I believe my neighbor murdered his wife, he would become a murderer; my believing it would make it so. If I kept changing my mind about it, he would become a murderer whenever I believe it and a non-murderer whenever I stop believing it. Or, if I believe my neighbor is a murderer and you believe that he is not a murderer, it would follow that he both is and is not a murderer at the same time. Worse still, if a proposition is true simply because I believe it, then (by definition) none of my beliefs could ever be false. But what if I *believe* that some of my beliefs are *false*? It would then be both true and false that some of my beliefs are false.

The difference between "*x is* the case" & "*I believe* x is the case".
Instead of asserting that "x is the case," we often say "I believe that x is the case." We should understand that these are logically different claims.

1. "Jesus rose from the dead."
2. "I believe that Jesus rose from the dead."

Proposition 1 is about ancient history. Proposition 2 is modern autobiography. Proposition 1 has everything to do with Jesus and nothing at all to do with the people who believe in Him. Proposition 2, on the other hand, is about a person who believes in 1. That someone believes that Jesus rose from the dead is a fact about that person only, not a fact about Jesus.

Notice what all of this implies. Proposition 2 might be true even when 1 is false. This would be the case if Jesus did not rise from the dead and yet the person believes that He did. Likewise, proposition 1 might be true even when 2 is false. This would be the case if the person who asserts 2 is lying (e.g., a non-Christian student trying to fit in at a Christian school).

This distinction is important for at least two reasons. In a debate, the pressing issue is not whether a person believes a proposition, but whether the proposition is true. People often attempt to nullify another's belief (e.g., the belief that abortion is wrong) by saying, "But others do not share that belief!" Yes, but the fact that people have conflicting beliefs is irrelevant to whether a belief is true or false. A belief has truth-value regardless of *who* believes it, or *how many* believe it, or how *firmly* they believe it. The issue is whether the belief is true. If abortion really is murder, and yet *no one* believes it is murder, the implication is not that abortion is no longer murder; the implication is that everyone is wrong! (For a similar real-life case, look up the phrase *Athanasius contra mundum*.)

Secondly, people try to avoid debate by "subjectivizing" a claim. In our skeptical, non-confrontational culture, people are hesitant to be right. Instead of simply asserting "Jesus rose from the dead," some try to cushion the claim by saying, "I believe that Jesus rose from the dead." Consider the practical difference this makes. If I say to someone, "Jesus rose from the dead," the person is likely to demand a proof. This puts me in the position of having to argue. If I don't know how to argue it, I may appear simpleminded or unreasonable. This could tempt me to tone down my claim by saying, "*I believe* that Jesus rose from the dead." Logically speaking, it no longer makes sense for the person to challenge me (unless they think I am lying about what I believe). By putting the focus on the fact that *I believe* that Jesus rose, my claim is much less significant and confrontational. After all, what does the person care if I believe that Jesus rose? That is an autobiographical remark, a fact about me only. What really matters, though, is whether *Jesus rose*. The statement "I believe that Jesus rose" might mean something like, "This is just my personal outlook on things, and not something I'm trying to impose on you." Tolerant people are likely to respond by saying, "Oh, that's cool" or "I respect that" or "To each his own." These slogans are so many ways of leaving us in our private little belief systems.

We need to understand, however, that the "I believe" qualifier doesn't ultimately shield us from critique. Since beliefs are propositional, and since propositions are either true or false, it follows that beliefs *themselves* are correct or incorrect. Therefore, a critic could rightly reply, "You are *mistaken* in *believing* that Jesus rose from the dead."

Our beliefs commit us to saying that the world is a certain way. One would not say "I believe that Jesus rose" unless one believed that *Jesus rose*; and about that issue, one is either right or wrong. This is why one cannot ultimately hide behind the hedge of the "I believe..." qualifier.

Why beliefs are not tastes or preferences: We are now ready to respond to the confused idea that beliefs could be matters of taste.

Like tastes, opinions have a subjective quality to them. To understand what "subjective" means in this context, imagine the pain of sitting on a cactus. Clearly the pain is in the person, not in the cactus; the pain is had by the person, not by the cactus. Since the person is the "subject" of the pain, the pain itself is "subjective," meaning that the pain is a property of one who has it. What is true of pain is true of opinion. They are both subjective. If I believe that Pluto is a planet, this opinion is "mine" in the sense that it is had by me, and your opinion is "yours" in that it is had by you. Like tastes, opinions have this somewhat personal aspect to them. But this is where the similarity between beliefs and tastes stop. As we will now see, their differences are far more important than their similarities.

Beliefs, unlike tastes, have propositional content. The first and most important thing to realize is that beliefs, but not tastes, have propositional content. We earlier said that to "believe" is to assent to a *proposition*. This means that *assent* is one thing, and the *proposition* to which one assents is another. Assent is the subjective side of belief. The proposition to which one assents is the objective side of belief. We can visualize it this way:

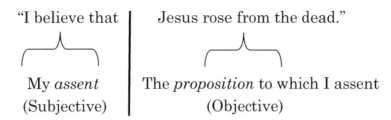

The diagram illustrates that we can detach the proposition "Jesus rose from the dead" from the personal and subjective part of the sentence ("I believe..."). It is crucial to recognize that beliefs have propositional content. Notice that the detached proposition "Jesus rose from the dead" *points us beyond ourselves to an alleged fact outside of ourselves*. The resurrection is either a fact or it is not. If it is a fact, the belief "Jesus rose" is true. If it is not a fact, the belief "Jesus rose" is false.

People who portray belief as a purely subjective matter (like tastes) are failing to distinguish (1) the subjective assent of the believer, and (2) the objective truth-value of the proposition believed. Though beliefs have a subjective aspect to them (one must assent), beliefs also have an objective aspect to them; they have "propositional content" (i.e., the proposition assented to). This proposition is *objectively true or false*. Belief is not, therefore, a mere expression of feeling or taste or personal preference.[12]

Tastes, on the other hand, do *not* have propositional content, so they do not have truth-value; nor, then, are they debatable. As noted, a proposition represents the world as being a particular way. But tastes, unlike beliefs, do not represent anything. If I happen to like ketchup, and you are disgusted by it, it makes no sense to say that I am correct and that you are incorrect. After all, what is there to be correct or incorrect about? The pleasure I get from ketchup is not true or false; it's just an experience of pleasure. Likewise, your aversion to ketchup is not true or false; it's simply a disagreeable effect of ketchup on your taste buds. When it comes to ketchup, we just experience it differently; we have different felt reactions to it. But neither of our reactions is the "correct" one. This is because tastes do not

---

[12] Some propositions initially *seem* to be a mere expression of taste. Suppose someone says, "Tom Brady is the all-time greatest quarterback." Though this is a belief, it has the appearance of being a taste or personal preference. To see why the appearance is deceiving, however, note that while it makes sense for us to reply, "That's your opinion," it does not make sense to say, "That's your taste." For the proposition "Tom Brady is the all-time greatest quarterback" is the sort of expression that can be true or false. It has truth-value. It's not like the expression "Yay Tom Brady!" or "Boo Tom Brady!" These exclamations are neither true nor false, since they only express likes or dislikes. The sentence "Tom Brady is the all-time greatest quarterback" is debatable, however, since (depending on its meaning) it is arguably true or false. For example, if "greatest" means most Super Bowl wins, or most major QB records, then it is true. If "greatest" means "my personal favorite," then the proposition "Tom Brady is the all-time greatest quarterback" becomes a mere expression of taste or feeling. But that's a strange way of saying it. One should simply say, "He's my favorite."

declare facts. This explains why tastes cannot be true or false and why they are not to be disputed.[13]

So back to the professor who insists that Jesus was a mythical figure. When he rebuffs the Christian student by saying, "That is just your personal opinion," this professor is missing the point. When the student says that Jesus rose from the dead, this proposition has nothing to do with the student. It has everything to do with Jesus, who rose from the dead or not. The fact that the student believes this proposition is irrelevant to whether the proposition is true.

Logically speaking, then, what *should* the professor have said? He only had two options. On the one hand, he could have replied, "Well, you are mistaken." In this case, though, the professor would need good reasons for denying the student's claims, which the professor may not actually have. The professor's other option is to tone down his original claim, by saying something like: "I suspect Jesus is mythical" or "Some people think he is mythical." These are much weaker claims. But at least they make logical sense, in that the professor now recognizes that Jesus either is or is not who Christians say he is. He is acknowledging, in other words, that this is not a matter of taste or personal preference.

The fallacy of "That's just your opinion": This slogan is the best example of what I earlier called the "subjectivization of truth." The person who uses this slogan is trying to collapse the truth-value of the belief into the person (or subject) who believes it. The sloganeer is speaking as if truth itself a purely *subjec*tive thing. You should now see why this slogan is so unintelligent. A belief can *never* be "*just* an opinion" or "*just* a belief." For you now know that (1) a belief has propositional content, (2) that a proposition is true or false, and (3) that the truth-value of the proposition is dictated (only and wholly) by the *objective facts*, which means that those facts are what they are <u>regardless</u> of what we think or feel. Therefore, whether Joe Blow is of the opinion that abortion is wrong is *totally irrelevant* to whether abortion is wrong.

Is there a quick way to help people understand all of this? Probably not. (If I knew of one, I would've shortened the previous reading!) But there are ways of helping them start. Here's a suggestion for you: The next time someone says, "That's just what you believe," respond by saying something along the lines of, "Well, but I also believe that JFK was shot" or "...that 2 + 2 = 4," or "...that Earth orbits the Sun." That is, state another proposition that you *know* they also believe. They will then reply with, "But that's different—that's just a fact; that's simply

---

[13] You might ask, "But don't tastes relay information about the world? For example, don't tastes tell us that something has a high salt content?" Well, the salty sensation is not, as such, a statement or proposition. The mind must interpret the sensation and judge that (using language) "This is salty."

true." It's at this point that you have them where you want them. All you have to say is, "Yes, it is a fact; yes, it is true; but it's also what *I believe*. Therefore, the issue is not what *I* believe or what *you* believe, but rather *which belief* is *true*.

The fallacy of "Don't impose your belief on me": This slogan suggests that we are forcing him to think or act in a particular way; it's as if we're loading him with a sack of rocks or enclosing him in a cage, when all we are really doing is uttering a sentence! To see why this slogan is nonsensical, suppose a teacher says to his class, "Caesar crossed the Rubicon," and that a student retorts, "Hey, don't impose your belief on me!" Why is this obviously silly? For one thing, the teacher is doing nothing more than declaring a fact. It's not as if he's forcing the student by gunpoint to believe it. In fact, if the student has a reason for doubting it, he can simply say on his test, "You taught us that Caesar crossed the Rubicon, but I'm still a skeptic."

Secondly, we know that either Caesar crossed the Rubicon or he didn't. If there is good evidence that he did, then we *should* believe it and we *should* teach others to believe it. Likewise, if a teacher says, "Jesus rose from the dead," this is either true or false. If there is good evidence, we should believe it; if there is no good evidence, we should not believe it.

The bottom line is this: Do people want to believe the truth or not? If they do, they should welcome open discussion and exchange of ideas. Remember: it's not as if they are being forced to believe what people say. This makes me wonder if the slogan "Don't impose your beliefs on me" is more of a defense mechanism, a way for people to continue believing what they *want* to believe *regardless* of the facts. (See Romans 1:18ff. for an example.)

Beliefs v. feelings: Over the last several decades Americans have changed the way they speak about their beliefs. Whereas we should say "I *believe* that such and such is the case," we now often say, "I *feel* that such and such is the case." To why these are different, contrast these statements:

> I feel hot.
> I feel that the defendant is guilty.

Contrary to popular discourse, feelings are not beliefs, and beliefs are not feelings. Beliefs are true or false; feelings are neither. We feel hot, we feel sick, we feel sad. We do not *believe* hot (or believe sick or believe sad). A feeling is a sub-rational sensation or emotional state. A belief is a rational assent to a proposition. Like tastes, feelings are non-propositional; they do not have propositional content. We are duped into thinking that they do because we make assertions *about* our feelings. The statement "I feel hot" is a proposition, but the *feeling of being* hot is not a proposition, and so cannot have truth-value. Your report about your feelings ("I am hot") is true or false, but not the feeling itself *as* a feeling; it just *is*.

This is why we cannot debate feelings. Suppose you tell your friends "I am hot" even though you are in a thoroughly air-conditioned room. They express a type of disbelief: "How can you feel hot? It's 65 degrees in here!" Your friends are not doubting that you feel hot (unless they think you are lying). They understand that your feelings are what they are. If you feel hot, you feel hot. There's nothing for your friends to dispute there. What they are *really* wondering is how it's possible for you to feel that way in such a cool room. There might be something wrong with you feeling hot in a cold room (perhaps you need to see a doctor?), but the feeling itself, as a sensation, is neither false nor true. This is why we should stop saying "I feel that gun control will not reduce violent crime" or "I feel that men evolved from apes." No one literally *feels* propositions; we can only understand them and assent to them.

This is not a mere verbal distinction without a practical difference. There are dangers of which we need to be aware.

First, this mode of speaking leads to irrational subjectivism. Feelings are purely subjective, like tastes or preferences. When a culture is accustomed to the language of "I feel that x is the case," it's conditioning itself to think about beliefs as purely subjective, and as non-rational or non-cognitive. People conclude that debate itself as a process of emoting and manipulating.

Secondly, this mode of speaking also tends to give equal *authority* to different beliefs. If I feel hot even though it's 65 degrees, I feel hot nonetheless, and it doesn't matter what the world is like or what anyone says to me. My feeling of being hot has a quasi "infallibility" to it.[14] I might be mistaken in *believing* that it is 89 degrees, but one cannot say I am "mistaken" in presently *feeling* as I ordinarily feel when it is 89 degrees. The more we talk about beliefs as feelings, the more inclined we are to accept people's false or irrational beliefs as valid, or to refrain from challenging them. We are unknowingly transferring the authority of people's feelings to their beliefs about the world. This is disastrous. Consider the difference between these two statements:

> I feel hot.
> I feel that the defendant is guilty.

---

[14] Since feelings are not true or false, it is technically incorrect to say they can be fallible or infallible.

In reality, the defendant is guilty or not, regardless of what anyone believes or feels. But what happens when a culture is accustomed to ascribing authority to their feelings, and to interpreting the world through the prism of those feelings? Feelings begin to take the place of *facts*. We no longer look to facts. We need only look to our feelings. I sat on a jury where one of the jurors, during the period of deliberation, appealed to her feelings as a basis for thinking the defendant was guilty. (How many people like her are serving as jurors across the country and what does this mean for the practice of trial by jury?)

What people need to hear nowadays is that their feelings are irrelevant to the facts and to truth-value of their beliefs. We need to stop "trusting our feelings" (contrary to the Jedi philosophy of Star Wars and to virtually every Disney movie made since the 1990s) and to start looking to facts.

As a side note, it's disturbing to think what today's schools are doing to youth. Students are being encouraged to find their own truth by relying on their personal feelings. By treating their feelings as sacred, we shield students from the facts themselves out of fear of offending them or threatening "their truth."

I teach at a school that works hard to correct this mindset. To this end, we have students write a senior thesis. One of the goals of this project is for students to find the truth about an issue, not by looking to their own personal feelings, but to whatever objective facts are relevant to the claim they're trying to prove. Given their younger age and relative lack of experience and knowledge, students are required to rely on sources *outside of themselves*, including tradition and sound scholarship. It is folly for them to "trust their feelings" when exploring topics like abortion, evolution, global warming, vaccination, gun control, just war, or even more personal and subjective topics like emotional or psychological disorders.

Belief v. desire: It's tempting to dismiss someone's belief (or unbelief) on the grounds that they *want* it to be true (or false). Atheists say to Christians, "You believe in God's existence because you want your life to have meaning." Christians say to atheists, "You don't believe in God because you want the freedom to live as you please." Interestingly, both accusations may be true. In fact, some atheists have openly admitted that they don't want God to exist, since that would create a sense of guilt for their sins and an anxiety over their death. Likewise, some Christians admit that they don't want to live in a world without meaning.

Even if desires can *influence* beliefs, desires do not determine whether beliefs are *true*. Beliefs remain true or false regardless of the believer's desires. I'm sure that many atheists *want* a world without God so that they can live as they please, without guilt and fear. But the way they want the world to be does not determine the way the world really is. If God does *not* exist, then the world is the way atheists want it to be. If God *does* exist, the world is not the way atheists want it to be. Either way, the atheists' desires are irrelevant.

It's worth noting that desire is not sufficient to create belief or unbelief. One's desire for a proposition to be true cannot, by itself, enable one to believe it is true. I wish a million dollars would suddenly appear in my bank account, but this desire is not enough to cause me to believe that it has happened. I know it's possible that someone could purposefully or accidentally put money into my account, but I have no *reason* for believing that anyone has. This shows that one's desire for a proposition to be true must be accompanied by some evidence (however slight) for thinking that it is true. In fact, people who say they *want* to believe in a claim find that they *cannot* do so, precisely *because* there is too much evidence against it.

Even if one's desire for a proposition to be true influences their belief in it, this would not necessarily be a bad thing; it could in fact *help* one find the truth. A defense attorney may strongly desire for their client to be innocent. This desire may motivate him to go the extra mile to form a powerful defense of a client who (it turns out) is in fact innocent. Likewise, a scientist who wants to confirm his theory will be motivated to persevere in his research. This is a benefit when the theory is true. But, of course, desires can also bias us to search in the wrong direction or to ignore or suppress evidence against our beliefs.

In sum, it is a mistake to center a debate around the desires of the disputants rather than the evidence or arguments for their sides.

SUBJECTIVE (THE BELIEVER)		OBJECTIVE (OBJECTS OF BELIEF)	
		PROPOSITIONS (DECLARATIONS OF FACT)	REALITY (FACTS)
Cognitive (rational)	Belief = Assenting to one of these propositions	"The preborn is a human being" ⟶ TRUE ⟶	The actual human status of preborns.
		"The preborn is not a human being" ⟶ FALSE ⟶	
Non-cognitive (non-rational)	• Taste • Desire • Feeling		

4) Plato on Chaining Down True Beliefs with Arguments

In one of Plato's dialogues we find Socrates discussing a philosophical puzzle. Suppose we are giving directions to a lost tourist, who is trying to get to the town of Larissa. Though we ourselves have never been to Larissa, we *think* that road A is the right one. We stress for the traveler that we are not *sure* about this. Even so, the traveler decides to venture down road A, which, as it turns out, leads to Larissa.

This example illustrates the possibility of having a true belief *without confidence* that the belief is true. This raises a question for Plato. What is the *value* of confidence if, in fact, we can have true belief without confidence? After all, the lost traveler would have arrived at his destination either way. Our lack of confidence made no difference in this regard. This seems to suggest that, as long as one happens to believe the *truth*, it does not really matter whether one is also *sure* that they are in possession of the truth.

Consider a weightier example. Imagine two pregnant women, both of whom think that abortion is murder, but one of whom is *sure* that it is and the other is very much unsure. Again, as long as the unsure woman refuses to abort her child, there seems to be no *practical* difference between the two. Right? Wrong.

The value of confidence in preserving true belief: Let's put the question in more general terms: If accepting that a true proposition *is* true enables us to travel the road of life, what does confidence *add*?

To answer this, let's start by noting that, as a general rule, people prefer true beliefs to false beliefs, especially when it matters most.[15] When one buys a used car, for instance, one prefers the truth about the car's reliability. But now think about the significance of this. If true beliefs are valuable for one to possess, it follows that they *remain* valuable for *only as long as* one *continues* to possess them. The problem is that true beliefs *don't always stay put*.

To illustrate this point, Plato mentions the Greeks' custom of chaining down expensive sculptures in their yards to protect them from theft. He proposes that the value of true beliefs is like that of sculptures: both are valuable, but *only as long as they stay put*.

It is obvious how sculptures can be stolen, but how exactly does one "steal" true beliefs? One cannot exactly *grab* a belief and run off with it. No, but one can undergo a change of mind, by being *persuaded out of* their true beliefs. As we grow

---

[15]From a Christian standpoint, it is erroneous to assume that men *always* prefer truth to falsehood. The Bible speaks of the deceitfulness of sin (Hebrews 4). Men have a tendency to "rationalize" their sinful lifestyle, by persuading themselves of what they know is not true. This is called "self-deception." See also John 3 and Romans 1.

older, we gain new insights which lead us to revise our beliefs. This is good when we exchange a false belief for a true one, as when a racist (for example) comes to realize that race is irrelevant to evaluating a man's character. But a change of mind can go in the wrong direction. Sometimes people *become* racists after listening to a lecture or reading a book. Here we have a case of a true belief ("Racism is false/bad") being replaced with a false belief ("Racism is true/good"). We can describe this change of mind metaphorically, by saying that the person's true belief about racism was "stolen." This is an apt metaphor, given that true beliefs are highly valued; we *want* to keep them.[16]

Proof as the proper cause of confidence: So how do we keep our true beliefs? Just as the Greeks chained down their sculptures, we must chain down our true beliefs, not with physical chains, but with *logical* chains. We must tie down our true beliefs with what Plato called a *logos* (i.e., an account, reason, or explanation). We will simplify Plato's point by saying that confidence should be secured by means of *proof*.

The confident Christian: For Christians, there are no true beliefs as valuable as those about the person and work of Jesus Christ. But these beliefs do not always stay put in the minds of those taught to believe them. Christians who go to college are confronted with intellectual challenges from hostile peers and professors. Many college professors make it their point to steal the beliefs of professing Christians. Anti-Christian philosopher and educator, Richard Rorty, made the following confession:

> "...I, like most Americans who teach humanities or social science in colleges and universities...try to arrange things so that students who enter as bigoted, homophobic, religious fundamentalists will leave college with views more like our own ... The fundamentalist parents of our fundamentalist students think that the entire 'American liberal establishment' is engaged in a conspiracy. The parents have a point. Their point is that we liberal teachers no more feel in a symmetrical communication situation when we talk with bigots than do kindergarten teachers talking with their students ... When we American college teachers encounter religious fundamentalists, we do not consider the possibility of reformulating our own practices of justification so as to give more weight to the authority of the Christian scriptures. Instead, we do our best to convince these students of the benefits of secularization. We assign first-person accounts of growing up homosexual to our homophobic students for the same reasons that German schoolteachers in the postwar period assigned *The Diary of Anne Frank*... You have to be educated in order to be a participant in our conversation ... So we are going to go right on trying to discredit you in the eyes of your children, trying to strip your fundamentalist religious community of dignity, trying to make your views seem silly rather than discussable. We are not so inclusivist as to tolerate intolerance such

---

[16] He explains this in the *Republic*, 413a-d.

as yours ... I think those students are lucky to find themselves under the benevolent domination of people like me, and to have escaped the grip of their frightening, vicious, dangerous parents ... I am just as provincial and contextualist as the Nazi teachers; the only difference is that I serve a better cause."

This is one reason why some who enter college as professing Christians graduate as skeptics, agnostics, and atheists. This happens partly[17] because these students never *chained down their true beliefs*.

"Personal opinion" as *unprovable* belief: There is another interpretation of the phrase "personal opinion" that we did not yet discuss, since it makes more sense to do so now. When one says, "That belief is just your personal opinion," they sometimes mean to say, "That belief *cannot be proved*." This presumably means that there is no way to tell *whether* it is true or false.

To be sure, the fact that a proposition has truth-value does not mean it is provable. When I traveled to Greece and stood amidst the ruins of Corinth, I wondered if the Apostle Paul stood on the same steps where I stood. The proposition "Paul stood on the same steps on which I am standing" was true or false. In fact, that proposition was at least plausible, since I was standing right in front of Gallio's "bema" seat (see Acts 18:12-17). Even so, if you overhead me saying, "Paul stood on these steps right here!" you could reasonably reply, "Maybe, but you cannot prove it either way." After all, maybe Paul stood a little to the right or left of where I was standing.

Is there buried treasure under my house? Did Paul write the letter to the Hebrews? Was the assassination of JFK a conspiracy? Questions like these might not be answerable. They certainly *have* an answer in the sense that claims about them are either true or false; but this does not mean *we* can always *know* the answer.

Some unprovable propositions are not worth debating (except as a mere intellectual exercise). Suppose there is literally no solid evidence for or against a proposition, e.g., "There is an even number of stars in the Universe." Clearly such a proposition is "unprovable" or "undebatable." In that sense, and in that sense only, such beliefs are like tastes or preferences. This is *not* because they have no truth-value (they do!); it's only because they cannot be proved or disproved.

So, can moral and religious beliefs be proved or disproved? Very scholarly books have been written on such topics. For example, there are excellent arguments for

---

[17]A complete explanation would take account of the person's spiritual condition: whether they are a genuine Christian, a member of a strong church, associating with the right friends, being nurtured in Christian community, and so on. Failure to reason through their beliefs is only part of the problem. The extent to which this is to blame will vary from person to person. For a fuller discussion of this subject, read *How to Stay Christian in College*, by J. Budziszewski.

the resurrection of Jesus. Even some non-Christian historians have conceded this much. They continue in unbelief for partly personal reasons (they don't want to follow Jesus) and partly for philosophical reasons (they don't think miracles are likely or reasonable). And yet they freely admit that the historical evidence is against them!

Secondly, even if some moral and religious beliefs cannot be proven, the same can be said of beliefs in math, science, history, psychology, economics, and so on, though no one infers that these subjects are matters of "personal opinion."

Finally, the question of whether any belief can be "proven" will depend on what we mean by "proof."

Sometimes the term is used in a very strong sense, to refer to evidence that is *certain, conclusive, unquestionable*. Some have held that claims like "God exists" (a religious claim) or "Murder is wrong" (a moral claim) are in this category. On the other hand, there are countless non-moral and non-religious beliefs that are not in this category, including much of what we're taught in history and science. Even those who think that there is good evidence for human evolution, for example, cannot seriously say that the evidence is "unquestionable." There are alternative ways of interpreting the evidence.

This means that there is also a weaker sense of "proof," which usually goes by the name of *probable* evidence. In this sense, one proves his belief with evidence that rational people consider reliable, even if it is not conclusive or unquestionable. This is the status of many of our historical beliefs (e.g., "Caesar crossed the Rubicon") and scientific beliefs (e.g., "A meteor caused dinosaur extinction"). Yet no one says of these beliefs, "That is just your personal opinion."

As we will see in Unit 4, the word "proof" can mean different things to different people. So the question of whether a claim has been proved, or can be proved, is itself a matter of debate. Interestingly, we will often need to prove our claims about what it means to prove our claims.

5) The Nature of Argument

Definition of "argument": We will start with a preliminary definition of "argument" as simply a *way of proving our beliefs*.

Arguments are not the only way to prove beliefs, nor even (in many cases) the best way. Suppose you hear that your math teacher, Mr. Marvolis, can juggle six flaming torches. Finding this hard to believe, you demand proof. In this case, the best possible proof is to simply *see* him juggle six flaming torches. But this sort of proof is *not* an argument. The second best option is to see a video or a photograph; but that is still not an argument. Now suppose your friend comes to you and reasons as follows:

> "During college and graduate school, Mr. Marvolis held a part time job as a circus performer. Moreover, plenty of people have claimed to see him do it. All of them relayed this in a straightforward, matter of fact manner. Furthermore, all of them are honest, and none of them had anything to gain by lying. Finally, it's not as if he performed a miracle. There are plenty of people in the world who can juggle six flaming torches, and some who can juggle even more."

Here we have an argument. Note how this evidence differs from the evidence of actually seeing him juggle. First, your friend is giving you proof in the form of *propositions*. He is not so much saying "look and see" but rather "hear and consider." Secondly, these propositions are *logically relevant* to thinking that the proposition about Mr. Marvolis is true. Thirdly, your friend expects that you should accept these reasons *in place of* the evidence of actually seeing your teacher juggle. Generally speaking, arguments are given when the fact in question cannot be directly inspected and verified.

We can now give a more precise definition of "argument" as *a set of propositions used to prove a point*.

Arguments consist of premises and conclusions: Every argument consists of two components: (1) the *proposition we are trying to prove*, and (2) the *propositions used to prove it*. The proposition we are trying to prove is called the "conclusion." The propositions used to prove it are called the "premises."

For any good argument, the conclusion is the proposition on which all the others converge. We can visualize it this way:

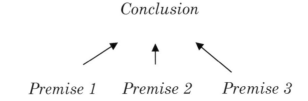

This suggests that premises can be thought of as supports for the conclusion. The premises are support*ing* propositions. The conclusion is the support*ed* proposition.

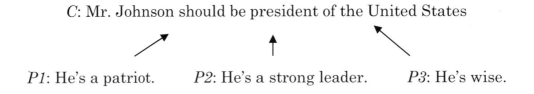

Though every argument must have at least one conclusion and at least one premise, it is possible to have multiple premises or multiple conclusions.[18] The following argument has one conclusion and multiple premises.

The next argument has one premise and multiple conclusions.

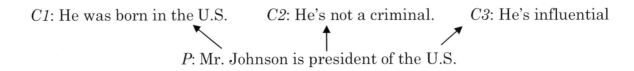

We said that an argument is a set of propositions (the premises) used to prove a point (the conclusion). Though the majority of arguments meet this definition, the two previous examples mean that the definition is potentially misleading, since some arguments have only one premise, and other arguments have more than one conclusion. More precisely, then, we could define an argument as a set of propositions consisting of *at least one conclusion* and *at least one premise*. For the sake of simplicity, however, we will stick to the previous definition of "argument" as a set of propositions used to prove a point.

---

[18] This means that arguments can dramatically vary in size, from two simple sentences (one premise and one conclusion) to book-length arguments involving hundreds of pages.

Arguments express inferences: Arguing involves *inferring*. To understand what this means, suppose it is true that (1) Mike is taller than Ted, and (2) Ted is taller than Fred. From these two propositions we can *infer* that Mike is taller than Fred. The amazing thing about an inference is its power to move us from the known to the unknown. Neither of the first two propositions (1) and (2) tells us anything about the relation between Mike and Fred. Proposition (1) pertains *only* to Mike and Ted, and (2) pertains *only* to Ted and Fred. And yet, *from* these two facts we have enough information to *move to* the *new* fact that Mike is taller than Fred. Inference can be visualized with an arrow.

If it is true that Mike is taller than Ted, and Ted is taller than Fred…

…Then it is true that Mike is taller than Fred.

A prominent philosopher, A.C. Ewing, shares a more entertaining example of an inference (in which the identities of the actual persons involved are disguised). Ewing writes,

> "There is a story that Mr. X., a man of high reputation and great social standing, had been asked to preside at a big social function. He was late in coming, and so a Roman Catholic priest was asked to make a speech to pass the time till his arrival. The priest told various anecdotes, including one which recorded his embarrassment when as a confessor he had to deal with his first penitent, who confessed to a particularly atrocious murder. Shortly afterward Mr. X arrived, and in his own speech he said: 'I see Father _____ is here. Now, though he may not recognize me, he is an old friend of mine. In fact, I was his first penitent.'"

If you followed the story, you inferred that Mr. X is a murderer. The story illustrates that inferences are *informative*. Even though the proposition "Mr. X is a murderer" is not contained in the story, we were able to infer it from the information given to us. We can think of an inference as a sort of *mental motion*, a movement of the mind, in which we go from one insight to another insight. We will define an inference as *the discovery of the truth-value of a proposition (the conclusion) by seeing its connection to some other proposition (the premise) whose truth-value is already assumed or known.*

We make inferences every day, often without realizing it. Suppose you are rummaging through your closet. You find a can sealed with tape. You shake it and hear the high pitch clinking of small metal pieces. You then *infer* the can is filled with coins. Or perhaps you find large clumps of your cat's hair on the lawn. You know a tomcat has been prowling the neighborhood at nights. So you infer that your cat fought the tomcat and perhaps took a beating. In these cases, your mind is moving from one insight to another, and it is doing so on the basis of a perceived connection between them.

The concept of inference suggests another way of thinking about premises and conclusions. In an inference, the premise is the proposition *from* which we move and the conclusion is the proposition *to* which we move.

Implication: The conclusion can also be called an "implication." An implication is a proposition implied by the premise. The proposition "Mike is taller than Fred" *implies* the proposition "Fred is shorter than Mike." The proposition "Fred is shorter than Mike" is the implication. We can use an arrow to symbolize implication:

- Mike is taller than Fred. → Fred is shorter than Mike.
- Sally is having a sneezing fit. → Sally has allergies or a cold.

Learn to distinguish the word "infer" from the easily confused word "imply." Only *minds* "infer" and only *propositions* "imply." We might say that, in an inference, the *mind receives* information, whereas in implication the *proposition sends* the information. So it is incorrect to say either (1) "The fact that all men are mortal *infers* that Socrates is a man" or (2) "From the fact that all men are mortal we may *imply* that Socrates is man."[19] We should rather reverse the two statements.

How arguments prove and persuade: To *prove* is to show that a proposition is true or likely to be true. To *persuade* is to move someone to accept (or assent to) the proposition. (We discuss the distinction in more detail further below.)

Let's consider one of the more common ways in which arguments actually persuade. Suppose we want to persuade someone of proposition x. The trick is to show him that what he already believes (say, propositions y and z) somehow *demands* that he should *also* believe proposition x. In this respect, arguments cause someone to believe what they do *not yet* believe, and they do so by means of what they *already* believe. Let's take a simple example. Suppose our friend believes the following proposition:

P1: "People should be allowed to do whatever they want as long as they do not physically harm anyone."

Now suppose we want him to believe the opposite proposition, namely:

---

[19] Though we often say something like "I meant to imply that..." what we're really saying is that our *statement* was intended to imply something.

> P2: "There are some actions that people should *not* be allowed to do even though those actions do not physically harm anyone."

We are trying to win his assent to P2; this is the conclusion we are trying to prove. This means we need to find premises for it, and preferably premises that he already believes. Ideally, we need to identify an action he knows will not physically harm anyone, but which he also believes people should not be allowed to do. We might ask him, "Would you be physically harmed if, day after day, someone followed you around in public and mimicked your every word or gesture?" He would have to say no. We might then ask, "Should people be allowed to do that to you?" Unless he is lying, the answer is again no. This means our friend has agreed to the following two propositions:

> P3: It does not physically harm anyone to follow a person around in public and mimic them.

> P4: People should not be allowed to follow others around in public and mimic them.

We are trying to make him see that propositions P3 and P4 demand that he *also* believe in proposition P2 above. We are making the proposition he did not believe appear as a *conclusion* of propositions he *did* believe. This is the goal of every argument: to win someone's assent to a proposition *x* (the "conclusion") *on the basis of their prior belief* in propositions *y* and *z* (the "premises").

The goal of argument—proof or persuasion? Is the goal of an argument to prove a conclusion, or is it to persuade someone into believing a conclusion? As noted above, proving involves *showing* that a conclusion is true or likely to be true. Persuading involves *moving someone to accept* the conclusion. Ideally, we prove *in order to* persuade.

Interestingly, it is possible to prove a proposition without persuading people of it. It is also possible to persuade people of a proposition without proving it. Persuasion can and often does result from proof, but not always; people may remain unpersuaded in the face of proof. Similarly, persuasion can and often does occur apart from proof. People can accept arguments that do not prove their points or reject arguments that do prove their points. This frequently happens in debates, where some people side with the more engaging speaker against the (objectively) superior reasoner. Proof and persuasion do not always line up.

6) Perceiving Arguments

To argue well, you must learn to *perceive* an argument *as* an argument. To understand what this means, consider some analogies.

In a movie called *The Gods Must Be Crazy*, an airplane pilot throws an empty Coke bottle out of his plane onto the sands of the Kalahari Desert, where a very primitive tribesman discovers it. He knows nothing of airplanes, bottles, or modern technology. The man picks up the bottle and stares at it with a look of complete confusion. He has no idea what it is. He takes it back to the village, where the tribesmen use it as a toy, a tool, a weapon, and a host of other things. When you or I look at this object, we know precisely what it is—a glass vessel made to hold the world's most famous soft drink product. What is strange, though, is that this man *sees* exactly what we see, but he does not see it *as* we see it; he does not *perceive* what we perceive; he does not *identify* it for what it really is. To take another example, imagine two men watching a wrestling match. One of these spectators is a former champion wrestler and a current coach. The other has never seen a wrestling match until now. These two men are seeing the wrestlers grappling and moving about the mat, but only the coach *perceives* the motions as specific "moves," "holds," and "tactics." Consider similar experiences from your own life. If you are an artist or musician, you have trained your mind to perceive what others do not perceive. An artist sees a painting and recognizes it as a Da Vinci. The inexperienced person next to him sees only a painting. He sees what the artist sees, but does not see it *as* the artist sees it; he does not *perceive* it for what it is. Or again, the musician hears a piece of music and recognizes it as Baroque or as Beethoven's Ninth symphony. The untrained person next to him hears what he hears but does not hear it *as* he hears it; he does not *recognize* it for what it is.

The same can be said of people trained in logical argumentation. They learn to perceive forms of speech *as arguments*. In contrast to the untrained person next to them, they don't merely hear people talking; they hear people trying to prove a point by means of other propositions; they don't just hear statements; they recognize them *as* premises or *as* conclusions. This power of perceiving arguments comes with study and practice. This lesson and the following will introduce some of the tools needed to do so.

Inferential indicators: To signify that two propositions stand in relation to each other as premise and conclusion, the English language contains "inferential indicators." These words are like clues, signifying that a given proposition serves as a premise or as a conclusion.[20] There will therefore be two types: "premise indicators" and "conclusion indicators."

Premise Indicators	*Conclusion Indicators*
Socrates is a mortal, *because* Socrates is a man.	I think. *Therefore* I am.
...*since* Socrates is a man.	... *Hence* I am.
...*for* Socrates is a man.	...*So* I am.
...*in that* Socrates is a man.	... *Consequently* I am.
...*given that* Socrates is a man.	... *It follows that* I am.
...*as* Socrates is a man.	... *Ergo* I am.

For example, the premise indicators in this passage from Romans have been underlined.

> "The wrath of God is being revealed from heaven against all the godlessness and wickedness of men who suppress the truth by their wickedness, <u>since</u> what may be known about God is plain to them, <u>because</u> God has made it plain to them. <u>For</u> since the creation of the world God's invisible qualities—his eternal power and divine nature—have been clearly seen, being understood from what has been made (Romans 1:18-20)

There are three premises in this argument: (1) "what may be known about God is plain to them"; (2) "God has made it plain to them"; and (3) "since the creation of the world…"

Notice that the second use of "since" ("For *since* the creation…") is not a premise indicator. Here it functions as a time-indicator, as in the statement "I have been a teacher since 1999." This means we cannot automatically assume that words which *can* serve as inferential indicators always *do*.

Arguments vs. explanations: In the statement "I don't have my homework because my dog ate it," the word *because* does not serve as a premise indicator. The clause "my dog ate it" is not a premise; it is an explanation. The student is not trying to *prove* that he doesn't have his homework; the teacher already knows that. The student is giving an account of this mutually agreed upon fact. Take the generic statement "*x* because of *y*." If y is a reason for someone to believe <u>that</u> x is the case, "because" is a premise indicator; but if *y* is an account for <u>why</u> *x* is the case (offered to someone who believes x), "because" is an explanation indicator.

---

[20]Inferential indicators are not *part of* the premises or conclusions themselves. They only point to the premises or conclusions.

The correlativity of premises and conclusions: It is possible to know that a conclusion is present even if there is no conclusion indicator, or that a premise is present even if there is no premise indicator. This is because the presence of one always presupposes the presence of the other. They are "correlative." Take the notions of cause and effect. For any pair x and y, if we know x is a cause of y, then we also know that y is the effect of x. Or take the notions of teacher and student. If Joe is Sam's teacher, then we know Sam is Joe's student. Likewise, the terms "premise" and "conclusion" presuppose one another. It is impossible for a proposition in a paper to function as a premise unless there is also a proposition functioning as its conclusion (and vice versa). In the paragraph from Romans, we can infer that the first statement (underlined below) is the conclusion, even though there is no conclusion indicator.

> "<u>The wrath of God is being revealed from heaven against all the godlessness and wickedness of men who suppress the truth by their wickedness</u>, since what may be known about God is plain to them,

Supplying missing indicators: Not every argument contains inferential indicators. The Second Amendment of the U.S. Constitution says this:

> "A well-regulated Militia, being necessary to the security of a free State, the right of the people to keep and bear Arms, shall not be infringed."

This is an argument, though it contains no inferential indicators. Which is the premise and which the conclusion? Sometimes it is intuitively obvious. But it's always helpful to supply an indicator to test your hunch. It makes most sense to read this argument as:

> The right to bear arms shall not be infringed *because* a well-regulated Militia is necessary to the security of a free State.

The premise is that a Militia is necessary. The conclusion is that the right to bear arms shall not be infringed. Here is another example from Paul's letter to the Romans:

> "There will be trouble and distress for every human being who does evil: first for the Jew, then for the Gentile; but glory, honor and peace for everyone who does good: first for the Jew, then for the Gentile. God does not show favoritism."

Paul is arguing that God will judge all men, Jew and Gentile, according to their works rather than their racial or ethnic status. The last sentence—"God does not show favoritism"—is best read as a premise. To test this, we can supply a premise indicator and then a conclusion indicator to see which one makes more sense.

- "…first for the Jew, then for the Gentile. *For* God does not show favoritism."
- "…first for the Jew, then for the Gentile. *Therefore*, God does not show favoritism."

It is not because there will be trouble for the Jew and the Gentile that God does not show favoritism (which is why the "Therefore" does not make sense); it is because God does not show favoritism that there will be trouble for both Jew and Gentile (and so "For" makes sense).

To take one more example, the following argument is from a Roman Catholic in response to the claim that Christians are "homophobic."

> "The term *homophobic* refers to fear of homosexuality. This term often is used by homosexual activists to end rational discussion of the issue by accusing their opponents of having an irrational fear. This is unjust. One can disagree with and be critical of a behavior without having a fear of it."[21]

The conclusion is "This [accusation] is unjust." Though there is no premise or conclusion indicator, we can test our hunch by seeing which indicator works best:

- "This is unjust. *For* one can disagree with and be critical of a behavior without having a fear of it."
- "This is unjust. *Therefore*, one can disagree with and be critical of a behavior without having a fear of it."

The first makes more sense. It is *because* one can critically disagree with homosexual behavior without fearing it, that it is unjust to call him "homophobic."

Backtracking: As a rule of thumb, when reading an argument, try finding a conclusion first. The conclusion is what the passage is designed to prove. Then backtrack to find the statements which most obviously support it. These will be the premises.

In a larger argument, such as an article or book, the author will often prove one overarching claim. We can call such an argument a "case," which is a relatively large set of premises converging on a single conclusion called the "thesis statement."

---

[21] http://www.catholic.com/library/gay_marriage.asp

If we can find this main conclusion first, we will then have a better idea of which statements serve as premises for it. Think of the main conclusion as the destination of a journey. One cannot know whether a road is the means to the destination unless one first knows where one is going. Likewise, one cannot decide whether a premise supports a thesis statement unless one first identifies the thesis statement.

7) Diagramming Arguments

Inferential structure: Premises can stand in several different relations to conclusions. We can display these relationships using diagrams, which will help us see the basic structure of an argument. Identifying the inferential structure of an argument is like putting together the pieces of a puzzle, or the parts of an engine, to see the function and connection of each part to the others. In each of the boxes below you will find an argument (in the top row of the box) and the diagram of that argument (in the bottom row). The arrows indicate the relationship between the conclusion and the premises. The statements to which the arrows point are the conclusions; the other statements are the premises.

Independent **premise support:** The simplest structure consists of one premise supporting one conclusion.

Socrates was a valiant soldier, for he fought heroically in the Peloponnesian War.

Socrates was a valiant soldier.
↑
He fought heroically in the Peloponnesian War.

The premise is "independent" because it does not rely on another premise to support the conclusion.

When diagramming arguments, it is not necessary to write out the statements. You may use letters to represent each statement. In this case, we might use 'V' to represent the conclusion "Socrates was a valiant soldier" and 'F' to represent the premise "He fought heroically in the Peloponnesian War." We then diagram the argument as simply:

V
↑
F

The following argument differs from the previous by the addition of one premise.

> Socrates is a great philosopher, for he was the father of moral philosophy. Moreover, he was a master debater.

> Socrates is a great philosopher.
> ↗   ↖
> He was the father of moral philosophy.   He was a master debater.

Here we find two different premises used to support the conclusion. If we use the letter "S" to represent the conclusion (for Socrates), and the letters "F" (father) and "M" (master) to represent the premises, we may diagram the argument this way:

Though two premises are generally better than one, one powerful premise is better than two (or more) weak ones. In this case, had we used *only* the premise "He was the father of moral philosophy" or *only* the premise "He was a master debater," the conclusion would not have been as strong. The addition of yet a third premise would add further support to the conclusion. Let's add the premise "He was committed to truth above reputation" and then represent it with the letter "T" (for truth) so as to get:

S
↗↑↖
F T M

Notice that whether we use one or more premises, each one stands on its own. This means that the degree of support any one premise gives to the conclusion *does not depend* on the other premise(s). Since each premise stands on its own in providing support for the conclusion, they are said to be *independent* of each other.

***Interdependent* premise support:** Some premises *work together* to support the conclusion. Here's a famous example:

> Since all men are mortal and Socrates is a man, it follows that Socrates is mortal.
>
> Socrates is mortal
> ↑
> ↗ ↖
> All men are mortal   Socrates is a man

To see why these premises are interdependent, first consider them as independent premises.

         1   **2**
Socrates is mortal   Socrates is mortal
     ↑   ↑
All men are mortal   Socrates is a man

In example 1, the premise "All men are mortal" does not fully support the conclusion "Socrates is mortal," since it does not, by itself, tell us that Socrates is a man. (Perhaps Socrates is an angel who never dies?) In example 2, the premise "Socrates is a man" likewise fails to support the conclusion on its own weight, since it does not tell us that men are in fact mortal.

If arguments 1 and 2 initially seem to work, this is because we unwittingly supplied missing information. In 1 we assumed that Socrates is a man. In 2 we assumed that all men are mortal. But in neither case was this information stated. Interdependent premise structure avoids this problem. Each of the interdependent premises complements the other by adding what the other lacks.

Technically, almost every premise needs another premise to support a conclusion.[22] Recall the earlier argument which used only one independent premise: "Socrates was a valiant soldier, for he fought heroically in the Peloponnesian War." Even here we are assuming that *whoever fights heroically in the Peloponnesian War is valiant*, an assumption which, if stated, would serve as a second and interdependent premise.

---

[22]The only type of premise that does not need another premise is one containing all the necessary information in itself. For example, from the premise "no men are women" we could infer "no women are men"; no other premise is needed. You will learn about these exceptions in your study of immediate inferences.

From now on, we will use numbers instead of letters to diagram arguments. To do this, simply number each statement as it appears in the flow of the argument. Take the previous example again:

Since all men are mortal and Socrates is a man, it follows that Socrates is mortal.

Number each statement as you read them, placing the number at the beginning of the statement.[23]

1 *Since all men are mortal and* **2** *Socrates is a man, it follows that* **3** *Socrates is mortal.*

Diagram the argument by placing the number that represents the conclusion on top, with the premises below it:

***Stacked* premise support:** Stacked premises are similar to interdependent premises. Both are used to reach the conclusion, but their relationship is not that of interdependence.

If **1** God is just, **2** He must punish sin. Therefore, **3** sinners are lost apart from grace.

---

3 Sinners are lost apart from grace.
↑
2 God must punish sin.
↑
1 God is just.

The diagram shows that the premise "God is just" supports "God must punish sin," which, in turn, supports "Sinners are lost apart from grace."

Notice that, in stacked arguments, one of the premises serves as *both a premise and a conclusion*. The statement "God must punish sin" is a *conclusion* in relation to "God is just," but a *premise* in relation to "Sinners are lost apart from grace."

---

[23] Keep in mind that some arguments—especially longer ones—may contain statements that are not logically relevant to the argument as such. These should not be numbered.

***Complex* premise support:** Any combination of the three previous structures is "complex." The following argument combines independent premise support, interdependent premise support, and stacked premise support. (However, it is not necessary for all three kinds of premise support to be included; two will suffice.)

Since **1** the Bible is inspired, it follows that **2** the Bible is infallible, since **3** whatever is inspired is infallible. Consequently, **4** the Bible must be authoritative.

---

4 The Bible must be authoritative.
↑
2 The Bible is infallible.
↑
↗ ↖
3 Whatever is inspired is infallible.   **1** The Bible is inspired.

8) Character in Argument

The previous lessons described the character *of* argument. We are now addressing character *in* argument, or rather the character of the argu*er*. It's been said that the study of logic, by itself, may create little more than "clever devils." We need to consider why this happens, and how we can avoid this trap in our own lives.

Arguing vs. quarrelling: Many people portray argument in a negative light. When we hear that two people "got into an argument," we tend to assume that they were angry with each other. It would be better, however, to call *that* a "quarrel." In its literal sense, "arguing" is a good thing. It's a form of rational discussion. It involves listening, defining, questioning, and offering reasons for one's beliefs. Quarrelling, on the other hand, is an angry exchange of A saying to B, "I'm right, and you're wrong" and of B saying to A, "No, *I'm* right and you're wrong!"[24] When parents tell their kids, "Don't argue with me," they probably do not mean what they are literally saying. What parents should say is, "Don't quarrel with me." G.K. Chesterton, a well-known Christian thinker, suggested that men quarrel because they do not know how to argue. Even so, a logic course will hardly keep us from quarreling. To the contrary, it can make us all the more quarrelsome.

Argument metaphors of Science and of Struggle: We said that arguing has the twofold aim of proving and persuading. We prove in order to persuade. This difference is hinted at in two metaphors commonly used to describe arguments: the metaphor of science and the metaphor of struggle.

Like the natural sciences, arguing involves discovering and displaying the truth.[25] Consider the emphasized terms below:

- My argument *shows* that the American Revolution was justified.
- His argument *revealed* that she's mistaken.
- A deductive argument *discloses* information contained in the premises.
- The philosopher gave a rational *demonstration* of God's existence.
- I try following the logic wherever it *leads*.
- I *examined* the theory of evolution.
- The trial attorney *uncovered* the defendant's guilt.
- A good debater *sifts the evidence* carefully.

---

[24] For a humorous example of this, see the online video skit called "The Argument Clinic."

[25] In fact, we should probably say that science itself is a form of arguing. This is particularly true in the case of the formulation and testing of hypotheses. One forms a hypothesis on the basis of evidence. In this respect a hypothesis is like a conclusion. One then seeks to confirm the hypothesis using other forms of evidence.

Since we prove in order to persuade, argument is often described as a sort of struggle:[26]

- He never *wins* an argument with him.
- She *demolished* his argument.
- He *attacked* every weak point in my argument.
- His criticisms were right on *target*.
- Your claims are *indefensible*.
- If you use that debate *strategy*, he'll *beat* you.
- He *shot down* all my arguments.

Sources of poor character in argument: The metaphors of struggle help us to understand why people become ugly in argument. Arguing can have the feel of being a *contest*. As with any competition, we prefer not only to win, but even more so not to lose. Friendly competition is fine. But it can easily degenerate into prideful stubbornness.

Moreover, the study of logic might puff up our egos. By learning how to argue, we may get a heightened sense of our intellectual abilities and a growing awareness of other people's weaknesses. We might find ourselves taking pride in our unproved thinking, even to the point of looking down on others.

It is also true that arguing can get very personal very fast. You have probably heard someone say, "Don't take this personally, but I think you're wrong." People say this because they know others get defensive in the face of disagreement. Why do arguments get so personal? *What we believe* cannot be totally disassociated from *who we are.* My beliefs are *my* beliefs. Your beliefs are *your* beliefs. Beliefs are part of who we are. They move us to feel and act as we do. To some extent, therefore, correcting another's belief is correcting *them* as persons.

Cultivating virtuous character: To fight vanity and arrogance, we must "humble ourselves before the Lord" (1 Pet 5). We must bear in mind, first of all, that our inborn intelligence, however great it may be, is not something for which we're ultimately responsible. Though we develop these gifts, even here we find God's grace at work: our desires, our abilities, our circumstances, and even our energy, are all made possible by His kindness toward us. In light of this, we *should* feel humility and gratitude for whatever talents we possess. Moreover, we must see ourselves as the Lord's servants. The study of argument should not be for the sake of serving or magnifying ourselves; it should be directed to helping others understand the truths that matter most.

---

[26] The examples are from *Metaphors We Live By*, by Lakoff and Johnson (p.4)

Pride and arrogance are not only wrong; they are ineffective and self-defeating. If you want to catch a fish, shouting and splashing are not advisable. Likewise, a loud or forceful voice, an angry or agitated spirit, a sarcastic or condescending tone, will only drive your audience away, not only from you, but from your message as well. We should not be surprised when people disregard *what* we say because of *how* we say it. Since we argue in order to persuade, an offensive approach to arguing is self-defeating. The Roman orator, Quintilian, asserted that a rhetorician is best defined as "a good man speaking well." This should be our goal.

Argument as a wholesome and necessary conflict: It is important *not* to infer that arguing should be free of passion or of a desire to win people over. The Apostle Paul said this about himself: "The weapons of our warfare are not of the flesh but have divine power to destroy strongholds. We destroy arguments and every lofty opinion raised against the knowledge of God, and take every thought captive to obey Christ" (2 Cor 10:4-5). Repeatedly throughout the book of Acts we find Paul trying to persuade men of the Gospel. He argued before the Jews at Pisidion Antioch (13:16-47), Iconium (14:1-3), and Antioch (15:2). He argued before the Gentiles at Lystra (14:15-17). He spoke "in such a manner that a great multitude believed" (14:1). Paul regularly sought to give a "defense" of the Gospel (26:1). This was his habit: "And according to Paul's custom, he went to them and for three Sabbaths reasoned with them from the Scriptures, explaining and giving evidence that 'This Jesus who I proclaim to you is the Christ'….And some of them were persuaded" (Acts 17:2-4).

Nor was Paul a disinterested thinker. He was deeply invested in his arguments. In Acts 26:27-29 we find Paul arguing with Agrippa, the king of the Jews, who responded to Paul with a question: "In a short time you will persuade me to become a Christian?" Paul replied, "I would wish to God, that whether in a short or long time, not only you, but also all who hear me this day, might become such as I am, except for these chains" (Acts 26:27-29). Arguing was no cool, calm, academic enterprise for him. It was an issue of eternal significance.

We should also note that, even when there is no clash of egos, argument still has the potential to get emotionally charged. When the Christian statesman, William Wilberforce, argued for the abolition of the slave trade, he was fueled by a passion for justice and the well-being of the African people, not by the love of applause or an inflated sense of his importance. Winning the argument was, literally, a matter of life and death. Wilberforce's debate was a conflict between *people*, not merely between abstract "positions." We might even go a step further and suggest that this was a conflict between good men and bad men. Many advocates of the slave trade knew how cruel and dehumanizing this institution was, but they were more concerned about money than men. The same is true of some abortion rights advocates today, who are more concerned to uphold a faulty ideal of personal liberty than the lives and rights of the preborn. This is not merely a clash of abstract and impersonal ideas; it is a clash of *wills*, a clash of *affections*; it is a contest between people who love the light and people who hate it, or, what is the same thing, between those who hate the darkness and those who love it (John 3).

This makes it all the more important to cultivate good character in argument. We'd do well to take Paul's exhortation to heart:

Colossians 4:5-6: Walk in wisdom toward outsiders, making the best use of the time. Let your speech always be gracious, seasoned with salt, so that you may know how you ought to answer each person.

2 Tim 2:22: So flee youthful passions and pursue righteousness, faith, love, and peace, along with those who call on the Lord from a pure heart. Have nothing to do with foolish, ignorant controversies; you know that they breed quarrels. And the Lord's servant must not be quarrelsome but kind to everyone, able to teach, patiently enduring evil, correcting his opponents with gentleness. God may perhaps grant them repentance leading to knowledge of the truth…

9) Sophistry (i) Its Origins and Nature

Realpolitik: A group of policy-makers on National Public Radio were discussing the 2012 presidential election. A month out from the election, the Republican candidate's polls were slipping fast. The panelists were debating what he needed to do to win. One of them suggested that he should "educate" the people about his policies. Another participant objected that this would have precisely the opposite effect. He insisted that the candidate should win people over *first*, and educate them only after he made it into office. The man claimed that this is how politics "actually works." This attitude is what we call *realpolitik*. According to the *Encyclopedia Britannica*, realpolitik is:

> "…politics based on practical objectives rather than on ideals. The word does not mean "real" in the English sense but rather connotes "things"—hence a politics of adaptation to things as they are. Realpolitik thus suggests a pragmatic, no-nonsense view and a disregard for ethical considerations. In diplomacy it is often associated with relentless, though realistic, pursuit of the national interest."

Rhetoric as the art of public persuasion: Realpolitik goes back to ancient times and to Greece above all. The Athenian citizens of the fifth century were members of a direct democracy. Unlike America, where citizens participate indirectly through elected representatives, the Athenians personally proposed, debated, and voted on their laws. In this context, the ability to persuade others was invaluable. For Athenians, the power of persuasion was first and foremost a political power. For them, the study of rhetoric focused specifically on political oratory. The Greek term *rhetorician* had the more restricted meaning of one who spoke to an assembly (called an *ekklesia*) of the voting citizens within the state (called a *polis*, or 'city-state'). Rhetoric was not simply the study of how to speak. (After all, mothers teach toddlers how to speak.) Nor was rhetorical ability merely the ability to "communicate information." (A math teacher informs his student, but he is not a rhetorician per se.) In Greece, a rhetorician was a *political speaker*.

Plato's worries about rhetoric: There are several features of public speaking that concerned Plato. First, the rhetorician spoke to a large audience, many of whom were uneducated, uncritical, and gullible. Secondly, the rhetorician spoke about very complex and controversial matters (e.g., whether to wage war). Evaluating these matters required a strong grasp of ethics, law, politics, economics, history, and psychology, which most citizens did not possess. Finally, the rhetorician was expected to persuade his audience in a relatively brief time (before the water clock ran out). In sum, the rhetorician was out to persuade the uneducated masses about complex topics in a short period of time.

For Plato, this was a recipe for disaster. He knew that, under these constraints, the most a rhetorician could hope to do was *persuade* people to *believe* a claim; he could not actually *prove* the claim. Most issues require painstaking research and critical thinking, as well as discussion and debate with others, especially with experts on the subject. Hopefully, a good rhetorician will persuade people of *true* beliefs. But how are people in the audience to *know* when the speaker's assertions are true? For even *false* propositions can *appear* to be true when spoken persuasively. How can the audience secure itself against believing error? As long as men do not know how to distinguish truth from the mere appearance of truth, there is always the risk of believing falsehoods.

This is especially disconcerting when the rhetorician is *trying* to deceive his audience. Athens was filled with talented but unprincipled "demagogues" (lit. "one who speaks to the people"). Plato knew that Athens lost the war due to demagogues. Socrates himself lost his life. Not even Socrates' brilliant speech seemed capable of overcoming these hurdles. But the biggest problem of all was the sophists.

Sophists: The sophists (lit. "wise men") were intellectuals who instructed aspiring politicians in the art of persuasion. The sophists knew that the ability to prove a claim is unnecessary if one can persuade people anyway. (Remember: one can prove without persuading or persuade without proving.) Sophists taught that the rhetorician should resort to *psychological manipulation* rather than rational demonstration. Like the panelist in the NPR conversation mentioned above, the sophists taught that one should concentrate on persuasion rather than proof. Win people first, educate them later (if necessary). It is no coincidence that some of these sophists were atheists and immoralists, who openly rejected the existence of moral law. For them, the power of rhetoric was morally unconstrained. It was a tool to be used to get power and keep it. This is realpolitik.

Sophisms: Sophists made an art of verbal manipulation. They formed arguments to persuade audiences of propositions without the support of good reasons. These arguments are known as "sophisms" or "fallacies" (from *fallacia*, lit. "trick", "deceit", "fraud"). We will define a fallacy as *a bad argument that appears to be good*.

Aristotle labored to combat the sophists. He wrote an entire volume entitled *Sophistical Refutations*, which enumerated some of the more common sophisms. Aristotle's list has undergone considerable expansion over the centuries.

The next several lessons introduce some of the simplest and most common sophisms. Before turning to these, it's worth noting that all of us use fallacious arguments from time to time, but not necessarily because we're trying to manipulate or deceive people. It's often because we are ill-equipped to detect them in our own reasoning. This is why we must learn to identify fallacies. But knowing what they are does not automatically prevent us from using them; we must also make a conscientious attempt to avoid them. Like so many other areas of life, the principles of logical thinking must be practiced.

10) Sophistry (ii) *Ad Hominem* Fallacies

The *ad hominem* (lit. "to the man") fallacy aims to discredit an argument by criticizing its argu*er*. This tactic may attack someone directly, by targeting a characteristic of the person himself, or indirectly, by focusing on a circumstance in his life. We can divide them as follows:

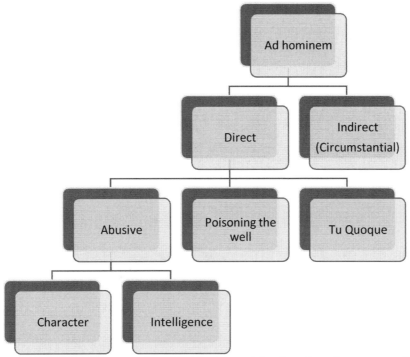

Direct attacks: Direct attacks divide into (1) *abusive*, i.e., appealing to defects in one's intelligence or character; (2) *poisoning the well*, i.e., appealing to one's alleged prejudice or ulterior motive; and (3) *tu quoque*, i.e., appealing to inconsistencies between one's words and one's actions.

Abusing intelligence: It may be tempting to think that the following statement is reasonable: "I would not place much trust in what Joe says; he is not the sharpest knife in the drawer." If an audience can be persuaded that someone is not intelligent or educated enough to be taken seriously, they'll be more likely to dismiss the person's argument. Some examples:

- "C'mon! No *rational* person could think such a thing!"
- "You *obviously* have not studied logic."
- "A child wouldn't have made *that* mistake!"
- "That's the biggest bunch of *nonsense* I've ever heard."

It is true that people resort to really bad arguments at times. Yet it is neither necessary nor helpful to insult them. Jesus taught us to do unto others as we would have others do unto us. We all want to be treated with consideration and respect. When we're in error, we desire to be graciously corrected. Moreover, we should not make the already difficult task of persuading people any harder than it needs to be. Nor is there any *logical value* in calling people names; this does not exactly constitute "evidence."

Abusing character: As with intelligence, so with moral character—it is tempting to think that one's character is logically relevant to his argument. This is why people use arguments such as this: "Joe's a chauvinist pig for thinking that women should not serve in the military." But the quality of one's *character* does not necessarily weaken (or strengthen) the quality of one's *arguments*. Suppose an axe-murderer argued this:

1) If God does not exist, murder is not morally wrong.
2) God does not exist.
3) Therefore, murder is not morally wrong.

Even though premise 2 is false, the argument makes sense; that is, the conclusion follows the premises. The fact that a murderer is making the argument does not make it fallacious. On the other hand, suppose Billy Graham, a model of moral integrity, reasoned this way:

1) If I preach the gospel, then God exists.
2) I preach the gospel.
3) Therefore, God exists.

This would be a really bad argument even if it came from a really good man.

Poisoning the well: Another ad hominem tactic is to discredit one's assertion on the ground that the asserter is *biased* (i.e., he *wants* the claim to be true). His bias is supposed to be the sole cause of his assertion, rather than evidence and solid reasoning. For example:

"He defends the morality of hunting only because he is a Texan."

Maybe he has good reasons for believing that hunting is morally permissible. Poisoning the well is sometimes done so as to suggest that biases always blind people from seeing facts correctly.

"Joe is a scientist, but he is also a Christian. Therefore, his theological bias will prevent him from seeing scientific truth."

Since the person (i.e., the "well") is "poisoned" by his bias or ulterior motive, it supposedly follows that his argument *itself* is contaminated. Suppose a pharmaceutical company is under fire for selling an anti-depressant, Escapenex, which some suspect causes bleeding from the ears. Realistically, owners of the company will be biased against evidence supporting this accusation and biased toward any evidence that refutes it. It is therefore tempting for us to dismiss the company's logical defense of Escapenex. The reality, however, is that their arguments might be very good. Their bias does not imply that their arguments are false or unreasonable. This is because the truth-value of one's claim is logically independent of one's bias. A bias *can* obscure our thinking, but it does not *necessarily* do so. For example, a scientist hoping for result x in his research is not necessarily unable to see result not-x, if and when that occurs. Furthermore, since *everyone* has biases of some sort, this criticism (if true) would make the search for truth impossible.

Tu Quoque (lit. "you're another"): It is very tempting to reject the position of someone who does not "practice what he preaches." For example:

Joe: "Smoking is bad for your health."
Bob: "Well, you smoke too!"

This fallacy is often expressed by saying, "Look who's talking!" Suppose that Bob, a professing Christian, is trying to persuade Joe of the Christian faith using good arguments. However, Bob himself fails to act as a Christian. Understandably, Joe will be tempted to dismiss these arguments. Logically speaking, though, hypocrisy does not disprove the truth-value of one's claims or the force of one's arguments, though it *will* make the person himself less persuasive.

Indirect attacks—i.e., circumstantial: This fallacy is committed when one attempts to undermine another's claim in light of some unsavory circumstance in one's life. In trying to undermine Jesus' claims, the religious leaders of his day criticized His hometown (Nazareth), as well as the people with whom He associated (tax collectors), neither of which is logically relevant to the truth-value of His claims.

Are there legitimate uses of *ad hominem*? One's intelligence and moral character are relevant in a court of law, where attorneys try discrediting expert or eye-witness testimony. True, disqualifying a witness does not *logically* make their testimony *false* (since a chronic liar might still tell the truth); but it is a sound policy where the innocent are in jeopardy of being found guilty.

11) Sophistry (iii) *Ad Populum* Fallacies

Are reason and emotion at odds? We often form beliefs and make decisions on the basis of how we *feel*. This explains why rhetoricians use the *ad populum* fallacy. The fallacy of *ad populum* (lit. "to the people") is the rhetorical trick of appealing to people's emotions *rather than* logically relevant evidence.[27] The *ad populum* fallacy occurs when persuasion is based on an emotional reaction *in place of* solid evidence and well-reasoned argument.

Note, however, that there is a difference between an *emotional argument* (which is often valuable) and an *argument based on emotion* (which should be avoided). The mere presence of emotion in an argument is not fallacious. It is possible to be both passionate and logical when defending one's position. The Old Testament prophets used strong emotive language, but they were not simply pulling the emotional strings of the people. Their method was to move the Israelites *by means of reasoned evidence* concerning the nation's rebellion against God. They did not rest their conclusions on emotion *alone*; they were not *bypassing* reason in the attempt to move the hearts of their audience. To immunize ourselves to the *ad populum* fallacy, we should not try to suppress our emotions, but to subject them to truth and logic.

On the other hand, there is great wisdom in practicing emotional restraint. Staying calm enhances our ability to concentrate and think clearly. It's better to err on the side of caution here. As a rule of thumb, it's advisable to save the passion for public speeches, while staying cool during discussion and debates.

There are as many *ad populum* fallacies as there are emotions. We will address three of them: fear, pity, and anger.

Appeal to fear (*ad baculum*, lit. "to the stick"): A biology professor said something like this: "Let it be known at the outset of this class that I will not tolerate arguments for Intelligent Design. Evolution is an established fact and I will not allow anyone to waste our time arguing otherwise." Needless to say, the critical students determined then and there to keep silent.

The appeal to fear has been called "the logic of kings." It is the resort to coercion as a means of persuasion. The suppression of beliefs in the Middle Ages is a case in point. Authorities provided their subjects with the following premise: "If you teach heretical beliefs, you will burn at the stake." Is this logical? Perhaps, if you're the king! Physical threats are only one type of fear-tactic. An employer might say to his

---

[27] Why call it *ad populum* rather than *ad passiones* ("to the passions")? Perhaps it is because the thinking of "the people" (pejoratively referred to as the "masses" or "herd") is often blinded by their passions.

employee, "I suggest that if you want to keep your job, you better start seeing things my way." The problem with *ad baculum* is the fact that one can fight an idea only with another idea. If I believe that X is the case, nothing will alter my stance except the belief that X is not the case, which should come from a good argument, not the edge of a sword.

Appeal to pity (*ad misericordiam*): A news segment on hand-gun regulation portrayed a distraught inner-city woman who lost her child to gun violence. In her agony, she railed against the National Rifle Association for supporting gun-rights. Nothing she said would have scored points in a formal debate; there was no evidence, no use of definitions, no clear or cogent reasoning. Even so, it is hard not to *feel* like siding with her in this instance. Likewise, we are all moved by commercials with starving children in Third World countries. The presumption of the organizations is that our pity will move us to dig deep into our pockets. The reality is that we *should* feel pity for these children.

So what's the fallacy? The feeling of pity, *by itself*, is not a rational basis for regulating guns or contributing to a particular charity. In the latter case, we must make several important calculations: What will be done with the money? How much of the money will go to helping the children? Will the children be taught Christian values or secular values? Do I have enough money right now, or am I racked by my own personal hospital bills or college debt? These considerations reveal that we should never act upon emotions *alone*.

Politicians and lawyers supply us with endless *ad misericordiam* fallacies. Politicians get federal funding for the poor by painting a pathetic picture of their conditions. But federally funded programs can become the enemy of the poor by encouraging dependency on government hand-outs, so as to trap them in poverty. Whether we should take pity on the poor is not the question. Nor is there any room for debating the need to fight poverty. But the end does not always justify the means. We must use informed and well-reasoned arguments, under the guidance of Scripture, to determine the most ethical and effective means of helping them.

The danger of basing our beliefs and actions upon feelings of pity is perhaps nowhere clearer than in a courtroom. We can only imagine how many guilty men have escaped justice because of the jury's pitying defendants (e.g., "He had such a difficult childhood!"). But in this context, the jury should be concerned with only one question: "Did he do it?" If so, they should convict him; if not, they should acquit him.

Appeal to anger (*ad iram*): It is bad enough when a jury *frees guilty men* on the basis of pity; it is far worse when they *condemn innocent men* on the basis of *anger*. What the appeal to pity is for the defense attorney, the appeal to anger is for the prosecutor. Righteous indignation is a forceful motive. It's the emotion of choice among leaders of political revolutions.

> "It's time to rise up against the tyranny of the government! Our rights have been trampled upon; we're overtaxed; we're over-policed; they run our lives and then make us pay for their service! We must stop these bloodsuckers!"

Adolf Hitler built an empire on this sort of fiery rhetoric. When we're persuaded that an act is unjust, there's a danger that we'll act more from heat than light. This is because our sense of justice does not always align with truth. False condemnation of others is way too easy at times.

12) Sophistry (iv) Fallacies of Distraction

A common sophistic tactic is to direct the attention of one's audience from the real issue or point of dispute. There are two fallacies under this category: (1) the *red herring* fallacy, where one essentially "changes the subject" midcourse, usually when unable to shoulder the force of an opposing argument; and (2) the *straw man* fallacy, which attacks a misrepresentation of an opposing view.

Red herring: Imagine a debate in which one person says that the U.S.' decision to bomb Japan was unjustified. His opponent, Mr. Red, replies:

> "I disagree. WWII was a terrible conflict. The war had gone on for many years and millions of soldiers were dying. Adolf Hitler was a tyrant needing to be stopped. His extermination of the Jews was a crime against humanity."

This might seem to be a relevant reply, since Germany and Japan were allies in WWII, but it shifts the focus from the issue at hand.

Red herrings are often inconspicuous. Calling people names (*ad hominem*) and appealing to their emotions (*ad populum*) are not exactly subtle. Red herrings, on the other hand, are sneaky. It is difficult to detect when someone is going off trail. An effective red herring will shift our focus away from the point of dispute without our noticing. Often times the new issue bears a close similarity to the original one.

The subtlety of red herrings, and the difficulty of detecting them, explains the name of the fallacy. It is borrowed from the world of hunting. When teaching foxhounds to track the scent of a fox, trainers try tricking the dog by dragging a bag of pungent fish (usually red herring) across the fox's trail. The trainer is trying to teach the dog to stay on the real trail in spite of the temptation (offered by the red herring) to veer off it. The same is true in the world of argument, where we're too easily tempted off the logical track in a debate. Like a well-trained dog, we must learn to detect where an argument veers off trail, by keeping in mind the opposing line of thought. We must fix in our minds on the exact point of dispute and then lock onto it. We must memorize the scent, as it were.

The red herring provides the debater with an effective means of not admitting defeat. As with competitive sports, where people want to win, so too in argument—people don't want to lose. This means they will sometimes resort to less than honorable ways of winning. The red herring is one of the most common of these tactics. To see how, suppose you are debating an atheist over God's existence. You say the world is obviously designed. He notes that the world is filled with brokenness and suffering, which is not what one would expect if designed by a good and wise God. You are not sure how to rebut this, so you say something like, "But what about all the people who believe in God?" This does not address the atheist's point about evil, but it might succeed in getting him off topic.

Here is an example of a subtler red herring. A well-known biochemist, Michael Behe, was arguing before a crowd of professors and students at Princeton. He argued that at least some aspects of the world reveal evidence of design, and that this should lead us to believe in a designer. During the Q&A period, a man in the crowd objected to Behe's reasoning. The critic tried refuting it with this argument (and I paraphrase):

> Dr. Behe, your argument is seriously flawed. For since you argue that a complex being implies the existence of a designer, and because the designer must itself be a complex being, it follows that *the designer must also have been designed*. But this means that designer's designer, who must also be complex, was likewise designed; and on and on it goes. You are thus left with an infinite number of designers. That, of course, doesn't explain anything.

Can you detect where he went off trail? Recall the point of dispute, namely, that there *is* design in the world. The critic's argument needs to disprove Behe's claim that design does *in fact* exist in the world. But the objection went completely off course. Whether there exists an infinite number of designers is irrelevant to whether there is design in the world. Had Behe replied by trying to prove that an infinite series of designers was not necessary, he would have been led off the trail by the objection.

Straw man: We commit this fallacy when we refute a misrepresentation of someone's actual position or, perhaps, a position they do not even remotely hold. Critics of the early church argued this:

> "Christianity is irrational and immoral, because the New Testament teaches that Christians are to eat the literal body and blood of Christ when they take communion."

This is a caricature of Jesus' teachings and of Christian belief and practice. Why call it a straw man? Just as a farmer convinces crows that his scarecrow is a real farmer, so the arguer convinces his audience that the refuted argument is the opponent's real argument, when in fact it's not; it's only a "straw" version of it.

Suppose professor Enosent drew conclusion x from premises a and b, and that professor Straugh wants to undermine Enosent's belief in x. But instead of attacking Prof. Enosent's actual premises, a and b, professor Straugh persuades his class that Enosent holds to x because of c and d, which are obviously false or unreasonable. By refuting *those* premises, he persuades his class that Enosent is wrong. This is a straw man fallacy.

A straw man might also be a *technical* misrepresentation of an opponent's view, as when definitions and subtle distinctions are missed, ignored, or misconstrued. In theology, for example, some reject what they imagine to be the Calvinistic doctrine of predestination, because they think Calvinism teaches that people are not free agents who are ultimately responsible for their actions. This is a straw man. Though Calvinists believe that God plans human history, they have sought to explain how this is consistent with human freedom and responsibility, which they wholeheartedly affirm. Non-Calvinists may disagree with these explanations, but they should at least recognize that Calvinists do not *deny* freedom or responsibility.

We should be careful before charging someone with the straw man fallacy. It's very easy to misunderstand others. Misrepresentations often result from a failure to carefully understand another's position, but this is not always the case. Maybe the person was a responsible thinker who took time to understand the opposing side but honestly failed to grasp it. Maybe *we* are at fault. Perhaps we did not make our claims clear enough. They may be accurately representing our misrepresentation of ourselves!

13) The Three Tests for Evaluating Arguments

If a fallacy is a bad argument that *appears* to be good, how do we determine when an argument *really is* good or bad? Well, there is a sense in which this entire book attempts to answer that seemingly simple question. For now, however, we can simplify the answer by noting three features that every good argument has in common. The remainder of this book will then explore each of these features.

To "evaluate" an argument is to determine whether it is *good* or *bad*. Every argument will have three sides. These are (1) the *evidential* side, pertaining to the truth-value of the premises; (2) the *inferential* side, pertaining to whether the conclusion follows the premises; and (3) the *semantic* side, pertaining to the meaning of the argument's terms. We will evaluate arguments according to this threefold test, which we can formulate as questions:

1) The Evidential Question = *Are the premises true?*
2) The Inferential Question = *Does the conclusion follow?*
3) The Semantic Question = *What do the terms mean?*

Sometimes an argument passes the Evidential Test while failing the Inferential Test. In some cases we may agree that the premises of an argument are true, and yet deny that the conclusion follows:

Premise: Generally speaking, men are physically stronger than women.
Conclusion: Therefore, women should not be allowed in the military.

Few would dispute the first premise. But that by itself doesn't make the conclusion follow. It's hard to see why a woman's relative weakness should keep her from serving in the military. Even if she shouldn't fight in frontline combat, there are other roles that don't involve carrying heavy gear or engaging in hand-to-hand combat.

Sometimes an argument passes the Inferential Test while failing the Evidential Test. In other cases we may agree that that conclusion follows and yet disagree that the premises are true.

Premise: Only men are capable of shooting guns.
Conclusion: Therefore, women should not be military snipers.

The conclusion follows the premise. For *if* it's true that women cannot shoot guns, they should not serve as military snipers. But the premise, of course, is false.

How the Semantic Test differs from the previous two tests: To determine whether a premise is true or whether a conclusion follows, it is necessary to first understand what the statements in an argument *mean*. The terms in the following argument, for instance, are *not clear enough* to apply the other two tests.

Premise: Young well-to-do white people tend to be liberal.
Conclusion: So most college students probably vote democratic.

Virtually every term in the premise is indefinite. How young is "young"? (Teens? Twenties? Both?) Is "well-to-do" an economic category or also a cultural category? How well is "well"? How white is "white"? Are we to picture people of English or Scandinavian descent, or also Portuguese and Russian descent? Is this a racial category, an ethnic one, or a cultural one? (This is an impractical category in a country as mixed as ours.) What is meant by "liberal"? (A political liberal? A social liberal? A moral liberal? A socialist? And it's not exactly clear what *those* terms mean either.) What does "tend" mean? Does it mean that these people have a faint inclination to be liberal but not quite a commitment? Does it mean most of them? If the latter, does it mean a little over 50% or more like 70%? Questions like these are easily multiplied.

The three questions are distinct but interconnected: The Semantic Test relates *only* to the meaning of the terms. (It is *not* asking whether any of the premises are true or whether the conclusion follows.)

The Inferential Test pertains *only* to whether the *conclusion follows* the premises. (It is *not* asking what the terms mean or whether the premises are true, though the Inferential Test is affected by one's answers to the other two questions.)

The Evidential Test pertains *only* to whether the *premises are true*. (It is *not* asking whether the conclusion follows or what the terms mean, though it is shaped by the other two considerations.)

As already noted, these three tests will structure the rest of the book. To determine whether the premises are true requires an appeal to evidence, which we'll explore in Unit 4 ("The Evidential Test"). But even if the premises are true, the argument is still bad if the conclusion doesn't follow. We must therefore determine whether and how the conclusion follows. This will be our focus in Unit 3 ("The Inferential Test"). But we cannot answer either of these questions unless we know what the terms in the argument mean. I would suggest that this is the fundamental issue in most real-life arguments. This is why we will first turn our attention to the study of meaning and definition in Unit 2 ("The Semantic Test").

Unit II:
The Semantic Side of Argument

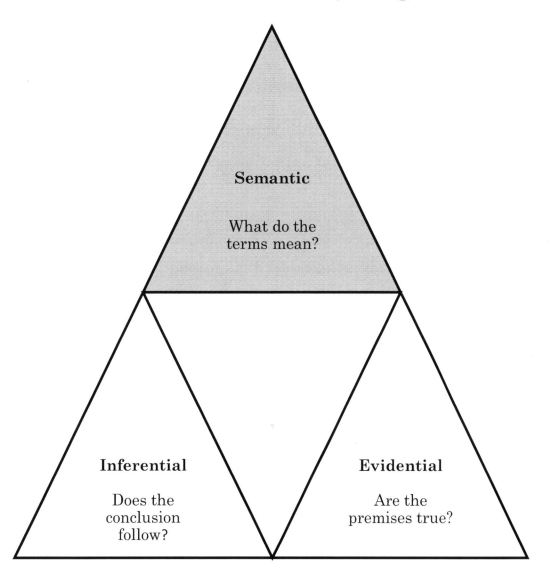

14) The Power of Words: Lessons from *1984*

In lessons 2 and 3 we critiqued slogans such as "That's not my truth" and "That's just your opinion" and "Don't impose your belief on me." If these slogans are so problematic, why do people keep using them? It's partly because they do not stop to think about what they are saying. They are not critically reflecting on the *meaning* of their *words*. As you will learn, this is arguably the most essential component of thinking well. This will be our focus in Unit 2, entitled "The Semantic Side of Argument." According to the Online Etymology Dictionary, the word "semantic" comes from the classical Greek *semantikos* (lit. "significant"), which derives from a verb that means "to show by sign, signify, point out, or indicate." In Unit 2 we will explore the nature of words, different forms of meaning, and a variety of methods for defining terms. But before we do, let's spend some time thinking about the *power* of words. Hopefully this will inspire you to master the lessons of Unit 2.

1984: In the first chapter of George Orwell's novel *1984*, he describes the futuristic world of Oceania, controlled not so much by the military or the police, but by *language*—by words, by slogans, by socially shared habits of speaking impressed upon the citizenry. The novel explores the tremendous power of words in shaping human thought and behavior.[28] It also raises a question: To control a *society*, is it enough to control its *speech*?

"The Ministry of Truth": The most powerful institution in Oceania is the "Ministry of Truth," which regulates "news, entertainment, education, and the fine arts." It would be more accurately named the Ministry of *Lies* or of *Mind Control* or of *Behavioral Manipulation*. In Oceania, truth is not the ultimate value, and so the society is not structured to pursue it and discover it. The chief end is to conform citizens to the "Party Line," to the values and vision of those in power. Most citizens do in fact follow them, since they've been brainwashed by news outlets, the entertainment industry, the educational system, and the academies and museums of the fine arts, all of which are controlled by the Ministry of Truth.

---

[28]Here's an interesting question: Do we *think* the way we do because we *speak* the way we do, or do we speak the way we do because we think the way we do? Philosophers like Wittgenstein have argued that our thoughts are essentially our words. He argued against the philosopher St. Augustine. While the former's *Philosophical Investigations* is a brilliant work, I don't think it ultimately escapes the Augustinian and Medieval distinction between words, thoughts, and things, which we will study in the next chapter.

"Newspeak": Though Orwell stresses the power of words to shape thought, he also recognizes the role of thought in shaping words. The Party leaders start with a vision of their ideal society and then create a new vocabulary and way of speaking to cause people to think and behave that way. The Ministry of Truth implements this "Newspeak" in schools, shows, and so forth, to trick everyone into thinking that they are *freely choosing* their beliefs and lifestyles.

Newspeak is at odds with the *old* language, or Oldspeak, used to express the ideas and beliefs of the past. To change the society, the Ministry must constantly repeat and praise the use of Newspeak, and to erase, censor, discourage, and even punish the use of Oldspeak. One of the lexicographers boasts,

> "By 2050—earlier, probably—all real knowledge of Oldspeak will have disappeared. The whole literature of the past will have been destroyed. Chaucer, Shakespeare, Milton, Byron—they'll exist only in Newspeak versions, not merely changed into something different, but actually changed into something contradictory to what they use to be."

For example, in Oldspeak words like "individual," "individuality," or "individualism" had the positive meaning of *thinking for oneself* or of *not mindlessly going along with the flow*. To discourage this dangerous mindset, the Party deletes these words and replaces them with new words possessing negative meaning. In this case they invent the negative word "ownlife," which means something like the *unacceptable habit of spending time by yourself*. Those suspected of ownlife are accordingly harassed.

"Thought Crimes" & "Thought Police": As the name makes plain, "thought crime" occurs in the mind, in the way one interprets the world and in one's attitude toward the world. It is not necessary to *do* anything to anyone (e.g., lie or steal or kill); it's only necessary to think in an undesirable way about someone. Thought crime, says Orwell, is "the essential crime that contained all others in itself." The crime consists of thinking in a manner contrary to the Party's established "orthodoxy" (lit. "right opinion").

In Oceania, it is not even necessary to openly voice one's thought crimes. For thought crimes can also be revealed by means of "facecrimes," where one's facial expressions betray their unspoken beliefs. It is for the "thought police" to determine this.

Ideally, Newspeak will reduce the burden on the thought police, by shrinking the citizens' vocabulary to the point that there is very little thinking left for them to be wrong about! As one of them says, "Don't you see that the whole aim of

Newspeak is to narrow the range of thought? In the end we shall make thought crime literally impossible, because there will be no words in which to express it."

"Reality Control" & "The Mutability of the Past": To maintain control over citizens' minds, the leaders of Oceania must also control the flow of information. Orwell calls this "reality control." For "if one is to rule, and to continue ruling, one must be able to dislocate the sense of reality."

To this end, the Party's top priority is to control the teaching of *history*. By reading *actual* history, citizens will discover that the beliefs and practices of past generations were totally at odds with their own. The veil of ignorance will be lifted and the Party's lies exposed. To prevent this from happening, the Party must suppress or destroy writings from the past (dump them down "the memory hole") and then *rewrite* History to conform to the Party's preferred narrative. In effect, the Party will "alter the past." The logic of this policy is explained this way: "Who controls the past controls the future: who controls the present controls the past." As Orwell says, "if all records told the same tale—then the lie passed into history and became truth." Of course, the past itself is not "mutable"; it's impossible to undo what has been said or done; but it *is* possible to change the next generation's *beliefs* about the past. It's simply a matter of deleting or whitewashing what happened, or of adding in things that did not happen. This is called revisionist history.

"Swallowers of Slogans": A prominent form of newspeak is what Orwell calls "slogans." A slogan can be a single word or a phrase or statement that is pithy, catchy, and memorable. Slogans are effective ways of implanting ideas in unthinking people. The most thoughtless citizens of Oceania are said to be "swallowers of slogans."

A well phrased and thoroughly repeated slogan can even override common sense. For example, virtually everyone (outside of places like Oceania) recognizes that men and women are very different. But the Party of Oceania manages to blur or erase this distinction by forcing it citizens to address each other with the gender-neutral term "comrade."

Three slogans are of particular importance to the Party, and all of them serve to redefine reality—"War is peace" / "Freedom is slavery" / "Ignorance is strength." When citizens are conditioned from childhood to *say* such things, and to say them *repeatedly*, and to *hear* others say them repeatedly, they gradually begin to believe them and to live them. These beliefs can even become obviously "true" to them.

Orwell does not believe that "reality control" can erase reality. Even the most indoctrinated citizens remain human beings possessed of reason. They continue living a real world that is constantly bumping into them. Reality limits what they can believe and how they can live. This means that they cannot fully and consistently believe, or live out, the lies they are taught. For example, though men are being taught to view women as simply "comrades," Orwell says that men continue to "instinctively" find themselves referring to them with female designations, such as "Mrs." Some facts are just too natural and evident to totally suppress or reinterpret. This leads to the next point.

"Doublethink": There remains an important sense in which the citizens *believe* what they do not believe. Orwell calls this "doublethink," which means:

> "To know and not to know, to be conscious of complete truthfulness while telling carefully constructed lies, to hold simultaneously two opinions which cancelled out, knowing them to be contradictory and believing in both of them, to use logic against logic, to repudiate morality while laying claim to it…"

The slogan "War is peace" is a contradiction in terms. When analyzed, it winds up meaning "Not peace is peace." Humans probably cannot self-consciously believe in contradictory claims at the same time. But we *can* believe in contradictory claims *for as long as* we are *not thinking about* them. To enable people to "swallow" such slogans, they must be kept from thinking critically (No "ownlife" allowed!). And since *everyone* is being taught to say and believe that "War is peace," believing it becomes much easier. People have a powerful impulse to believe what they think everyone else believes; they tend to think that there must be something right about it. (How can so many people be wrong?) Plus, there's also this little thing called "peer pressure," or what the Bible calls "fear of man." Keep in mind, as well, that citizens in Oceania have been taught these slogans from *childhood*, back when their minds were least critical and most susceptible to believing nonsense. People normalized in nonsense are least likely to see it as such. This is why the Ministry of Truth is so concerned with *controlling childhood education*, be it their "textbooks" and "spelling books" or their "plays" and "telescreen programs."

"Orthodoxy is Unconsciousness": Much of Newspeak involves reworking or redefining the ideas used in Oldspeak. For example, "freedom" was one of the noblest and most essential words in Oldspeak. The Newspeak slogan "Freedom is slavery" is obviously meant to bias citizens against the word, by making it appear as positively bad. But a more effective strategy will be to rid society of dangerous words like "freedom" altogether. If the Party plays its cards right, "Even the literature of the Party will change. Even the slogans will change. How could you have a slogan like "freedom is slavery" *when the concept of freedom has been abolished?*" (Emphasis added.)

Eventually, "The whole climate of thought will be different. In fact, there will be no thought, as we understand it now. Orthodoxy means not thinking – not needing to think. Orthodoxy is unconsciousness." When the Party's "orthodox" language and corresponding belief system is fully worked out, it will strangle reason and freedom of thought to death. Logical thinking will almost disappear.

This lesson raises some interesting questions: Could Oceania become a reality? Can you think of where in history something this has already occurred? Are there any similarities between Oceania and present-day America? What must Americans do to avoid becoming Oceania? As far as you are concerned, the study of semantics will play an important role in protecting yourself against the Newspeak of our own day, whatever that may look like.

The semantic side of argument is so crucial, in fact, that Cicero said, "Every rational discussion of anything whatsoever should begin with a definition in order to make clear the subject of dispute."[29] We cannot pronounce an argument "good" or "bad" unless we first *understand* it. This is why the semantic test is so critical. We often cannot apply the inferential and evidential tests *until we fix the meaning* of the argument by means of the semantic test. This will become clear as you think through the following lessons.

---

[29] Cited in *Elements of Argument: A Text and Reader*, by Annette T. Rottenberg, p.57

15) Words, Thoughts, and Things

The nature of signs: A man encounters this street sign while driving down the road and then immediately slows down. He recognizes that this symbol indicates that a curvy road lies ahead. Though he does not yet see the curved road, he *infers* that it exists because of the sign. He understands that the sign is *pointing beyond itself* to some other fact. That is what a sign *is*. As Augustine says, "a sign is anything which, over and above the impression it makes on the senses, causes something else to come into the mind as a consequence of itself."[30] He noted that "A sign is what shows both itself to the sense and something else besides itself to the mind"[31]

Intentional and unintentional signs: Intentional signs are purposeful ways of signifying something to someone else. Blowing a kiss signifies an affectionate farewell. Shaking our heads from side to side means "No." An unintentional sign is something that *just happens* to signify something else. Smoke signifies fire. Dark clouds signify the likelihood of rain. Deer tracks by a riverbed signify the presence of deer. The migration of birds signifies a change in the season. Runny noses signify allergies, a cold, or flu. Heavy eyelids signify tiredness. All these things have significance—they signify something—though their significance is not intentional (e.g., deer do not leave tracks *in order* for us to infer their presence).

Words are intentional signs: When Paul Revere cried out, "The British are coming!" he used *words* to intentionally signify that the British soldiers were marching on the town of Concord. Like smiling, waving one's hand, or nodding one's head, words are a sort of intentional sign,[32] though a far more complex and informative type of sign. According to Augustine, words serve "to bring forth and get across to the mind of another what is going on in the mind of the one who gives the sign."[33] In signifying, words "establish an understanding" (*constituere intellectum*) in the mind of another.[34] Signs are used to either establish one's own understanding in the minds of others (we call this teaching) or to establish the understanding of others in one's own mind (we call this learning).

---

[30] See Mortimer Adler's *Syntopicon* (Vol. II), 730
[31] Cited in Paul Vincent Spade, 64 [www.pv**spade**.com/Logic/docs/**thoughts**1_1a.pdf]
[32] By 'words' is meant both the spoken word and the written word. (The medieval scholastics called the "spoken word" the *terminus prolatus*, and the "written word" the terminus *scriptus*.) Spoken words are physical sounds produced by the passage of air through the throat. Written words are physical images made on a tablet, wall, animal hide, or sheet of paper.
[33] Spade, 83
[34] Spade, 63 and 73

Words signify thoughts about things: Suppose a reporter interviews you about a crash you witnessed. You say, "A 2008 Volkswagen ran a red light at high speed and t-boned the Buick crossing the intersection." Your *words* are signifying your *thoughts about the things* you saw and heard.[35] Your *words* are the English symbols—"Volkswagen," "ran," "red," "light," etc. Your *thoughts* are your memories and interpretations of the crash. The *things* are the intersection, the stoplight, the two cars, their impact, and so forth.

The priority of thoughts and things to words: In the summer of 2001, Andrea Yates was tried for the crime of drowning her five children in a bathtub. When the news broke, Americans reacted with disbelief, wondering how anyone could do such a thing. Many assumed that she must have been insane. In fact, Yates was eventually found "not guilty by reason of insanity." Instead of life in prison (or the death penalty), she was committed to a mental health hospital.

Defense attorneys often use the insanity plea to secure a reduced sentence for their clients. What is interesting, however, is that there is no definite agreement on the *nature* of insanity. What *is* it exactly? Notice, here, that the principal question is not what the *word* means, but what the *thing* itself is. What exactly is the mental condition we call "insanity"? This is a crucially practical question. If a person is insane, and yet the jury decides they are sane, the defendant may receive too severe a punishment. On the other hand, if the person is sane, but the jury decides they are insane, the defendant may not be punished severely enough. In either case an injustice occurs.

In the Yates trial, the *word* "insane" was batted around by the defense attorney and the prosecuting attorney. The defense argued that the word applied to his client. The prosecuting attorney argued that it did not. The jury sought to determine who was correct. But the *word* "insane" was not the main issue. The real issue was the *thing* signified by the word, the mental condition of insanity. If the defendant *really is* insane, the word applies to her; if she is not insane, the word does not apply. But to determine if she is insane (the thing itself), everyone in the trial must first have the *idea* of what it is to be insane. Only then can they determine whether Yates conforms to their idea of insanity. After all, one must know what one is looking for before one goes looking for it. Suppose you are told to go out in the woods to find a "blik." If you have no *idea* what a "blik" is, how will you know when you've found it? Likewise, if the attorneys and the jurors have no clear idea of what it is to be insane, how can they know if she is insane?

The problem of different thoughts about the same words/things: The reality is that people do not always have the *same idea* in mind when using the

---

[35] In an indirect sense words signify your *thoughts* about those things, your memories and understanding of what happened. Your words signify both thoughts and things.

same word. This means they are not always talking about the *same thing*. Here are three different notions of insanity.

| **Idea 1**: *the inability to feel natural and proper affections* | **Idea 2**: *the inability to apply the standards of right and wrong* | **Idea 3**: *the inability to distinguish fact from fantasy* |

Suppose the defense conceives of insanity as involving the loss of natural affections (Idea 1). He argues that she is insane, since he thinks it's obvious that she lost her natural motherly feelings for her children. The prosecutor, we'll say, thinks of insanity as an inability to apply the standards of right and wrong (Idea 2). He argues that she is not insane, because he has evidence that Yates knows perfectly well how to distinguish right and wrong. Suppose the jury has yet a third notion of insanity in mind, as a condition involving the inability to distinguish fact from fantasy (Idea 3). The jury will therefore want to know if she was able to identify the children as her children, or if she was hearing "the voice of God" commanding her to kill them, or if some other such distortion in her thinking was occurring. Notice that though they are all using the same *word,* they each have different *ideas* of what this word signifies.

This illustrates a frustrating but important fact about human communication: using the same *word* does not guarantee that everyone is *thinking* of the same *thing*.

How should we resolve this difference of perspective? The least of our concerns should be with the *word* "insane." This is an arbitrarily invented symbol. Spanish speakers use the word *loco*. Germans (if I am not mistaken) use the word *verrückt*. This shows that words are mere tools or instruments put into the service of thoughts about things; we *use* words to communicate our thoughts about things.

The most pressing concern is to determine the defendant's mental condition when she performed the dreadful act. But this requires that everyone in the courtroom—jurors and attorneys—first get clear on how *they conceive* of this condition. They must first make clear their ideas or thoughts. Suppose they do so, and that, as a result, they now realize there are three different ideas of insanity floating about the courtroom. Now what? Whose idea is correct?

Before answering this question, we should note an interesting fact. Even if everyone in the court agreed on what mental condition the woman is actually in, this, by itself, would only tell us whose *idea* of insanity applies to this woman, not whether she really is insane. Let's say she was not hallucinating (Idea 3), that she was able to apply the standards of right and wrong (Idea 2), but that she had lost all motherly feelings for her sons (Idea 1). In this case, a type of agreement can be reached among the three parties. The prosecutor could then grant that the defendant *is* "insane" according to the defense attorney's definition. The defendant could agree with the prosecutor and the jury that she is *not* "insane" according to *their* definitions.

But none of this would tell us whose *idea is correct*, or whether she *really is* insane. It would only tell us that she is insane *according to one person's definition* and not insane according to another's definition.

Does this mean we cannot ultimately know whether she is insane? Are we left with a sort of "relativism," which makes her insane according to some people's definition but not according to others? If so, how can we judge justly in a court of law? For surely a just judgment is a true judgment.

To resolve the dispute, all three parties need to find some common ground about the meaning of insanity. For instance, all agree that insanity a mental condition that is *relevant to determining whether someone should be held responsible* for their actions; that is, insanity is a mental condition that impairs one's ability to act in a morally or legally responsible way, and which excuses (or lessens the severity of) an otherwise criminal action. Having established this bit of common ground, the three parties can now test one another's ideas (Ideas 1, 2, and 3) to see which one (or which combination of them) would strip a person of responsibility.

Frankly, Idea 1 seems mistaken, since many criminals have abnormal affections. Moreover, through repeated acts of violence and cruelty, criminals harden themselves and reduce their empathy for others. These corrupt feelings do not excuse them, however. If anything, it makes them even more deserving of punishment. Idea 2 seems problematic for a similar reason. A life of extreme crime can dull or darken the conscience, making it difficult to reason in a morally sound way. The Bible speaks of people who, through habitual sin, began calling good "evil" and evil "good." If a person erodes their moral discernment and affections, they should be held accountable for their offenses in the same way as a drunk driver who kills a pedestrian; he's responsible for being in the condition that led to the behavior. What about Idea 3? If one is hallucinating from an involuntary brain disorder, such that one cannot distinguish reality from fantasy, fact from fiction, it makes more sense to excuse that person. Supposing this to be the correct idea of "insanity," and that everyone in the courtroom agrees, they could then determine whether Yates was in this mental condition when she killed her children. If so, they would call her "insane" and treat her accordingly; otherwise, they should not.

16) The Meanings of "Meaning" (1)

Propositional meaning (i.e., *what* is said rather than *how* it is said): The nature of *meaning* is a topic that extends well beyond the narrow confines of logic. It's a central theme in forensics (the meaning of a broken window), archeology (the meaning of an artifact), music (the meaning of a Romantic symphony), art (the meaning of Raphael's "School of Athens"), and a wide range of other studies. In logic, however, our concern is limited to the meaning of arguments, and specifically to the meaning of *propositions*.

Roughly speaking, propositional meaning is *what* someone says rather than *how* they say it. Suppose a farmer says, "I am going to kill the cow." The *propositional* meaning is what the farmer asserts—that he is going to kill the cow. But this is not the *only* meaning. There is also a *non-propositional* meaning communicated by the farmer's context and the manner in which he asserts the proposition. If he is going to slaughter the cow for food, he will make the statement in a calm, matter-of-fact manner. But suppose, instead, that the cow keeps breaking out of its pen and eating the farmer's crops. The farmer now says, "I am going to *kill* the cow!" The context and delivery convey that he is angry. But they do not change the propositional content, which is simply that he is going to kill the cow. When evaluating arguments, our focus should be on what is said rather than how it is said.

The difficulty of determining propositional meaning: It can be challenging to discover what a proposition means. For instance, when it comes to interpreting the U.S. Constitution, scholars and Supreme Court Justices often disagree on what the text means. Take the Second Amendment: *"A well regulated Militia, being necessary to the security of a free State, the right of the people to keep and bear Arms, shall not be infringed."* What is the meaning of this text? Is it:

(1) The words themselves, regardless of the author's intentions?
(2) The intention of the authors, as something over and beyond the words?
(3) How the original audience understood those words, regardless of what the author's themselves meant?
(4) The understanding of whatever generation of Americans is debating the Second Amendment?
(5) Some combination of the above?

Our answer to these questions will change the meaning of the text. Take the word "Arms." If we interpret this according to (2) or (3), this word would signify 18th century muskets, not modern bazookas or machineguns. But if we interpret "Arms" according to (1), it would mean any and every weapon, or at least any and every hand-held weapon (in contrast to, say, a cannon).

The source of the difficulty: As already noted, words are inventions of men; they are tools or instruments for communicating thoughts about things. So the meaning of words will ultimately depend on who uses them. But people do not use words clearly or consistently. For the sake of simplifying, we can distinguish two word-users: (1) the *society* that uses the word,[36] and (2) any given *individual* within that society. This distinction accounts for two different senses of the question, "What does this word mean?" The question can be interpreted as asking:

(1) What is a society's officially agreed upon meaning(s)?
(2) What do *you* mean by it?

We answer (1) by consulting the dictionary, and (2) by consulting the individual. The dictionary meaning is called the "lexical" meaning of a word. This will be our primary focus in the subsequent lessons.

Lexical meaning—its value, problems, and limitations: We often assume that the lexical meaning of a word like "dog" or "insane" or "marriage" (or pretty much any other word) is the *correct* meaning, the meaning to which our language *should* conform. But this is not quite right. To see why, contrast these lexical meanings of "marriage":

- *Noah Webster's 1828 edition*: "The act of uniting a man and woman for life; wedlock; the legal union of a man and woman for life. Marriage is a contract both civil and religious, by which the parties engage to live together in mutual affection and fidelity, till death shall separate them. Marriage was instituted by God himself for the purpose of preventing the promiscuous intercourse of the sexes, for promoting domestic felicity, and for securing the maintenance and education of children."
- *Encarta (2013)*: a legally recognized relationship, established by a civil or religious ceremony, between two people who intend to live together as sexual and domestic partners.
- *Merriam-Webster's online (2016)*: the relationship that exists between a husband and a wife; a similar relationship between people of the same sex.

---

[36] This gets complicated, as a given society will often evolve. The American "society" *of 2000* is very different from that of 1800. Is it the same society? If not, can we speak of how "American society" uses a word?

Now, if the role of a dictionary is to tell us the nature of things, i.e., how the world truly is, we are then faced with an impossible problem: some dictionaries flatly *contradict* each other. (The second and third contradict the first.) This means that, as descriptions of the nature of things, at least one of these meanings cannot be correct.[37]

One possible reply is to deny that dictionaries are meant to describe the nature of things. Perhaps the role of a dictionary is *only* to tell us how a society *uses* a word. If a society uses a word in different ways over time (as in the case of "marriage"), these dictionaries are not really contradicting each other; they are merely reporting different uses of the word "marriage" *at different times*.

This suggestion has some merit, but it cannot be the whole story. When Noah Webster defined marriage in 1828, he was not *merely* informing his readers of how *Englishmen* happened to use that word. He meant to tell us what marriage really and truly *is*. He meant to describe the *thing* itself signified by the word "marriage." Consider the modern dictionary. The *Encarta Dictionary* (2013) defines "sun" to mean "the star at the center of our solar system around which Earth and the eight other planets orbit." Is this merely reporting how English speakers use the word "sun," or is it describing what the sun itself really is? Plenty of English speakers did not know (and still do not know) that the sun is a star or that there are nine planets in the solar system. Yet they know full well how to use the word "sun"—it's the big, bright, hot, yellowish orb that rises and sets every day. For them, "sun" does not mean all of what this dictionary definition means. Interestingly, though the *Encarta* definition of 2013 was supposed to be a factual statement, it is no longer factually correct. According to scientific consensus, Pluto is no longer a planet.

There is another reason for thinking that lexical meanings are often meant to represent reality. Dictionaries are used as authoritative *factual sources* in cultural debates, legislative processes, and courts of law. Suppose a disagreement occurs regarding the nature of a biological cell. We might resolve the disagreement by consulting a dictionary. Encarta defines a cell as "the smallest independently functioning unit in the structure of an organism, usually consisting of one or more nuclei surrounded by cytoplasm and enclosed by a membrane." Here we have a straightforwardly factual statement. This definition is not *merely* reporting how society uses the word "cell." For one thing, most people do not have this very technical meaning in mind when they use the word. (Many of us don't even understand the definition once we read it.) More significantly, though, if dictionaries merely report how a society uses the word "cell," it would not be legitimate for us to cite it as evidence about the *nature of a cell* itself. A debate

---

[37] What is true of 'marriage' is true of less controversial terms as well. For instance, the lexical meaning of scientific terms changes with time as well.

about a cell is *not* a debate about how a society uses a word; it's about the nature of the *thing* itself we call a "cell."

Using dictionaries: We can draw several conclusions from the above discussion. First, it is not always clear what the function of a dictionary is supposed to be. Is it to indicate the social usage of *words* or is it to indicate the nature of *things*? The answer, it seems, is yes! Lexicographers (those who write dictionaries) do both. There is an understandable reason for this. Insofar as dictionaries record how society uses a word, it follows that they are (to some extent) recording the nature of things, since a principal function of our words is to signify the nature of things.

Secondly, it's not always clear when a dictionary is talking about the nature of things or only about the use of a word. One must rely on critical common sense and a good education to decide.

Thirdly, all of this means that dictionaries are biased, fallible, and potentially misleading sources, which cannot be accorded more authority than they deserve. Dictionaries are produced under the pressure of companies and institutions with financial goals, political agendas, and ideological commitments. Take the recent (re)definitions of "marriage" above. Many English speakers across the world continue to think of marriage as a union between opposite sexes. (Some of them *refuse* to think of a same-sex union as a "marriage.") Even so, this has not stopped dictionary companies from modifying the definition to be inclusive of so-called "gay marriage." Note well what this means: here we have a case of dictionaries *disregarding* common usage in order to promote an agenda. No one recently "discovered" that marriage is *really* just a union between any two consenting people, including homosexuals. Nor is the redefinition an attempt at reflecting standard social usage, since same-sex unions *contradict* society's standard meaning of "marriage." The best explanation is that the dictionary companies have jumped on the recent social bandwagon.

Incidentally, the previous example shows the power of words to shape the worldview of a culture. It is likely that the radical redefinition of marriage will recondition future generations to take the new view *for granted*, as a view that is just "obviously" true. It will also change what they think marriage *really is*.

Fourthly, we must be careful when using a dictionary to prove our beliefs about the nature of things. As noted, the entry in the dictionary might only be about word usage rather than the nature of things; and the definition might be illegitimately biased. But there is another reason: not all dictionaries are created equal. Some dictionaries are more accurate and authoritative than others. For example, the *Oxford English Dictionary*, consisting of 20 massive volumes, is superior to the *Encarta Dictionary* used for casual word processing. Moreover, some dictionaries are written for specialists in a subject matter, such as science or philosophy. These technical dictionaries provide more precise meanings than one finds in popular dictionaries. Whenever possible, one should rely on technical dictionaries over and against popular ones. For instance, in the previous lesson we referenced three meanings of "insane." This was not a debate about the mere use of the word "insane." It was a disagreement about what it is to *be* insane, about the *thing itself*. Now, how might these three parties seek to resolve the dispute? A standard dictionary seems an obvious place to turn. But, having browsed half a dozen of them on my own, I found that they do little more than tell us what we already know, namely, that insanity is a mental disorder which, in a court of law, reduces (or removes) one's responsibility for an otherwise criminal act. These definitions fail to indicate the *criteria for knowing* when one is insane. This is where a technical dictionary comes into play, such as a legal or psychological dictionary. While this is an improvement on a standard dictionary, not even this is a foolproof method of getting to the nature of insanity. We might find that in some cases (like the case of insanity) not even the experts agree. Even scientific, psychological, and legal dictionaries are subject to contradiction and constant revision.

Where does this leave us? The point is not to discourage us from using dictionaries; but we need to use caution in how we rely on them. Insofar as we are trying to get to the nature of things, dictionaries should not be viewed as anything more than a clue or helpful starting point for inquiry. The Greek philosopher, Plato, said that reality leaves tracks in language. Dictionaries record these tracks. When it comes to discovering the truth about "things" (in contrast to "words"), we must *ultimately go to the things themselves*.

Real meaning, nominal meaning, and their truth-conditions: Going back to the distinction of Words, Thoughts, and Things, "real meaning" refers to the *nature of Things*, and "nominal meaning" to our *use of Words*. Take the word "dog." The real meaning of "dog" is *what it is to be* a dog. The nominal meaning of "dog" is *how the word "dog" is used* by people. This may appear to be a distinction without a difference, since it seems that the two meanings always coincide. But you now know this is not the case. We already considered the meaning of "marriage." Let's think about another example—"human."

The *real* meaning of "human" is whatever it is to be a human, whatever we essentially are. The nominal meaning of "human" is whatever people use the word to mean (as in the case of lexical meanings). Some people use the word "human" to mean a highly evolved species of the genus of primate.[38] Others use the word "human" to mean the only creature to bear God's image, a creature who did not evolve and who is not a mere animal. Here we have two different nominal meanings, or two different ways in which the word "human" is used by large

---

[38]Wikipedia defines "human" as "the only living species in the Homo genus of bipedal primates in the Hominidae, or great ape family."

segments of the populous. And yet, only one of these nominal meanings can be the real meaning, since only one of them describes what humans really are.

The truth conditions for real and nominal meanings are very different. Real definitions are true if, and only if, they define things to be what they actually are. If humans are specially created divine image bearers, it is true to define them that way, and it is false to define them as highly evolved members of the primate genus. On the other hand, what makes it true that a word has a nominal meaning is that people do in fact use it that way. If people use the word "human" to signify highly evolved members of the primate genus, then it is true that this is (at least one) of the nominal meanings of "human."

We need to be clear in how we ask definitional questions. When asking about the meaning of "human," there are really two different questions:

1. Is this what *most people mean* when they *use the word* "human"?
2. Is this what the *things* signified by the word "human" *really are*?

The first is asking for nominal meaning, and the second for real meaning. The answers to these questions *might* be one and the same in some cases, but clearly not in all cases. We see, then, that is not a distinction without a difference.

17) The Meanings of "Meaning" (2)

For the purposes of reading, discussing, and writing, it is useful to distinguish a word's "denotative meaning" (or denotation) and its "connotative meaning" (or connotation).

Denotation: To teach a toddler the meaning of words, we usually start by *pointing to examples* of the things signified by our words. We point to a particular dog (e.g., your neighbor's poodle) and say "Dog." We point to a particular car and say "Car." This is one way of teaching the *denotative* meaning of those words. The denotative meaning of the word "dog" would be the *members of the class* signified by that word. This includes any *one* member of the class (my dog), any *sub-class* (poodles), or *all* the members of the class together (every dog).

Connotation: The *connotative* meaning of a word is *the set of characteristics common to all members of the class* signified by the word. According to one dictionary, the connotative meaning of "dog" is a *carnivorous animal with prominent, canine teeth and, in the wild state, a long slender muzzle, a deep-chested muscular body, a bushy tail, and large, erect ears."* Each dog shares these characteristics with every other member of the class.

In logic, connotative meaning is more important than denotative meaning. This is because, logically speaking, the connotative meaning of a word is *the* meaning of a word. Let's consider why.

Suppose we are trying to explain the meaning of the word "scientist." We might initially answer by giving its denotative meaning. We might say, "People like Galileo, Dalton, or Darwin." But this is not quite right. Galileo is *a* scientist, but he is not *the* meaning of "scientist." If he were, then Dalton and Darwin could not also be the meaning of "scientist."

Suppose we try improving our answer by saying that "scientist" means "Physicists, chemists, and biologists." This is still inadequate. Are these really the only three types of scientists? What about archeologists, anthropologists, and computer engineers, just to name a few other options? Moreover, even if all scientists are physicists, chemists, and biologists, we still don't know what these three groups *have in common*. What attributes are shared by all three that make them (and not others) "scientists"?

To see why this is important, suppose one were to extend the list of scientists to include astrologists, witchdoctors, and psychotherapists. If we challenged this list, we must first specify the characteristics had by scientists that are not (presumably) had by astrologists, for example. In short, we must give its connotative meaning.

Here is the connotative meaning of "scientist" according to one source: *an academic dedicated to the accumulation and classification of observable facts in order to formulate general laws about the natural world.*[39] This nicely describes what physicists, chemists, and (to a lesser degree) biologists have in common. I am pretty sure this excludes witchdoctors!

Inverse relation of connotation and denotation: It is a basic principle of logic that the *connotation of a word determines its denotation*. In other words, the connotation of the word determines the *number of things* (or range of things) to which the word refers. Suppose that, in a classroom of thirty students, we ask them to raise their hand in response to these questions:

1. How many of you are *male*?
2. How many of you males *play sports*?
3. How many of you males play *water* sports?

Suppose fifteen students raise their hands in reply to question 1. We can predict that, in reply to question 2, some of those hands will go down, and that still more will drop in response to question 3. This illustrates the principle that connotation determines denotation. The connotation in question 1 is "male students." This connotation denotes fifteen students. The connotation of question 2 is "male students who play sports." This denotes a smaller class of students. By adding "water" to the connotation, the denotation shrinks even further. In sum, we find that as *connotation increases, denotation decreases*. To visualize this, let the circles below represent classes with members.

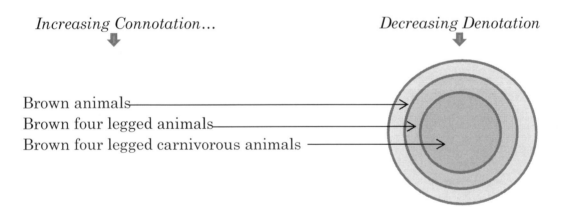

The reverse is also true: *as connotation decreases, denotation increases*. In other words, there is an "inverse relation" between connotation and denotation.

---

[39] https://wikis.engrade.com/genscimod1

Connotation signifies things and/or thoughts: We said that the connotative meaning of a word is the common nature, or set of attributes, characterizing the things signified by the word. But we must qualify this claim. As we will now learn, it is misleading to *equate* the connotative meaning of a word with the common attributes of things. This is because we sometimes use words to signify the "common characteristics" of objects that *do not actually exist*.

Though unicorns do not exist, we can still state the connotative meaning of the word—i.e., *a mythical animal usually depicted as a white horse with a single straight spiraled horn growing from its forehead*.[40] Though unicorns do not exist, we still have the *idea* of what they would be if they did exist. In that respect, the word "unicorn" does not signify *things*; it only signifies *thoughts*. Earlier we said that the connotative meaning of a word is the common attributes of things in a class. This way of putting it suggests that we are talking about the *real* attributes of *real* things. But that is precisely what we do not want to imply when describing imaginary objects like unicorns. Likewise, mathematicians regularly define ideal geometric figures, such as circles and triangles, without necessarily suggesting that these ideal entities exist. For even if no perfect circle exists, it remains true that we have the *idea* of a "circle" as *a plane figure enclosed by points equidistant from a common center*.

There is a strange consequence to all of this: if a word's denotative meaning is the particular thing(s) signified by the word, it follows that some words (like "unicorn") do *not have* a denotative meaning, though they do have a connotative meaning. To take a more relevant example, when atheists speak of God, they do not wish to be understood as talking about an actually existing being; they are only talking about the *idea* of that being. Atheists grant that "God" connotatively means *a good, wise, and all-powerful supernatural being who created the world*. But atheists deny that "God" actually denotes anything. For them, the word "God" (like "unicorn") signifies a *thought* only, not a thing.

Literal (logical) connotation v. literary (psychological) connotation: When people use the word "connote" or "connotation," they are usually *not* thinking of what we are calling "connotative meaning." More likely, people think of connotation as an idea or emotion we tend to *associate* with a word, some positive or negative feeling or attitude. For many, the word "terrorist" connotes a Muslim or person of Middle Eastern descent, though it does not *mean* that. Likewise, for some, the word "capitalist" connotes a greedy, heartless person obsessed with getting rich, though the word does not *mean* that.

For the sake of clarity, we will distinguish these two senses explicitly. What we earlier called the "connotative meaning" of a word we will call its *literal*

---

[40] Encarta Dictionary

connotation. Insofar as a word has some associated meaning, we can call this its *literary* connotation. A word's literal connotation is its standard *logical* sense. Its literary connotation would be any *psychological* association people give to the word, associations which may differ from person to person.

Let's consider some examples. The word "success" literally connotes *the achievement of a plan or attempted action*. But for many in our culture, the word literarily connotes *financial* achievement. Many will understand the statement "I met someone who is very successful" to mean "I met someone who makes lots of money." (In fact, for some people it is almost a contradiction in terms to say that a person is poor but successful.) Similarly, the word "teenager" literally means nothing more than *a youth between the ages of thirteen and nineteen*. In our culture, the word "teenager" often carries a *negative* literary connotation, suggesting someone who is shallow, self-centered, idle, indulged, and prone to rebellious behavior. What is interesting, however, is that this literary connotation does not exist in some non-Western cultures like Africa or Central America. Those cultures have plenty of literal teenagers, but not nearly as many literary teenagers.

18) The Problem of Ambiguity

"Ambiguity" means the *susceptibility of a word to be understood in more than one way*. This amusing interchange from *The Hobbit* provides an example:

> "Good morning!" said Bilbo, and he meant it. The sun was shining, and the grass was very green. But Gandalf looked at him from under long bushy eyebrows that stuck out further than the brim of his shady hat.
> "What do you mean?" he said. "Do you wish me a good morning, or mean that it is a good morning whether I want it or not; or that you feel good this morning; or that it is a morning to be good on?"
> "All of them at once," said Bilbo. "

Bilbo's use of "good morning" is ambiguous. From Gandalf's standpoint, it could convey any one of four meanings.

The word "ambiguous" comes from the Latin verb *ambigere*, which means "to wander about."[41] It's an apt image. An ambiguous word does not have a stationary meaning within a given context; at one time it means x, but at another time y; its meaning moves around, as it were, making it difficult to nail down. Ambiguity is a primary obstacle to clear and effective argumentation.

Connotative ambiguity—logical (literal) and psychological (literary): Ambiguity plagues both the literal and literary use of words. We already addressed the ambiguity of the literal meaning of "insane": (1) the inability to feel natural and proper affections; (2) the inability to apply the standards of right and wrong; and (3) the inability to distinguish fact from fantasy. Or take the word "Christian." The following are a few of the different literal conceptions people have in mind:

- One who has been baptized
- One who is born again
- One who goes to church
- One who assents to the doctrines of Christianity
- One who actually practices the doctrines of Christianity

Ambiguity can also plague literary connotation. The word "Christian" has positive and negative associations in society. Some people have a favorable attitude to the word. For them, it invokes the thought of someone who is compassionate, truthful, thoughtful, chaste, self-controlled, service-oriented, and so forth. For others, "Christian" carries the negative connotation of being hypocritical, legalistic,

---

[41]*Being Logical: A Guide to Good Thinking* (p.16).

intolerant, ignorant, or self-righteous. Ambiguity of literary connotation presents huge obstacles to persuading people. Suppose one wants to persuade an audience that homeschooling is superior to public schooling. This could be easy or difficult, depending (in part) on the psychological associations of the word "homeschooler." For some, the word has negative literary connotation, suggesting a poorly socialized child. For others, it has the positive connotation of an academically advanced student. To make our arguments more persuasive, we need to anticipate the negative literary connotation of our words, avoid them when possible, and clarify them when necessary.

Denotative ambiguity: When someone tells us they own a "dog," this might trigger the image of a *type* of dog (e.g., an image of a midsized, longer haired dog like a retriever, rather than a Great Dane or a Chihuahua). The word "Christian" might denote different *particulars*, e.g., the Apostle Paul, Billy Graham, the Pope, a neighbor, an aunt or uncle, or the members of a local congregation. Or it might denote different *sub-classes*, such as Greek Orthodox, Roman Catholic, Protestant, Lutheran, Reformed, Anglican, Baptist, Methodist, Charismatic, Fundamentalist, etc. If my denotative notion of "Christian" is the Apostle Paul, and your definition is a mere "church-goer" (who thinks and lives just like non-Christians), we will have two different notions of "Christian." The same is true of sub-class denotation: there may be a deep divide between Greek Orthodox Christians and Southern Baptist Christians.

Types and tokens: To appreciate why ambiguity is such a problem, and to see how many ways it shows up in discourse, we need to explore the distinction between "types" and "tokens." Count the words in this question:

"How much wood would a woodchuck chuck if a woodchuck could chuck wood?"

If you counted thirteen, you are thinking about word-*tokens*. If you counted nine, you are thinking about word-*types*. We will define "type" to mean a standard sequence of letters (or sounds) that gets used repeatedly. By "token" we will mean a particular instance, or instantiation, of a type. A *type* is an ideal, norm, standard, or pattern. A *token* is a particular, which shows up at different points in space and time. Take the word "wood" in the question. If we think of it as a token, it is just a particular blotch of ink on the paper in front of you, showing up first on the left side of the sentence and then again at the end of the sentence. As a blotch of ink, a token cannot be repeated. If it were physically possible, you could lift those marks off the page and move them somewhere else, but even then you are not "repeating" those marks; you are simply *relocating* them. But if we think about the word "wood" as a type, norm, or ideal, we can think of it being used countless times. A word-type is a *pattern* according to which any set of particular ink marks are formed, ordered, or sequenced.

These remarks apply as well to the spoken word, though here we're dealing with physical sound waves rather than visible ink marks. Millions of people have sung "Silent Night" at many different times and places. While the pattern of the song gets repeated in every case, no token of the song can be repeated. Let's suppose that the Mayberry Boys Choir sang it at 8:00 PM, on December 24th, 1968, at the First Baptist Church of Mayberry. For those few historic minutes, the sound waves produced by the choir carried through the church and then dissipated, never to be heard again. Like all token-instances, they were unique, particular, one-time events. However, that one instance conformed to the same type or pattern of song to which we all conform whenever we sing it.

The type-token distinction applies to all of life. Imagine that you are presently holding a pencil. The pencil in your hand is a member of a set or class of pencils that look just like it. The same is true of a particular rose, or particular tiger, or a particular car. A dozen roses, for instance, consists of twelve distinct roses, each of which is the same as the others, since they are all members of the same class. The world is populated with categories of things, such as stars, planets, trees, insects, cells, molecules, bodily organs, and so on. All the particular individuals we see or experience belong to a class. For any given class of things, we can call the particular individuals "tokens," and the commonly shared nature the "type." The human heart is a type, and your heart is a token instance of that type. My favorite type of car is the 1971 Pontiac Firebird. One day I hope to buy a token of that type.

Token ambiguity: In actual writing, debate, and conversation, men always reason by means of word-*tokens*. This is very significant. Since words are tokens of types, *it is easy to (mistakenly) assume that our words must mean the same thing in each token instance*. If one person says a woman is "insane" and the other person denies that she is "insane," it would seem that they must mean the same thing, since they are tokening the *same word-type*. But their different token instances might have different meanings. In the language of the previous lesson, they might be *thinking* about different *things* when they use the same *word*.

The meaning of a word-token will depend, in part, on the *intentions* and the *context* of the word-user. It is possible for two people to instantiate the same word-type with *different intentions*. The word-type may take on slight variations of meaning in the mouths of different people at different times, depending on *who* is using them, *when* they are using them, and *how* they are using them. This shows that word-types, in their token instances, are fluid and flexible.

Words are instruments for communicating thoughts about things. The key, then, is to discern what a given word-user is *thinking about* when he or she uses the word. As noted earlier, the question "What do you mean by...?" is trying to get at what a particular word-user has *in mind* when *he* uses a word. We ask the question because we realize that the direction or focal point of *his* thought gives *his* word-tokens their meanings.

We need to be careful not to oversimplify here. The meaning of a word-token is not determined *solely* by the user. When a competent English speaker uses a token of a type, he generally aligns his usage to the standard usage of English speakers. The word-type "dog" will not be used to mean a color, for example, as in the sentence "My favorite color is dog." Generally speaking, the socially accepted meaning of word-types constrains our use of tokens.

Type ambiguity: We said that one word-type, which presumably has one meaning, might express different meanings in different token instances, depending on the intentions of the users. But we must also recognize that some word-types are *already* ambiguous, even as word-types; they have a sort of "built-in" ambiguity. We will now consider some examples.

Equivocal types: The most straightforward examples are called "equivocal" words. A word-type is equivocal if it is socially recognized to have two (or more) *categorically different* and *unrelated* meanings. The word-type "bat" can refer to a flying mammal or to an instrument used in baseball. Likewise, the word "content" can signify that which is inside something ("The content of her letter worried me"), or a satisfied state of mind ("I am content"). Most equivocal word-types are easily recognized in everyday usage. The statement "Jim swung the bat" could be interpreted in two different ways, but context and common sense are usually enough to decide.

Analogical types: A word-type is analogical if it is socially recognized to have (at least) two *distinct but similar* meanings. To take just two examples, the word "evolution" can mean a process of change or development (e.g., the evolution of music from ragtime to rock n roll) or the biological theory of Charles Darwin. These meanings are distinct but similar. Even the more specific biological sense of "evolution" can have different meanings. Sometimes it means change within a species (diversification of canine into wolves, coyotes, etc.) and sometimes it can mean change across species (e.g., wolf-like creatures to whales). Thankfully, people will sometimes try to avoid the confusion by using the words "microevolution" and "macroevolution." Sadly, there are not always specific words to help us avoid these ambiguities.

For example, sometimes "evolution" in either of the previous two senses can mean a God-directed process (theistic evolution) and sometimes it can mean a totally undirected process (atheistic evolution). Notice that these latter two meanings are contradictory. The following conversation helps explain why conversations can become so confusing.

> A: I believe in evolution.
> B: So you're an atheist?
> A: No, I'm a Christian.
> B: But Christians believe that God created and controls the history of life.
> A: Right, and I do.

Person B is probably using the atheistic definition of evolution. (There are many other meanings of "evolution" and "creation" that we could specify, but this is enough to make the point.)

Let's take one more example. Here are two (of many) different meanings of "tolerance" and "intolerance":

	Older Meaning	Newer Meaning
Tolerance	Respecting another's civil right to believe or practice what others consider false or immoral.	Accepting other people's different beliefs and practices (i.e., not judging them to be false or immoral)
Intolerance	Not respecting another's civil rights to believe or practice what others consider false or immoral.	Not accepting other people's different beliefs and practices (i.e., judging them to be false or immoral).

Suppose a Christian says that Jehovah's Witnesses are wrong to believe and practice their doctrine that forbids them from receiving blood transfusions. The Christian would be "intolerant" in the newer sense of the term. But suppose, further, that the Christian says that JWs have the civil right to believe and practice this doctrine. The Christian is "tolerant" in the older sense. What's really fascinating here is that the Christian *cannot* be "tolerant" in the older sense *unless* he is "intolerant" in the newer sense. This shows that the older and newer meanings of "tolerance" are at odds with each other.

Univocal types: Some word-types are not ambiguous, since they have only one meaning. The word-type "Fibromyalgia" means only one thing, i.e., a medically unexplained condition of chronic pain. These word-types have "univocal" meaning (lit. "one meaning"). As a rule of thumb, we can say that a word-type has univocal meaning if, in standard social usage, it is assumed to mean the same thing in every token-instance. Other examples of univocal word-types might be: "Japan," "refrigerator," and "coconut." For some words, however, it can be difficult to decide whether it is equivocal, analogical, or univocal.

It can be difficult to distinguish univocal and analogical meanings. Consider the word-type "genius." Both Shakespeare and Newton are said to be geniuses. But one was a poetic genius and the other was a mathematical genius. The similarity is in their extraordinary intellects, of course, but there seems to be an important difference in their intelligence.

So is "genius" analogical or univocal? I would argue that it's analogical. As long a word-type can take on different meanings (especially if they're different enough to cause mistakes in reasoning), it's best to view that word-type as analogical. For example, try to identify what is happening in this dialogue:

A: What do you think "genius" means?
B: My calculus teacher said that Newton was a genius.
A: Why?
B: Because he had one of the best mathematical minds in history.
A: But my literature teacher said that Shakespeare was a genius.
B: Well, then he too must have had an exceptional mathematical mind.

Person B's conclusion is false, since Shakespeare was not mathematically minded, as far as we know. But person B's reasoning makes sense if "genius" has *only* to do with mathematical thinking (in which case it's univocal). But person A's teacher is using "genius" in a different way. Person B's false conclusion resulted from failing to understand that "genius" has more than one meaning.

Another way of approaching this is to define "genius" broadly enough to cover both men (and others besides, such as Bach, Da Vinci, Kant, etc.). One Internet definition says this:

Genius = a person who is exceptionally intelligent or creative, either generally or in some particular respect.[42]

Suppose we use the first part of this to define "genius" as *a person who is exceptionally intelligent*. As a connotative definition, this would seem to have univocal meaning. It would cover Newton and Shakespeare and Bach and many others. But notice that this definition has only one meaning because it is so very general; it ignores and leaves out the fact that human intelligence varies in very significant ways. Since we don't have different words to mark the different forms of intelligence, we wind up using the one word "genius" to cover them all. The problem, though, is that, in real-life conversation, people often *narrow* the meaning

---

[42] https://search.yahoo.com/search?fr=mcafee&type=E214US1214G0&p=define%3A+genius

of "genius" to mean *only one type* of exceptional intelligence, like Person B did. In effect, they are using the word "genius" *differently* than others, differently than even those who use it in the dictionary sense above. This may explain why the Internet dictionary of "genius" adds the italicized qualifier:

"a person who is exceptionally intelligent or creative, either generally *or in some particular respect.*"

It's the various "particular respect(s)" that makes "genius" analogical in actual usage.

Similarly, suppose that Ned uses "dog" to mean *only* poodles, and that Alex uses "dog" to mean every species of dog. In this case, though there is overlap in their use of the word "dog" (both are using it to include poodles), there is also a big difference. For Ned, "dog" does *not* mean Retrievers, or Collies, or any other animal apart from poodles.

Let's ponder another example to test out our understanding. Suppose that a teenage boy, while on a youth retreat at the beach, meets a beautiful girl named Sara, who teaches him how to surf. The boy comes home from the trip excited and says:

        [1] "I love surfing."
        [2] "I love Sara."

One might initially think that "love" is used univocally to mean a *passion for* something or someone, such that "I love *x*" = "I am passionate about *x*." But the more we think about it, the more we see that these are distinct types of passion. Though he professes to "love" both surfing and Sara, this cannot mean the same thing. Unless he is strange, the boy cannot love Sara in the *exact same sense* as he loves surfing (and vice-versa). In [2] "love" = "romantically attracted to." In [1] "love" = "thrilled with." We are dealing with analogical meanings of "love"—similar but distinct.

Secondly, sometimes a seemingly analogical word-type is better thought of as equivocal. Consider this use of "love":

        [3] "To follow Christ is to love one's enemies."

In this case, "love" cannot possibly carry the meaning of [1] and [2] above. The common denominator of [1] and [2] is an *attraction* to something or someone because of a *pleasure* derived from them. But no one is attracted to their enemies as such. If anything, it is precisely the reverse—we are antagonistic toward them. Moreover, the "love" of [3] pertains to *how one treats another person*, not to how they *feel* about them. To "love" an enemy is to forgive him and show kindness to him, and to do so in spite of the lack of love for them in sense of [1] and [2]. We can "love" in sense [3] even when we have *no* "love" in sense [1] and [2]. This suggests that "love" is equivocal. What it means in [3] is categorically different and unrelated to its meaning in senses [1] and [2]. But this is debatable.[43]

Finally, some word-types can be *both* equivocal and analogical, though in different respects. Take the word "bank" in these three cases:

> [a] He robbed the bank.
> [b] I fished along the river bank.
> [c] Don't bank on it.

As used in [a] and [b], "bank" is equivocal. As used in [a] and [c], "bank" is analogical.

---

[43] One could argue that "love" in sense [3] *might* be linked to the other two senses in this regard: to "love" in sense [3] is to treat someone *as if* one loves them in senses [1] and [2]. But this seems to be a stretch. One could also argue that Christ-like love involves genuine affection for one's enemy, not merely benevolent action toward him; one must *feel* sympathy, compassion, and a genuine concern for him. If this is right, then "love" in sense [3] is a mixture of analogical elements and equivocal elements. The element of affection is similar to what is involved in [1] and [2]; the element of gracious action is categorically different.

19) Denotative Definitions

Role of definition: Given the problem of ambiguity, we will often find it necessary to indicate exactly what we mean by a term. This is the function of a definition. To define a word is to indicate its meaning. The word "definition" comes from a Latin term which means "to limit" or "to set boundaries to," the same term from which we get "definite" and "definitive." Definitions *set limits* to how a word is to be understood.

Difference between denotative definitions and connotative definitions: Since definitions indicate a word's meaning, and since the meaning of a word will be its *denotation* or its *connotation*, it follows that there are two ways of defining—denotatively and connotatively. Denotative definitions convey a word's denotation, and connotative definitions convey a word's connotation.

A denotative definition does not describe an entire class; in fact, it does not "describe" anything. A denotative definition *signifies only some members* of a class, by either *pointing* to those members or by *naming* those members.

A connotative definition, on the other hand, is used to *describe an entire class*, by specifying the *attributes* shared by all the members of a class. The connotative definition of "dog" is a *carnivorous animal with prominent, canine teeth and, in the wild state, a long slender muzzle, a deep-chested muscular body, a bushy tail, and large, erect ears*.

Three types of denotative definitions: Denotative definitions sub-divide into the numbered boxes below:

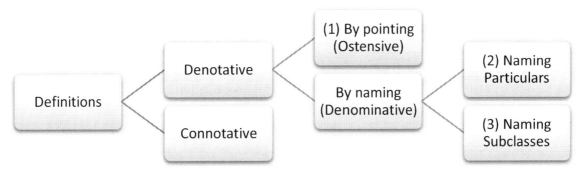

Suppose a foreign exchange student asks you what is meant by the word "dog." Since his English is so poor, you decide to point to an example of a dog and say, "*This* is what I mean by 'dog'." You are not defining the *category* of "dog" (which requires a connotative definition); you are only signifying one member of the category. This is called an "ostensive" definition. To define a word ostensively is to point at an individual member of a class and say, "This is what I mean by…" You might also pick out a photo or picture of a dog, or even draw an image of a dog.

But what if no dog is present at the time you are asked to define the word? You could resort to another method of denotative definition, by simply *naming* some of the members in the class the exchange student may already know. You might say, "Lassie is a dog; Benji is a dog; Pluto is a dog." Like the ostensive definition, you are indicating particular members of a category. Unlike ostensive definition, you are not "pointing" to them; you are rather picking them out by naming well-known examples.

You might also name a *sub-class* of the category, e.g., collies, shepherds, spaniels, terriers, poodles, etc. Here, too, you're using names, but common names rather than proper names.

We can distinguish these latter two methods by calling the first "enumeration by particulars," and the second "enumeration by sub-classes." Both denote by *denominating* (or naming) members.

The uses of denotative definitions: Denotative definitions can be used to clarify, correct, and construct connotative definitions.

For clarifying: First, denotative definitions can be used to *clarify* the *scope* of connotative definitions. Suppose two people agree that "immodesty" (as it applies to dress) has the connotative meaning of *overly revealing, sexually suggestive, and publicly indecent*. This definition is helpful, but it leaves plenty of room for disagreement about particular instances. There is still room for ambiguity. We can clarify the scope of the connotative meaning by offering concrete examples. We might point to someone and say, "*That* is an example of overly revealing, sexually suggestive, and publicly indecent dress." Or we might specify sub-classes (i.e., certain types of shorts, tops, etc.).

To take another example, in psychology there is a condition known as "multiple personality disorder" (or MPD). As the name itself suggests, the connotative meaning of MPD is "*a dissociative disorder involving a disturbance of identity in which two or more separate and distinct personality traits (or identities) control the individual's behavior at different times.*"[44] The scope of this definition is ambiguous. There is a sense in which this characterizes all of us. In Romans 7:14-25, the Apostle Paul refers to an internal struggle between two forces (two "selves," as it were) competing for control of his life. This is a universal experience. We sometimes think, feel, and act in ways that are profoundly contrary to how we think, feel, and act at other times. We can be gentle *and* harsh, compassionate *and* cruel, honest *and* deceitful, humble *and* arrogant, etc. In terms of the definition above, we

---

[44] Take from the *National Alliance on Mental Illness*.
http://www.nami.org/Content/ContentGroups/Helpline1/Dissociative_Identity_Disorder_(formerly_Multiple_Personality_Disorder).htm

experience the "disturbance of identity" from "distinct personality traits" that "control" our "behavior at different times." Does this mean that we all have MPD?

Suppose two people are debating the scope, or application, of the connotative meaning of MPD. One of them thinks it applies to the average person (for reasons I stated above), while others think it has a far more restricted meaning, such that only a very small percentage of people have MPD. Clearly these two people are interpreting the connotative definition differently. The latter could clarify his understanding of MPD by giving a *paradigm example* of someone he believes to be suffering from MPD. Suppose he gives the example of Ed. What makes Ed a paradigm case are the following two traits: First, Ed alternates between acting out two contrary and self-conscious identities, by calling himself "Bob" and "Sam." When Ed assumes the identity and behavior of Bob, he is a gentle, quiet, pleasant fellow, who enjoys painting, classical music, and horseback riding. When Ed assumes the role of Sam, however, he becomes a loud, angry, obnoxious person who likes cheap beer, heavy metal, and cage fighting. Secondly, when Ed becomes Bob, he has no memory of being Sam; and when he becomes Sam, he has no recollection of being Bob. It is now clear that *this* conception of MPD does not apply to the average person. Nor is it what the Apostle Paul was describing in Romans 7.

For correcting: Secondly, denotative definitions can be used to *correct* connotative definitions by showing that the connotative definitions are too narrow or too broad. Let's briefly consider what is meant by "too broad" and "too narrow." First, a connotative definition is too narrow if it excludes things that should be included. If one defined "triangle" as *a plane figure enclosed by three equal line segments*, this would leave out scalene triangles and isosceles triangles. Secondly, a connotative definition is too "broad" if it includes members that should be excluded. If one defined "triangle" as *a plane figure enclosed by line segments*, this would include squares as well.

To take an example of an overly-broad definition, let's revisit the definition of MPD above: "*a dissociative disorder involving a disturbance of identity in which two or more separate and distinct personality traits (or identities) control the individual's behavior at different times.*" This definition arguably *does* refer to the average person. Most of us experience the "disturbance of identity" from "distinct personality traits" that "control" our "behavior at different times." But surely we do not, on that account, have what is *really* meant by MPD (e.g., Ed). This means that the definition above is too broad and must be revised. It would be more accurate to define MPD as something like *a mental disorder causing one to alternate forgetfully between two (or more) contrary, controlling, and self-consciously possessed identities.*

Now for an example of a definition that is too narrow. Suppose one defined "patriot" as *someone who militarily fights for his country*. One could challenge and correct this definition for excluding sub-classes of people who fight for their country in *non*-military contexts, as do statesmen (who defend the Constitution) or teachers (who train their students to loyally serve their country). By offering examples like these, one can correct narrow definitions in the same way one corrects broad definitions.

For constructing: Thirdly, denotative definitions can be used to *construct* connotative definitions. Here too one starts with paradigm examples. This is what we did with the case of Ed. Assuming he is a paradigm example of someone with MPD, we can *describe* him—i.e., his specific MPD characteristics—and then use that description to represent the entire class of people with MPD.

Take the definition of "hate crime." When this legal concept was first introduced into public discourse, the goal was to increase the severity of certain types of crimes, along with the severity of their punishment. It is bad to harm someone simply because you do not like his behavior. It is worse to harm him because you do not like his race. If a white man kills a black man who stole from him, that is the crime of murder. If a white man kills a black man because he is black, this is said to be a hate crime. This means that the latter case will involve a more severe punishment than the former.

The objections to hate crime policies are numerous. For our purposes we will focus on only one—*defining* it. One problem is that proponents of hate crime laws do not settle with this definition; they have in fact broadened the definition to include crimes motivated by hatred toward *religious beliefs* (e.g., Muslims) or *sexual practices* (e.g., homosexuals). But let's say we want to uphold the race-based definition while rejecting the other two. We will need to identify a relevant difference between race-based crimes and the other two. One option is that race is an involuntary trait, while one's religious beliefs and sexual practices are (arguably) voluntary. We might then re-define "hate crime" to mean *harming others on account of their involuntary characteristics*. This could include people with birth defects and mental handicaps.

Now notice what we have done: we used racially motivated hate crimes as the *paradigm* for constructing a connotative definition of "hate crime," a definition that includes more than "race-based" crimes, while excluding other candidates for "hate crime."

Shortcomings of denotative definitions: As valuable as they are, there remain several limitations with denotative definitions. First, in the case of ostensive definitions, it is not always obvious what *exactly* one is pointing to when defining (e.g., defining the football term "bootleg" and pointing to a complex offensive play on a field).

Secondly, many words denote things to which we cannot point, such as categories or classes (e.g., one can point to a particular dog, but not to the class or category of dog or dogness). We cannot point to invisible objects (e.g., God, angels, one's mind, numbers, logical laws, etc.). We cannot point to abstractions like "duty" or "love" or "law" or "happiness." Nor can we point to what we mean by terms like "and," "but," "or," and "therefore."

Thirdly, though ostensive definition can convey a word's "reference" (i.e., that to which one is referring), it cannot convey the "sense" in which one is referring to it. The problem of referring to the planet Venus is a famous example. The word "Venus" picks out one object to which we can point. But since this planet can be seen in both the morning and the evening, it is referred to as both the "Morning Star" and the "Evening Star." These two terms have the same reference, since they refer to the same object, but they do not have the same sense, in that "Morning Star" means "the planet Venus *as viewed during the morning*" and "Evening Star" means "the planet Venus *as viewed during the evening*." As these definitions reveal, the meaning of "Morning Star" is slightly different from the meaning of "Evening Star." The example shows that we cannot pick out, by ostensive measures, the *full meaning* of the words in question. It also demonstrates that a word's *denotation* (i.e., what it refers to) is not always identical to its *meaning*.

The two denominative methods of denotation have problems of their own. They both depend on the audience's prior knowledge of particulars (e.g., Lassie) and subclasses (e.g., collies). But we cannot always depend on this assumption.

Finally, all three forms of denotative definition are always narrow and so potentially misleading. To point at a chihuahua and say, "That is a dog" could be understood as meaning "This and only this animal is a dog." Likewise, even if your friend knows what "collies" are, this does not indicate what is common to all dogs. This is the fundamental limitation: none of the three forms of denotative definition *represent the common nature* shared by differing members of the same class. This is why we need connotative definition, which will be our focus in subsequent lessons.

20) Rules for Testing Definitions (1) Equivalence

[For the list of all nine rules, see the chart on p.138]

Structure of connotative definitions (definiendum and definiens): Every connotative definition consists of two components: the definiendum and the definiens. The definiendum is the *word to be defined*. The definiens is the *set of words used to define* the definiendum.

If we look up the meaning of the definiendum "isthmus" in the dictionary, we find the following definiens: "a narrow strip of land, bordered on both sides by water, connecting two larger bodies of land." The definiens is a string of familiar words (i.e., narrow, strip, land, bordered, sides, water, etc.) used to convey the meaning of the (perhaps) unfamiliar word "isthmus." We can picture it this way:

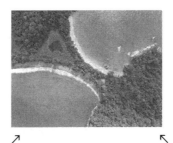

↗   ↖

[Definiendum]   [Definiens]

Isthmus   a narrow strip of land, bordered on both sides by water, connecting two larger bodies of land.

The logic of a connotative definition: Notice, first, that the *definiens is the connotative meaning* (or connotation) of the word "isthmus." Secondly, the connotative meaning of the definiens informs us of the *denotative meaning of the definiendum*; that is, the string of words on the right tells us what the word on the left refers to.

The use of the photo is somewhat misleading, since it could suggest that the definiens refers to only the particular isthmus in the photo. In fact, the definiens refers to the *whole class* of things signified by the definiendum. A more accurate picture would represent the class as a circle, containing *all* isthmuses and *only* isthmuses:

(All and Only Isthmuses)

↗   ↖

[Definiendum]   [Definiens]

Isthmus   a narrow strip of land, bordered on both sides by water, connecting two larger bodies of land.

The word "definition" comes from a Latin term meaning "to limit" or "to set boundaries to." The Latin word *definiendum* means "about to be limited" and *definiens* means "limiting." This is because the definiens restricts the reference of the definiendum, by telling us what it can *and cannot* refer to.

All the members of the denoted class (and only those members) are called the *denotata*.[45] Both the definiens and the definiendum refer to the denotata, but they do so in different ways: the definiendum *names* the denotata; the definiens *describes* them.

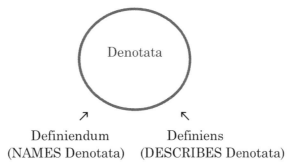

Ideally, the definiens and the definiendum *should have equivalent denotation*.[46] This means that the definiens should denote *all* the members of the named class and *only* those members. Negatively put, the definiens should denote neither more nor less than what the definiendum denotes. We may therefore place an equal sign between them:

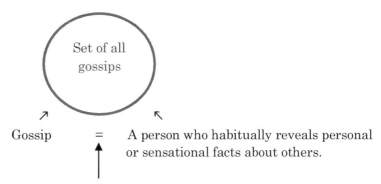

(The = means all *non*-gossips are *outside* the circle and all gossips are *inside* the circle.)

---

[45] We will also use the words 'denotatum' (a singular noun) and 'denotata' (its plural form). The following expressions are synonymous:

-The word "dog" *denotes* x, y, and z.
-The *denotation* of "dog" is x, y, and z.
-The *denotative meaning* of "dog" is x, y, and z.
-The *denotata* of "dog" are x, y, and z.

[46]To be precise, they only have identical *denotative* meaning. It is possible for terms with identical denotative meaning to have distinct "senses," e.g., the terms "Morning Star" and "Evening Star" denote the same thing (the planet Venus) and yet they have distinct senses to them: "Morning Star" = Venus as it appears at one time and "Evening Star" = Venus as it appears at another time.

We can think of a connotative definition, then, as a method for limiting the denotation of one term (the definiendum) by means of other terms (the definiens) that have *equivalent* denotation. We can translate this fact into two foundational rules for testing definitions.

Rule 1: The definiens should denote all that is denoted by the definiendum; it should not be "narrow": The connotation should denote *all* the things denoted by the word. If it fails to do so, it should be rejected for being too narrow. Suppose we define "triangle" as *a plane figure enclosed by three equal line segments*. This is too narrow, since it does not cover scalene and isosceles triangles. Another way of phrasing Rule 1 is to say that the definition *should not exclude from the class what should be included in the class*. If we define "boat" as "a motorized vehicle designed to transport cargo over water," this would be too narrow, since it does not denote some of what the definiendum denotes, such as non-motorized boats and passenger boats. In one of Plato's dialogues, the *Theaetetus*, the word "knowledge" is initially defined as *the sensations of the five senses*. Socrates rejects this definition for being too narrow, since it excludes the intellectual knowledge of logic, math, and morality. For example, it is not by mere sense-perception that we know that "Justice is a virtue" or that "Contradictory statements cannot both be true."

Rule 2: The definiens should denote only what is denoted by the definiendum; it should not be "broad": This is the flipside of Rule 1. The connotation should cover *only* the things denoted by the word. If it covers more, it should be rejected for being too broad. In other words, it *should not include in the class what should be excluded from the class*. By defining "triangle" as *a plane figure enclosed by straight lines*, this would include non-triangles (e.g., squares). To define "boat" as "an object designed to float on the water" is too broad, since the definiens refers to buoys as well. They both include in the class what should be excluded from the class.

Note that sometimes a definition can be both too broad and too narrow. For example, to define "beer" as "an amber, alcoholic drink" is both too broad (since that includes amber wines) and too narrow (since it excludes light and dark beer). To help remember the difference, "broad" means the definition is *overly-inclusive* (it includes what should be excluded) and narrow means that the definition is *overly-exclusive* (it excludes what should be included).

Rules 1 and 2 entail that the definiendum and definiens should be interchangeable. A good definition is like a math equation. In the expression *2 + 2 = 4*, the equal sign indicates that the expression *2 + 2* means the same as *4*. We can therefore switch the expressions around to become *4 = 2 +2*. This does not add new meaning or lose original meaning. Likewise in the case of connotative definition: if the definiens means exactly what the definiendum means, the definiendum means exactly what the definiens means.

We will call this the "convertibility" rule. This principle follows from Rules 1 and 2. Taken together, Rules 1 and 2 state that the definiens must denote *all* the members and *only* the members denoted by the definiendum. This results in the definiendum and the definiens having *equal denotation*. But if they have equal denotation, the definiendum and the definiens can be "converted," which is to say, switched around (or interchanged) with each other.

A definition is *in*convertible if the definiens denotes *more* or *less* than what is denoted by the definiendum. This is why we can put Rules 1 and 2 in negative terms, by saying that the definiens should *not* be "broad" or "narrow."

To test a definition according to these rules, place "all" in front of the definition and in front of its converted form. If both turn out true, the definition passes the test. If either one is false, the definition fails the test. Say we define "man" as "a sentient creature." To test this we need to write two propositions:

All men are sentient creatures.
All sentient creatures are men.

The first is true. The second is false. Therefore, the definition is not convertible.

21) Rules for Testing Definitions (2) Informative and Positive

Rule 3: The definiens should be informative; it should not be circular (i.e., restating the definiendum explicitly or implicitly): We said that a good definition should be convertible. By itself, however, this rule cannot guarantee good definitions. The rule is necessary but it is not sufficient. To see why, suppose we defined "cat" to mean *a feline*. This is convertible, since all cats are felines and all felines are cats.[47] The problem, of course, is that this is not *informative*, since it merely restates the definiendum. A definition should take one "from the known to the unknown." The point of seeking (or providing) a definition is to discover the meaning of the definiendum. But if a definition is uninformative, it is not taking us anywhere; it leaves us at the starting line. Let's explore this problem in a bit more depth by contrasting the following two statements:

1: A cat is [a cat].
2: A cat is [a feline].

Both statements are true but neither one is informative. We might initially explain the problem by saying that the definiens *means the same thing* as the definiendum. But this is not an accurate explanation of the problem. For you now know that the definiendum and definiens *should* have identical meaning. To get clearer on the exact problem, then, let's contrast 1 and 2 with a more satisfying definition of "cat":

3: A cat is [a carnivorous, purring mammal that usually has short fur, retractable claws, a long tail, and great dexterity].

In this definition, the definiens means the same thing as the definiendum (like 1 and 2 above), but it is also informative (unlike 1 and 2). This is partly because the definiendum in 3 does not reappear among the words in the definiens. But the same can be said of 2, since the definiens of 2 does not (literally) repeat the definiendum either. What exactly is the difference between 2 and 3? We know the definiens of 2 ("feline") is a *synonym* of the definiendum "cat." The problem with using a synonym is not that the synonym means the same thing, since (once again) every good definition involves equivalent meaning; the problem, rather, is that a synonym is not a *description*; it is *merely another class name*. In other words, a synonym does

---

[47] Some use 'feline' as a more general category of 'cat,' but this practice is not always observed. For the sake of making a point, I am assuming they have the same meaning.

not, as such, have any logical *connotation*. Definition 3 *characterizes* the members of the class. It tells us what kind of thing cats are and how they differ from non-cats.[48]

Even dictionaries sometimes fall prey to this use of synonyms. One dictionary defines "life" as "the quality that distinguishes a vital and functional being from a dead body." The problem is that "vital" is a synonym of "life." (The English "life" comes from the Latin *vita*, from which we get "vital"). Interestingly, elsewhere the same dictionary defines "vital" as "existing as a manifestation of life." This means it is defining "life" and "vital" in terms of one another.[49]

Non-informative definitions are often called "circular" definitions.[50] I once heard an argument for abolishing poetry from the high school curriculum. The person who proposed this was asked to define poetry. She replied by saying, "You know, poetic writing." Suppose we asked her what "poetic" means. Had she replied, "You know, poetry," this would have been going in circles. As you will learn from experience, this circular method of defining terms is very common.

With these points out of the way, we should observe that there are two cases in which it is appropriate to use synonyms.

First, sometimes we may use *loose* synonyms, which are words with analogical rather than univocal meaning. For example, suppose we define "ownership" as *having a right to possess a thing*. The terms "own" and "possess" have similar but not identical meaning. The word "own" is a legal or moral term, whereas "possess" is a physical or spatial term. One can own what they do not possess (think of a woman in relation to her stolen purse), or possess what they do not own (a thief in relation to that same purse). We must think hard to determine whether a definition involves a loose synonym.

---

[48]Perhaps it will help to think about it this way. Definitions 1, 2, and 3 involve the same definiendum, "cat." As a definiendum, the word "cat" is simply the name of a class. Therefore, the most we know is that it denotes *a* class of things. It does not tell us *which* class of things. Now consider the definiens in each of the three definitions. The problem with 1 is obvious: it expressly restates the class name ("a cat is a cat"). But definition 2 is *also* a class name, and therefore suffers the *same problem* as 1. Though "feline" is a different word-type than "cat," it does not, by itself, give us any more information about the nature of the things denoted by "cat" than the word "cat" itself does. The only new information we get from definition 2 is that we can use the class name "feline" to denote the same things denoted by "cat"—whatever those things happen to be. Only definition 3 describes or characterizes the things denoted by the class term "cat."

[49]We must not be hasty to criticize dictionary definitions with being circular. For example, some dictionaries define "happy" as "expressing or suggestive of happiness." This would appear to be circular, since "happiness" is just the noun form of the adjective "happy." Yet the dictionary also defines the noun "happiness"—i.e., "the state of well-being and contentment." This definition is not circular. But suppose the dictionary defined "happiness," instead, as "the state of being happy," and "happy," in turn, as "expressing or suggestive of happiness." In this case the dictionary would have locked us into a circular definition, in which two words are defined in terms of each other.

[50]They remind us of arguments that go in circles, e.g., the Bible is true because the Bible says it is true, and whatever the Bible says is true, because the Bible is true. This argument does not take us beyond where it starts. Likewise, circular definitions do not increase or advance our understanding of a term's meaning.

Secondly, sometimes we can use a strict synonym to help others understand how a word is being used. If my child asks what "feline" means, I may reply that it means the same thing as "cat." The context permits this. I am not trying to give the real connotative meaning of "feline." I am only helping the child understand how the word is used. It's simply a handy teaching device, especially when we cannot come up with a satisfying connotative definition. This would not be appropriate if we're arguing a thesis in a term paper or debate, where the real connotative meaning of a term is in dispute.

Rule 4: Do not define the indefinable: Sometimes we encounter concepts that defy definition. Take the word "consciousness." We cannot say, for example, *the state of being conscious*, since that is a circular definition. Nor can we say *awareness*, since that is (arguably) a strict synonym (like trying to define "cat" as *a feline*). Nor will it help to describe it as *a mental state*, or *a property of the mind*, since we will eventually find ourselves forced into defining "mind" in terms of consciousness. Nor will it do to say that it is *a property of the brain*, since that does not tell us what kind of property it is; at best, it tells us where consciousness is located (if that even makes sense). The only thing left is to list some of the properties of consciousness. We might say that it is immaterial (i.e., non-physical), but this claim (even if true) tells us what consciousness is *not*, not what it *is*. (We will address this problem in connection with rule 5 below). What sort of thing *is* consciousness? It does not seem to have anything in common with bodies, e.g., shape, weight, solidity, locomotion, color, texture, taste, sound, or smell. And yet we all seem to know what we mean by the word "consciousness." As conscious beings, we experience what it is to be conscious every waking moment of our lives.

There are other words that may (or may not) be definable. Some think the terms "existence," "good," "pleasure," and "one" are indefinable. A more concrete example is "yellow." We can say that it is a color—but so is red; or that it is a softer and lighter color—but so is pink. We might say that it is the primary color between green and orange in a rainbow. But not even this really works. Suppose we give this answer to someone who has seen green and orange but has never seen yellow. Telling him that yellow is between these colors does not convey, to his mind, what we have in our minds by the term "yellow." Or suppose we give the "scientific" answer, by saying that "yellow" is the visual sensation caused by light stimulating the L and M cone cells of the retina about equally, with no significant stimulation of the S cone cells.[51] Someone born blind might understand this scientific definition without knowing what the rest of us mean when we say, for example, that "the sun shone a lovely yellow hue." In everyday discourse, "yellow" signifies a particular color which all sighted people experience, but which no one can define connotatively.

---

[51] This is a simplified version of a Wikipedia definition.

We can only give denotative definitions to sighted people, by pointing to particular patches of yellow.

Indefinable ideas are sometimes called "primitive notions." If a term is indefinable or primitive, we will find ourselves using circular definitions to define it (e.g., "life" is a *vital* quality). To take another example, some define "cause" as *that which brings about an effect*. But what is an "effect"? That which is brought about by a cause.

Rule 5: As a general rule, the definiens should be positive (stating what things are) rather than negative (stating what they are not). It is tempting to define terms by contrasting them with other terms. We might say that a boy is *not a man*; that an atheist is *not a theist*; that a Protestant is *not a Catholic*; and so on.

Logically speaking, these statements are not nearly as informative as they initially seem. To see why, suppose you were told that "snollygoster" does not refer to a reptile. Does this tell you what it *is*? Does it tell you whether a snollygoster is a car, a planet, or type of potato chip? The statement "*x* is not *y*" implies that *x* could be *anything other than y*, any one of a virtually infinite number of things. Knowing that a snollygoster is *not* a reptile still leaves you far away from knowledge of what it is. In fact, a snollygoster is a politician guided by personal interest rather than moral principles.

"Theism" is typically defined as the belief that there exists one transcendent God who is all-good, all-wise, and all-powerful. A "theist" is someone who believes in theism. What, then, is an *a*theist?

Suppose we use the negative definition "not a theist." Does this work? No, it doesn't. First of all, panentheists do not believe in God—they believe that God is the personal governing force within the world, like a soul in a body. Polytheists do not believe in God—they believe that there are many gods, all of whom are finite. Agnostics do not believe in God—they believe that there is not enough evidence to either affirm *or deny* the existence of God or the gods. Therefore, none of these three groups are theists. But if we define "atheist" as someone who is *not* a theist, it follows that panentheists, polytheists, and agnostics are also atheists. The problem is that none of them *are* atheists. Atheists, in fact, reject pantheism, polytheism, and agnosticism as well as theism. An atheist is one who *denies the existence of divine being(s) of any sort*, whether many gods or one God, whether they be in the world (panentheism) or outside the world (theism).

Secondly, there is a sense in which "not a theist" could be taken to mean literally *anything other than* a theist, which includes swimming pools and dirty socks. We may as well say that an atheist is "not a watermelon" or "not an intercontinental ballistic missile." Why are we tempted to say that an atheist is not a theist, but not to say that an atheist is not a watermelon? It's because our background knowledge enables us to read meaning *into* words and statements that are not necessarily contained in them. Some English speakers know that the Greek letter alpha ("a") could be used to mean *not*, *non*, or *un*. This enables them to interpret "atheism" as "*not* theism" or as "the negation of theism." But this still doesn't tell us what "theism" means. However, since many English speakers already know what "theism" and "theist" mean, they infer that "atheist" means one who denies God's existence, in contrast to someone who denies the existence of unicorns.

But remember, atheists also deny pantheism, polytheism, and agnosticism. This means that we should define an "atheist" as someone who *denies the existence of divine or supernatural beings of all sorts*, whether God, gods, angels, or what have you.

We might wonder whether it's possible to define "atheist" *positively*. Maybe an atheist is someone who believes that *Nature exists*. This definition is positive. The problem, though, is that theists (and polytheists, panentheists, and agnostics) *also* believe that Nature exists. The atheist, in contrast, believes that *only* Nature exists.[52] But the word "only" is now serving a negative role; it means *and nothing else*. All of this shows that atheism is, by definition, a negative term; it involves a *denial*. We must define it negatively.

One last point: How should we define *opposites*, such as "up" and "down"? Can we define "up" as "not down"? No, since "not down" could just as well mean "to the side of." It would be better to define it as "the *opposite of* down." This only works, though, when someone has a prior knowledge of what "down" (and "opposite") mean. We could try to define "up" positively, as "that which is above" or "over," but what do those terms mean? They seem to be correlative, like "cause" and "effect."

Some words are defined negatively as opposites of other words, when, in fact, it's not clear that they are opposites at all, or (at least) what they are opposite *of*. For example, is "joy" really the opposite of sadness, as people often say? Why not think of joy as the opposite of anger too? A little reflection reveals that "joy" is a positive term (i.e., the *feeling of gladness*, perhaps?). There are many words that people mistakenly define in terms of their opposition to other words (white as opposite of black, or wife as opposite of husband). We need to carefully consider if this is right to do.

The exception to Rule 5: privations should be defined negatively: Many things in the world are *privations*. A privation (e.g., blindness) is not merely the absence or lack of something; it is the absence of something that *ought to be present* (i.e., the ability to see). Cats lack the ability to breathe under water; but, since they are not meant to possess this ability in the first place, their lack of it is not a privation, i.e., a defect or disorder. A lame cat, on the other hand, has a privation.

---

[52] To be accurate, panentheists and even polytheists think that only Nature exists, but they believe that God or the gods are somehow in and part of Nature. Therefore, atheists should really be called Materialists, not Naturalists.

Terms like "blind," "paralyzed," "sick," and "bald" signify the absence of what ought to be present. This means it is impossible to define them *without* using negative terms. Blindness *is* the *in*ability to see.

22) Rules for Testing Definitions (3) Essence and Accidence

Rule 6: The definiens should signify essential attributes; not accidental ones. The previous rules are necessary, but they are still not sufficient. Suppose we define "dime" as *the lightest U.S coin*. This definition is convertible, since the dime is the lightest U.S. coin, and the lightest U.S. coin is the dime. But convertibility only means that the definition is not *false*. Secondly, the definition is also informative. There is nothing circular about it. Finally, it is also positive. It does not say, for example, that a dime is not a quarter. Though this definition follows all the previous rules, it is still a poor definition. The reason is that the characteristic of being the lightest U.S. coin is not the most important defining characteristic of the dime. This definition omits what is *essential* to being a dime, namely, having the value of ten cents.

We will define "essence" to mean *a thing's most important defining characteristic(s)*. To state a thing's essence is to convey the *epitome* of the thing. It is to convey its primary or cardinal nature, its "core" or its "heart and soul." The medieval thinkers called a thing's essence its "quiddity." It is that which is most responsible for making a thing what it is, and for distinguishing it from other things similar to it. If we identified the most important defining characteristics of the denotata signified by the words "car" and "boat" and "plane," we would *not* describe their color, their weight, their price, or the material of which they are made. We would describe their function (i.e., to transport people or cargo) and the medium by which they travel (i.e., land, water, air). Again, if we had to identify the most important defining characteristics of the denotata signified by the word "human," it would not be weight, height, age, country of residence, skin color, political persuasion, or athletic accomplishment. We would think, rather, of more important traits like rationality, freedom, creativity, moral responsibility, and dignity. These are more defining of what it is to be human.

Whatever is non-essential is called "accidental." A thing's accidental attributes are the characteristics it just happens to have in addition to its essential attributes. I am essentially a human, and accidentally an American, a Caucasian, and 200 lbs. Likewise, a boat might just happen to be made of wood rather than fiberglass. A circle just happens to be the most difficult plane figure to draw by hand.

How do we determine what is essential to a thing? There are at least two considerations to bear in mind.

First, we can think of an essential attribute as an *indispensable* attribute, as an attribute *without which* a thing would no longer be what it is supposed to be. Strip away my height, my weight, the color of my skin, and I remain a human. Take away my limbs, or my ability to see or hear, and I remain human (a disabled human, perhaps, but still a human). But take away my freedom, my rationality, or my conscience, and suddenly my humanity seems compromised. These qualities seem to be indispensable to what it is to be a human.

And yet, even here we need to proceed with caution. Are people who are in a coma or "persistent vegetative state" (PVS) no longer *human* just because (as far as we know) they are no longer able to reason or to make choices? What about someone born with severe mental disabilities, or an elderly person with extreme dementia? What about someone who is insane, or a so-called sociopath or psychopath? Are they no longer human? What about the preborn? To answer these questions, we need to make two distinctions.

First, we need to distinguish (1) the way God originally created humans and intended them to be (see Matthew 19:8), and (2) the way they actually are as fallen human beings. The former is our *essence*. The latter is not. Humans are sinful but they were not created that way; they are fallen. Think of the Roman Colosseum as it now is contrast to the way it was originally constructed. Is it still the Colosseum? Yes and no. Or consider some make of car from the 1980s, such as the Chevy Camaro IROC-Z. Except for the ones that have been restored or kept in storage, the specimens still driving are worn down, dented, or otherwise defective. They are no longer in the original condition as when they rolled off the manufacturing line. Analogously, humans are now corrupted by sin. But is this their essence? No. Being sinful is not who humans essentially are (by Creation). Yet it is who they have become (by the Fall). Likewise, dementia and insanity are unnatural departures from who we *essentially are* as humans. We are not supposed to think or feel that way. But damaged humans are still humans, just as damaged Camaros are still Camaros.

Secondly, in the case of the preborn, God intended for humans to grow and pass though stages of development, from conception to adulthood. A preborn child in the first trimester cannot make moral choices, nor can a one-month-old child out of the womb. A one-year-old child cannot live (what Socrates called) an examined life, but neither can a three-year-old. Simply put, babies and children are not adults. (Surprise!) But does being a *young* human make one a *sub*-human? The question is self-answering. The ability to reason and to make significant moral decisions is what God has made humans to do *when He makes them able to do it*. It is part of their essence, as human beings, to *grow into* self-governing adults. The fact that they have not arrived implies nothing about their humanity, but a great deal about their maturity.

Moving on, we can think of an essential attribute as *intrinsic* (or inherent) to the thing. We often think of gold as a valuable metal. But the value of gold is not intrinsic to it. If people did not value gold, gold would no longer "have" value. But it *would* continue to have the same color, texture, weight, composition, and so forth.

These are its intrinsic properties. Or suppose we defined "triangle" as the *most popular plane figure* or as *the easiest plane figure to draw*. Neither one informs us of what it is to be a triangle; they inform us of something extrinsic to the triangle, something about us and our relation to triangles. Or again, suppose we define "triangle" as *the shape of the side of a pyramid*. This is true, but it still does not say anything about the intrinsic properties of the triangle itself; it's only a statement about the properties of pyramids.

A classic example of the intrinsic-extrinsic contrast comes from Socrates' analysis of "piety" in the Euthyphro. When Euthyphro defines "piety" as *what is dear to the gods*, he is not telling us what piety *itself* is—intrinsically. He is only telling us what effect piety has on the gods, which is something extrinsic to piety.

In sum, it is not enough to describe any attribute a thing happens to possess. A good definition must also signify the essence of the denotata; it must state *essential* attributes, not accidental attributes.

23) Excursus: Aristotle's Method of Specific Difference

We said that a thing's "essence" is its most important defining characteristic(s). This is an admittedly vague definition. It is difficult to state this in a satisfying way. In what follows we will explore the classical explanation of essence, first given by Aristotle and later developed by medieval philosophers. This is roughly the same account one finds in traditional logic texts. As we'll see, it is part of a classical theory of the nature and the standards of definition.

From Aristotle's day onward, many intellectuals taught that every attempt at describing a thing will involve one (or more) of five types of "predicate." (A predicate is a word we use to say something about another thing; it is how we describe, characterize, or categorize it. In the proposition "Dogs are animals" or "Dogs are barking animals" the words "animals" and "bark" are predicates.) Within this theory, there are five types of predicates corresponding to five types of attributes possessed by things. These predicates have been variously named the "Five Words," the "Five Universals," the "Five Types of Universals" or, more commonly, the "Five Predicables." The following statement includes all five:

"Socrates is a pug-nosed rational animal capable of questioning."

The subject of the statement is an individual named Socrates. The complex predicate of the statement is "pug-nosed rational animal capable of questioning." This complex predicate ascribes a number of attributes to him, all of which he actually possessed. But this complex predicate can be broken up into five distinct types of predicate, what are called: (1) "species," (2) "genus," (3) "specific difference," (4) "properties," and (5) "accidents."

		"Species" \ "Essence" ("definition" proper) ↓		
Socrates	pug-nosed	Rational	animal	capable of questioning
↑	↑	↑	↑	↑
Individual	**"Accident"**	**"Difference"**	**"Genus"**	**"Property"**

In the remainder of this lesson we will examine each type of predicate, and then consider how they are used to construct definitions.

Essence (i.e., "Definition" Proper): Thomas Reid, an eighteenth century Scottish philosopher, summarized Aristotle's understanding of definition as follows:

"He considers a Definition as *a speech declaring what a thing is*. Everything *essential* to the thing defined, and nothing more, must be contained in the definition. Now, the essence of a thing consists in these two parts: first, *What is common to it with other things of the same kind*; and, secondly, *What distinguishes it from other things of the same kind*. The first is called the *Genus* of the thing, the second is its *Specific Difference*. The definition, therefore, consists of these two parts."[53]

In its classical sense, a "definition" is not just any *definiens*, but only the one that signifies a thing's *essence*. An individual's essence is the *specific kind* of thing it is. If the question were posed to us, "What is a tiger?" we might give the general reply, "A tiger is a cat." This is what the tiger shares in common with things of the same kind. But since there are other sub-classes of cats, such as lions and panthers, defining a tiger as a "cat" fails to *differentiate* tiger from other cats, which is to say, it fails to tell us how a tiger differs from things very much like it. A full definition must indicate the *specific kind* of cat a tiger is. Again, to the question "What is a river?" we might reply, "A river is a body of water." Though true, it is not specific enough, since oceans, bays, lakes, and ponds are also bodies of water. To indicate the essential nature of a river, we must show how it differs from these other bodies of water; we must show the *specific kind* of body of water a river is.

As Thomas Reid stated, a specific kind will ideally consist of two parts: the genus and the specific difference. In fact, we can express this point in terms of an equation: (specific kind = genus + specific difference).[54] To understand a thing's essence or specific kind, we shall have to consider the two parts composing it.

Genus: Whenever one class of things falls under a larger class of things, the larger class is said to be the "genus" of the former. A genus is *a super-class*.

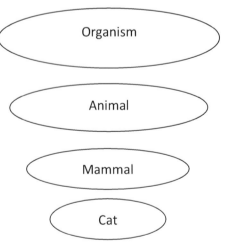

In the diagram to the right, we find that every member of the class of Cat is also a member in the larger class of Mammal, which is therefore called the "genus" of Cat. Every member of the class of Mammal is a member of the genus of Animal, which, in turn, falls under the higher genus of Organism. Since the category of Organism is the greatest in size, it is the highest genus in this hierarchy. This ascending level of categories is what we call a hierarchy of genera (the word "genera" is plural for "genus").

In reply to the earlier question "What is a tiger?" we do not find ourselves tempted to say, "A tiger is an organism." While this

---

[53]*A Brief Account of Aristotle's Logic*, Chapter 2, Sect. 4.
http://uk.geocities.com/frege@btinternet.com/joyce/reid_aristotle.htm
[54] This will be revised with "proximum genus."

is true, it is far *too general* an answer, which means that the class of "organism" is *too high* up the ladder of genera.[55] Given the vast number of things that fall under the huge category of Organism, to say that a tiger is an "organism" would not relay its specific nature. The category "animal" would be better, and "mammal" better still, but even these are too general. When we think of a tiger or any other thing, we naturally think of what is called its *most proximate genus*, which is the nearest genus of the thing we're defining. In the diagram above, the most proximate genus of tiger is Cat, rather than Mammal. On any hierarchy of genera, the most proximate genus will be the category directly under which is the thing to be defined. We earlier said that a genus is one of two parts of a definition, the other being the specific difference. To be more precise, we can now say that a definition must consist, not simply of a genus and specific difference, but of a *most proximate genus* and specific difference. So we can refine the equation given above by adding: "specific kind" = most proximate genus + specific difference.

Specific difference: We can define "specific difference" to mean *any attribute that differentiates one species from other species in the proximate genus*.[56] Let's explore this idea in depth. We earlier said that, whenever one class of things falls under a larger class of things, the larger class is the "genus" of the smaller, and the smaller class is the "species" of the larger. In this view, a species *just is* any subclass. But this is not quite the classical understanding of the word "species." It is important to understand why. Consider the three bubbles below. Those who make "genus" and "species" inter-definable will say that the category Dog is a genus in relation to Coyote, but a *species* in relation to Mammal. In the classical view, however, only Coyote is a species.

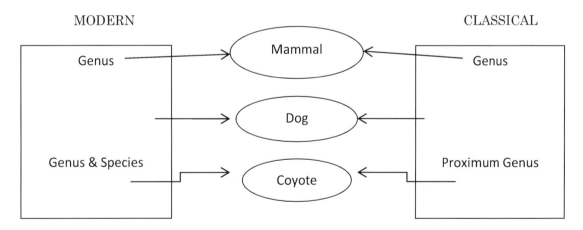

In the classical view, the term "species" is reserved for the bottommost level in a hierarchy of genera. Every level above the species is a genus of some sort. The

---

[55] The words 'general' and 'generic' come from genus; 'special' and 'specific' come from species.
[56] Some allow the specific difference to be an entire *set of attributes*.

highest genus in a given hierarchy is called the *summum genus*. Each lower level genus is called a *subaltern genus*, or *sub-genera*. The genus directly above the species is called the *proximum genus*. This is clearer in the case of triangles.

Hierarchy	Names
Figure	summum genus
Plane figure	subaltern genus
Closed plane figure	subaltern genus
Closed plane figure with line segments as sides	subaltern genus
Closed plane figure with three line segments as sides	proximum genus
Closed plane figure with three line segments as sides, none of which are congruent	*scalene* species of triangle
Closed plane figure with three line segments as sides, only two of which are congruent	*isosceles* species of triangle
Closed plane figure with three line segments as sides, all three of which are congruent	*equilateral* species of triangle

In the chart, triangle is a proximum genus of scalene, isosceles, and equilateral. In the common view (but not the classical view) a triangle could be considered a species relative to the subaltern genus of "closed plane figures with line segments as sides." That is, a triangle is under the same class as squares, and is therefore just one of many "species" of this class. In the classical, view, however, triangle is not a species; it is only a proximum genus.

Notice what this implies about the meaning of "specific difference." In both views, what differentiates triangles from squares is the *number of sides*. In the common view (but not the classical view) the number of sides is the specific difference, since (in the common view) triangles are a species along with square, and the number of sides is what differentiates them from squares. In the classical view, "triangle" is not a species but rather a proximum genus. The species are "scalene," "isosceles," and "equilateral." What differentiates the species of triangles—scalene, isosceles, and equilateral—from one other is the *number of equal sides*, which makes this the specific difference that distinguishes the three forms of triangle.

What is the practical point of this contrast between the classical and common views? The reason is this. Aristotle was after the *specific* natures of the *objects we experience*. In his (classical) view, a species is the essential nature of the *things we actually experience in the world*. You will never experience a merely generic "triangle" in the world; you will only ever experience a scalene, an isosceles, or an equilateral triangle. There is no such thing in the world as an object that is *merely* a closed plane figure with three line segments as sides. Rather, there are only closed plane figures with three line segments as sides, such that all of the sides are equal (equilateral), or only two of them are equal (isosceles), or none of them is equal (scalene). Or, consider the difference between a wolf, a coyote, and a collie. We say they are all "dogs." Why not settle with that? Why create the distinct names "wolf," "coyote," and "collie"? The reality is that we never see dogs *per se*; we always see *specific kinds* of dogs—e.g., wolves, coyotes, etc. We call all of them "dogs" because they share generic features. Yet (and this is the key point) these dogs always exist *as* species—as collies, as wolves, as poodles—and never as dogs *per se.* In other words, the essential nature of a coyote is not dogness (since that is shared by other kinds of dogs) but coyote-ness. Each coyote shares a specific nature with other coyotes, and which is had only by other coyotes.

You should also bear in mind that since the term "species" signifies the essential nature of the things we experience, it follows that the word "species" signifies *the only category in a hierarchy that cannot be further subdivided.* Sometimes it's not entirely clear where to stop the sub-divisions. Coyotes are a very specific form of canine, yet scientists have subdivided them into a variety of further subspecies based (mostly) on geographical location (e.g., western, eastern etc.). But wherever the division stops, there is where we find Aristotle's notion of a species. Suppose the eastern coyote is a true species. It would then follow that it cannot be further subdivided; there would be no *species* of eastern coyotes, only numerically distinct *individuals*. Likewise, we cannot further subdivide the class of equilateral triangles or the class of Great Danes.

By defining specific difference as that which differentiates one species from other species under the same proximate genus, the implication is that there are two or more species under a proximate genus. Consider the genus Dog. Most books subdivide the class into at least five species:

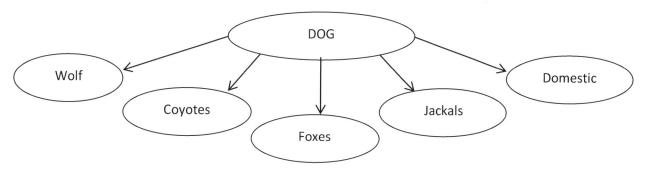

To justify this division, there must be both (1) something fundamentally similar among all the different kinds, and (2) something basically different between each kind. It is obvious that these five types of animals do in fact share a basic set of attributes, such as structural appearance and behavioral patterns. Though domesticated breeds vary widely from one another (this being a result of controlled modification by dog-breeders), even the Shih Tzu and Irish Wolfhound share the same anatomical form. These basic similarities lead us to classify all the otherwise distinct groups under one genus—dog. But it is also obvious that each of the subclasses differs from the others in significant ways. Therefore, just as the generic similarities lead us to group them into one major category, so the specific differences lead us to distinguish them from one another.

The most famous example of a specific difference is that of "rational" in the classical definition of "man" as "rational animal." The Greeks held that man is a kind of animal. So the term "animal" signified the proximate genus of man. What differentiates men from other species of animals is the attribute of rationality.

Now consider this definition ("rational animal") in light of what we have said so far. We said that a thing's definition = the specific kind of thing it is, and that the specific kind = the most proximate genus + specific difference. Therefore, a thing's definition = the most proximate genus + specific difference. Now, if the most proximate genus of man is "animal," and if "rational" is what essentially distinguishes him from other animals, it would follow that "rational animal" *just is* what "man" means. "Rational animal" is thus the *definition* of "man." "Man" = "rational animal."

It will be helpful, before moving on to the other two Predicables, to wrap-up the preceding discussion with a summary. We started by noting that, according to the classical view, a definition is a statement of a thing's essence or essential nature. We then added that a thing's essence is the *specific kind* of thing it is. The synonym is "species." Next we learned that a specific kind comprises two parts: the *most proximate genus* and the *specific difference*. We can display all these relations with the following equivalent expressions:

- Essence = Species = Specific Kind
- Specific Kind = Most Proximate Genus + Specific Difference
- Definition = Statement of a thing's essence
- Therefore, Definition = Statement of Most Proximate Genus + Specific Difference

Here is one final example. The definition of "trimaran" is "a three-hulled boat." Displayed diagrammatically, we find that the species is the essence or essential nature of a trimaran. Therefore, trimaran = a three-hulled boat.

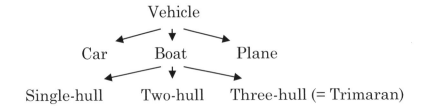

Generic and specific attributes: So far we've distinguished genus and species. By extension, we may also distinguish the *attributes* associated with each one. As a rational *animal*, Socrates shares a set of attributes possessed by other members of the genus Animal, such as the five senses and a nervous system. Since all members in the genus Animal share these attributes, they are accordingly called "generic attributes," i.e., *attributes shared by all members of a genus*. But as a *rational* animal, Socrates shares the attribute of rationality with only the members of his specific kind, i.e., Man. It is thus a specific attribute, i.e., an *attribute shared by all and only those members of a given species.*

Properties: A property is *any attribute that belongs exclusively to an essence or species*. The capacity to ask questions is a property of men, since it belongs only to rational nature, and only men have a rational nature. No other animal can ask questions because no other animal has a rational nature. The capacity for laughter and romantic sentiment are also properties of men. According to the classic account, a property differs from a specific difference by being an *extension* or *outgrowth* of that specific difference. The specific difference of rationality enables Socrates to behave in ways in which non-rational animals cannot. Because Socrates is *rational*, he is *able to construct a geometry proof* (this being one of many "properties" of men as men).

Accidents: The term "accident" literally means *that which happens to* something. That Socrates just happened to possess a pug nose has nothing to do with him being a rational animal. (If it did, then all rational animals would have pug noses.) The pug-nose attribute is one that Socrates, as a man, just happened to have. It is an "accident." Though we speak of different types of men—e.g., black and white, Chinese and Japanese, rich and poor, virtuous and vicious—these are not literally different *species* of man. These are accidental distinctions among men. Race, ethnicity, wealth, religion, etc., are all accidental predicates. Collies and Great Danes are different species of the genus dog, but so-called "Negroes" and "Caucasians" (to use the older language) are not different species of man. "Man" itself signifies a species. It does not signify a genus, and so it cannot be divided into species. Therefore, any differences among members of a species will be "accidental" differences. This is true of black and white people, rich and poor, etc.

For some time, tigers were divided by habitat into Bengals, Siberians, and so forth. Recently this classification was rejected as accidental, since it was based on differences of mere habitat. This would be like dividing Man into South American species and North American species.

Whereas generic and specific attributes are vital to the *whatness* of a thing, and therefore relevant to its definition, accidental attributes are not. It is impossible to be a man without being an animal or rational; but it is possible to be a man without being black or white, rich or poor, etc. Therefore, while we can debate whether "properties" should be used in a definition, we should all agree that accidental attributes should never be used.

Challenges with the Aristotelian standard of definition: This lesson began as an introduction to one (of many other) rules for testing definitions, what we called the "Essentiality Rule." Our attempt at defining the word "essence" led us into a lengthier discussion of the classical, Aristotelian standard of definition, often called definition by specific difference. This is because of the way in which the Aristotelian definition conceives of an "essence." It is a much more technical notion of essence than what we introduced at the beginning of the lesson. We defined an "essence" as that which is a thing's most important, defining characteristic(s). The Aristotelian definition is not at odds with this explanation. Aristotle would surely agree with it. The problem is that it is not precise enough to tell us what *constitutes* a thing's essence. His analysis provides one widely accepted answer.

The Aristotelian method is probably best thought of as an ideal to try following when possible. Experience suggests that it is not always easy to apply, that it is sometimes artificial and clunky, and that, in some cases, there might be better ways of defining terms. The remainder of this lesson will briefly note some of these limitations.

In some cases the method of proximum genus + specific difference seems fairly easy to apply. To generate the definition of "triangle," one begins by finding the proximum genus of triangle, in contrast to the summum genus or subaltern genus. We simply ask a series of logically progressing questions. What is a triangle? Answer: a *figure* (summum genus). What kind of figure? Answer: a *plane* figure (subaltern genus). What kind of plane figure? Answer: a plane figure *bounded by straight lines* (proximum genus). How many straight lines? Answer: *three*. This last answer gives us the "specific difference" that separates triangles from other plane figures bounded by straight lines (e.g., squares, pentagons, etc.). We now have our definition: *a plane figure bounded by three straight lines*.

This very clear and elegant example might mislead us into thinking that *every* class of things can be defined in this way.

It's not always obvious that there *is* a proximate genus. Contrast these definitions of "square."[57]

- "square" = "a plane closed figure that has exactly four sides all of which are straight and equal to one another and whose interior angles each measure 90°"
- "square" = "an equilateral parallelogram containing four axes of symmetry"

Which is the correct proximum genus—a "plane closed figure" or an "equilateral parallelogram"? It's not clear that there is a "right" answer here.

Assuming we have a proximate genus, it's not always obvious that there is one correct way of dividing a proximum genus. Now contrast these definitions of "square."[58]

---

[57] Taken from Norman Swartz. *www.ucd.ie/artspgs/semantics/swartznsc.pdf*
[58] Taken from https://www.sfu.ca/~swartz/definitions.htm

- "square" = "a plane closed figure that has exactly four sides all of which are straight and equal to one another and whose interior angles each measure 90°"
- "square" = "a plane closed figure having four straight sides and whose diagonals are both equal in length to one another and bisect one another at right angles"
- "square" = "a straight-sided, plane, closed figure, every diagonal of which cuts the figure into two right isosceles triangles"

All of these seem to be equally legitimate ways of defining a square. Or let's take an example from biology.

Let's try defining a platypus. Plato and Aristotle would have been scandalized by this creature. These thinkers sought to cut nature at its joints, by finding a place for everything and then putting everything in its place. But a Platypus? This mind-bending critter shows that things are a bit more complicated. A Platypus is considered a mammal, but it doesn't give birth to its young—it lays eggs. On top of that, it has the tale of a beaver, the bill of a duck, and the feet of an otter. If that isn't weird enough, it is also venomous. So what is its proximum genus? What is the specific difference? Encarta defines "platypus" this way: *an egg-laying water mammal with a snout shaped like a duck's bill and webbed feet*. In an Aristotelian analysis, "mammal" is a subaltern genus of this definition. "Water mammal" is a smaller subaltern genus. "Egg-laying water mammal" is the proximum genus. Among mammals, the platypus' attribute of laying eggs is shared with only one other creature, the echidna. So both the platypus and the echidna would be under the proximum genus "egg-laying water mammal." One problem with this definition, however, is that echidnas are not *water* mammals. We should therefore revise the proximum genus to "egg-laying mammal." But what is the thing that differentiates the platypus from the echidna? Being in water versus on land? Why not just as well say "having a bill" versus "not having a bill"? Or having webbed feet versus not having webbed feet? Or being venomous versus not being venomous? The obvious problem is that the platypus is the only egg-laying mammal that is aquatic, and the only one that has a bill, and the only one that has webbed feet, and the only one that is venomous. Which of these are the specific differences? All of them? None of them? Questions like these are hard to answer.

In some cases, a thing's nature seems to be the sum total of otherwise common attributes, in which case we can only pile up non-specific differences. For example, try to define "seagull." Its subaltern genus would be "bird." But what is its proximum genus? Would it be semi-aquatic? Even if we could nail down a proximum genus, what is the specific difference to distinguish it from other birds in that category? This is hard to answer. When we think about it, it seems we can only identify characteristics shared by a wide range of other birds, e.g., they inhabit coastal sea areas, have webbed feet, relatively long and thick beaks, relatively long wings, and usually have gray and white plumage. Every one of these characteristics can be ascribed to many other species of birds. The most we can do, then, is create a unique conglomeration of attributes capable of picking out seagulls.

Some things seem utterly indefinable using the method of specific difference. As noted in the previous lesson, some terms (e.g., consciousness) do not appear to be definable at all. If that is true, then they do not have a proximum genus and a specific difference.

24) Rules for Testing Definitions (4) Clarity and Brevity

Rule 7: The definiens should be as precise as possible; it should not contain vague, ambiguous, or figurative terms. Since a definition should take us from the known to the unknown, it follows that the known (i.e., the definiens) should be as clear as possible. If the definiens is not clear, we cannot tell whether the definiens is too broad or too narrow, nor whether it signifies essential attributes or only accidental ones.

Avoiding vague terms: A good definition is like a perfectly focused photograph: the appearance of the object in the photograph is crisp, clear, and definite. Conversely, a bad definition is like an unfocused photograph: the edges and contours of the objects in the picture are blurred and indistinct; they are *vague*. The following words are examples of vagueness:

> The man is *tall*.
> The plane is *slow*.
> The house is *big*.
> It was a *hot* day.
> The rope is *strong*.
> He slept a *long* time.

Vague words are not meaningless. They are indefinite because they are *open-ended*.[59] How tall is "tall"? Suppose you had to divide people into two classes, tall and non-tall. Would you know who to place into each class? If we picture a class of things as a circle, with members inside and non-members outside, we can contrast vague and clear classes this way:

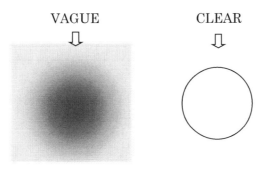

---

[59]Vagueness and ambiguity shade into each other. For example, the following italicized words could be considered both vague and ambiguous: "Democracy is *good*" and "That is an *interesting* comment."

As the image illustrates, it is not always easy to determine where the borders of a vague concept end or begin. Consider this definition of "judgmental"—*inclined to make judgments, especially moral or personal ones.*[60] Suppose we represent the categories of "moral" and "personal" as circles, and then ask ourselves what goes into them and what falls outside of them. Am I being "judgmental" for noticing that my son mowed the lawn unevenly? According to the above definition, the answer will depend on whether his lawn-mowing performance is "moral" (or non-moral), or whether it is "personal" (or non-personal). But where exactly are the borders or parameters of "moral" and "personal"? How do we know when something is "in" the circle or "outside" of it? It's hard to tell.

We might also think of vagueness in terms of a linear scale. If we used the example of "bald," we can imagine a dense head of hair on one side and a totally hairless head on the other.

"Not bald"   "Bald"

Abnormally thick head of hair	1,000,000 hairs?	100,000 hairs?	10,000 hairs?	1,000 hairs?	1 hair?	Not a single hair
	←					

At which number do we move out of the bald segment of the scale and into the non-bald segment?

It is worth distinguishing quantitative and qualitative vagueness. Sometimes vagueness can be overcome by *quantitative* description. If an elevator sign read, "This elevator cannot hold *many* people," we would probably not ride in it. But since this is a quantifiable term, it can be clarified by a numerical description. Similarly, instead of sending out a flyer saying, "Looking for tall lads to play basketball," the coach could specify an acceptable range of height, say, from 6'2 upward. But many vague terms cannot be quantified, because they express *qualitative* ideas, e.g.

> America is the champion of *freedom*.
> Americans tend to be more *religious* than Europeans.
> Liberals are more *progressive* than conservatives.
> Democrats are all about *change*.
> Conservatives believe in *traditional values*.
> Modern music tends to be *simplistic*.
> People need to respect each other's *privacy*.
> Children need to be taught to do what is *right*.
> The teacher is *severe* with his students.
> That kid is *hyperactive*.

---

[60] From *The Free Online Dictionary*

These terms cannot be clarified by quantitative analysis. It would not make sense, for example, to rate "judgmentalism" on a numerical scale, as if a 7.8 is too judgmental, but a 5.5 is not. What would 7.8 judgmentalism *look like*?

It is not necessarily wrong or inadvisable to use vague terms in everyday discourse. Sometimes the context makes them sufficiently clear. But even in their clearest uses, vague terms have only *approximate* meaning, and so will always stand in need of further clarification. This is why they should not be used in definitions, the precise goal of which is to clarify our words.

Avoiding figurative terms: Suppose we define Christian "faith" as *leaning upon the promises of God*. To "lean" is literally to rest one's upper body on a physical support, such as a shovel or kitchen countertop. Yet the analogy is easy to see. Since faith is a form of trust, i.e., *reliance* on another's promise, there is a sense in which one is "leaning" on that promise.

The problem with figurative definitions is not that they are wholly false, but that they are only partly true and so potentially misleading. Suppose we define "woman" as *the softer sex*. As in the case of "faith," this metaphor might be true in some sense. But it leaves us *guessing* about which sense is in view. As a metaphor, it is prone to ambiguity. In this case, "softer" might mean any one (or more) of the following:

1. Women are physically weaker than men.
2. Women cannot endure as much pain and suffering as men.
3. Women are more empathetic, compassionate, and nurturing than men; not as indifferent to the needs and sufferings of others.
4. Women are more emotionally sensitive, vulnerable, or defensive (e.g., their feelings are more easily hurt, or they have a harder time getting over personal offenses).
5. Women are less individualistic than men, i.e., more dependent on relations with others (e.g., on feeling loved).
6. Women are less clever, calculating, or analytical than men.

Option 1 is clearly true. Option 2 is certainly false without some sort of qualification. (Think childbirth.) Options 3-5 are probably true (also subject to qualifications, I suspect). Option 6 is plainly false, unless the terms "clever, calculating, or analytical" carry the literary connotation of being colder, less emotional, more machinelike, in which case option 6 is smuggling in the meanings of options 3-5.

Rule 8: As a general rule, the definiens should be concise. We can rephrase this rule as: *do not use more words when fewer words is possible*. If a definition can be shortened without losing necessary meaning, then by all means shorten it. This is a hallmark of good definitions. In this case, what makes it "good" is not its clarity or accuracy, but the ease with which it can be used or memorized. To ensure the definition covers everything meant by the definiendum, it is tempting to construct definitions consisting of multiple sentences. But this results in a definition as awkward to read as it is difficult to memorize. True, it might be necessary to sacrifice brevity for the sake of clarity. A long definition that communicates the full meaning of a term is preferable to a shorter definition that does not. But again, we should do this *only* when necessary.

The example of defining "Worldview": As this is the rule with which students have the most difficulty, let's practice it by comparing definitions of "worldview" from various authors, arranged from shortest to longest. (Look them over carefully before reading the subsequent comments.)

1. *"a set of beliefs about the most important issues…"*[61]

2. *"a system of assertions that makes sense out of total experience."*[62]

3. *"the widest view which the mind can take of things in an effort to grasp them together as a whole from the standpoint of some particular philosophy or theology."*[63]

4. *"a set of mental categories arising from deeply lived experience which essentially determines how a person understands, feels and responds in action to what he or she perceives of the surrounding world."*[64]

5. *"a commitment, a fundamental orientation of the heart, that can be expressed as a story or in a set of presuppositions (assumptions which may be true, partially true or entirely false) which we hold (consciously or subconsciously, consistently or inconsistently) about the basic constitution of reality, and that provides the foundation on which we live and move and have our being."*[65]

Definition 1 makes the mistake of sacrificing clarity to brevity. The definition is succinct but vague. What exactly are "the most important issues"? —Most important to whom? Most important in what respects? Some might consider politics,

---

[61] From Ronald Nash, a contemporary Christian apologist.
[62] From David Wolfe, a contemporary Christian epistemologist.
[63] From James Orr, a late 19th century Scottish Presbyterian theologian/apologist.
[64] From Wilhelm Dilthey, the late 19th century "father" of worldview thinking.
[65] James Sire—contemporary Christian popularizer of worldview thinking (Old & New definitions): Old: "A world view is a set of presuppositions (or assumptions) which we hold (consciously or subconsciously) about the basic makeup of our world."

economics, and environmental matters the most important issues, while supposing that theology and religion hold little importance.

Definition 2 appears to remedy this problem with "total experience." And yet, we are not told *whose* total experience? Presumably the author means the totality of *human* experience, and not merely his experience or the American experience. Another problem with 2 is the word "system." This might be too narrow, since it suggests that a worldview must be a very formal and well-defined set of interconnecting ideas. If that is what makes a worldview, then most people do not have a worldview, since most people do not consciously hold to a "system" of belief.

Definition 3 is subject to the same criticism. By adding "from the standpoint of some particular philosophy or theology," the implication is that only an intellectual has a worldview. Perhaps the definition would be better if left at: *the widest view which the mind can take of things in an effort to grasp them together as a whole.*

Definition 4 uses the word "categories" instead of "beliefs" (def. 1) and "assertions" (def. 2). The exact difference is unclear. Def. 4 also adds two interesting elements missing from the previous ones. First, he thinks that the personal *origin* of one's worldview ("from deeply lived experience") is an essential aspect of what it is. Perhaps. But do we really need to know where a worldview comes from, or how it is formed, in order to know what it is? Secondly, he thinks the personal *effects* of a worldview on one's experience and lifestyle are also essential. This might be an improvement on the other definitions. By defining "worldview" as a matter of thought, ideas, and beliefs, those definitions might be criticized for being too intellectual. One problem with definition 4, however, is the extraneous language at the end—"*and responds in action to what he or she perceives of the surrounding world.*" This could be shortened into "…and acts." In light of these points, we might revise this definition as: *a set of mental categories which essentially determines how a person understands, feels, and acts."*

Much can be said about definition 5. First, notice that it uses a different genus than "beliefs" or "categories." For this author, a worldview is a "commitment." This is definitely too narrow, if not altogether false. Surely "worldview" pertains as much (if not more) to how we understand, perceive, or interpret reality. We might be committed to our understanding of things, and our understanding of things might make us committed people, but this can only be one element of a worldview at best. Secondly, it is not clear what the additional phrase "a fundamental orientation of the heart" means, or how it relates to "commitment." Is it another way of saying "commitment" or is it saying something more? It seems that "fundamental orientation of the heart" goes deeper than "commitment." In any case, by using both descriptions the author lengthens the definition for no compelling reason. Thirdly, the author's heavy use of parenthetical comments is both helpful and unhelpful. The first one is unnecessary. Most readers would readily understand that presuppositions can be true or false. By adding this, the author makes an already wordy definition painfully long. The second remark is a helpful corrective to definitions 1-2, which suggest that one must consciously hold to a set of well-defined doctrines. It seems right that everyone has a worldview even though they may not have thought it through themselves or do not understand all its assumptions and implications. The phrase "constitution of reality" is unnecessary; it would suffice to say "reality." The final part of this definition—"on which we live and move and have our being"—is literary overkill. In light of these comments, the author could probably revise the definition to: *the fundamental orientation of the heart, expressing itself as a story or set of presuppositions about reality, which one holds consciously or subconsciously, consistently or inconsistently, and according to which one lives."*

Admittedly, it is easier to criticize a definition than to construct one. But let's try it anyway. What we want to do is incorporate the best insights of these definitions as succinctly (and elegantly) as we can. We can begin by identifying the most essential elements. First, it seems that a worldview is most basically a type of *explanation* or attempt to *make sense* of things. It can be thought of as an answer to some set of questions. Secondly, it is an attempt to answer questions about reality *as a whole*, not merely one sphere of reality. It is not a partial explanation of things (as we get in biology or economics); it is a complete or comprehensive explanation, though not exhaustive. (An exhaustive explanation would explain every little detail of our lives.) Thirdly, a worldview aims to answer all of the *ultimate* questions about reality, questions such as:

- Why is there something rather than nothing?
- How did the Universe form? Is there anything beyond the Universe?
- What is man? How did we get here? Why are we here? Are we different from the animals? How should we live? Is there anything beyond death?
- Is there is Supreme Being behind it all? A God (or gods)? If so, what is he/she/they like, and how do we relate to him/her/them?
- Why is there good and evil?
- How do we go about answering these questions? *Can* we answer them? What is it to "know" anything?

Fourthly, these questions are not unique to just one group of people in one period of time. These are the questions asked by thoughtful people from every nation and generation. They are Mankind's ultimate questions. Fifthly, it seems right to say that there are a limited number of plausible answers, or "standard" options, to these questions. There are seven billion people on earth but not seven billion worldviews. Some have argued that there are really only two major contenders—theism (which Christians believe) and naturalism (held by atheists). In any case, some of the other standard worldviews are animism, polytheism, pantheism, panentheism, agnosticism, skepticism, and nihilism. These worldviews tend to shape or color one's answers to all the other questions of life, from questions about the nature of family and gender, to questions about politics, economics, and entertainment. A classification of worldviews quickly runs into "variations on themes," which is to say, essentially similar perspectives differing on points of minor detail. It's safe to say that, for any given person you meet on the streets, he or she is likely to fit (more or less) into one of these worldviews. They might not know that, of course, but they have assuredly learned to interpret the world by means of it.

There remains only one other issue to resolve. Is the *effect* that a worldview has on our lives essential to the meaning of "worldview"? In other words, is a worldview *merely* an ideology or intellectual outlook? We are not asking *whether* worldview affects us. Surely it influences how we live. It determines what we are willing to watch or listen to, what we are willing to believe, how we spend our time and money, who we befriend, how we vote, whether we marry or divorce, how we define happiness and pursue it, and so on. What we are asking is whether a worldview's life-changing impact is essential to what it is. Think about this question in terms of the distinction between "essences" and "properties" in the previous lesson. Man's ability to calculate numbers, or to laugh at a joke, is a consequence of his being a rational being; that is, rationality is his *essence*. But the ability to calculate or to laugh is a *property*. Similarly, perhaps the life-determining impact of a worldview is a property of what a worldview is, rather than part of its essence.

This is a difficult question to answer. Let's call the two perspectives the *intellectual* understanding of "worldview" and the *existential* understanding of it. Our answer to this question will determine which definition we find satisfying. If one opts for the intellectual version, the following definition is probably a good one:

a standard set of answers to mankind's ultimate questions about reality

If, instead, we insist upon an existential version, we may want a definition like this:

a standard explanation of reality in terms of which we live

The main point, though, is that both definitions have the advantage of brevity. Each one compresses the desired elements into a concise definition. We could also try to combine the two as follows:

a standard set of answers to mankind's ultimate questions about reality and in terms of which he lives

You may have noted that these definitions omit several of the elements found in definitions 1-5 above. We made no reference to *feelings* (def. 4), to *commitments* and the *orientation of the heart* (def. 5), or to whether the one holds to a worldview *consciously* or *consistently* (def. 5), or to how worldviews are formed from *deeply lived experience* (def. 4). In terms of the prior lesson, we might argue that all these elements are best thought of as properties (or even accidents) rather than essential characteristics. In that case we do not need to include them.

Finally, the fact that we do not include them *in* a definition does not mean that we cannot talk about them *after* our definition. In fact, when arguing a case, it is often necessary to provide *further explanation* of one's definition, by giving commentary and analysis of it. It also frees us to make our definitions more concise, since we do not need to worry about cramming into the definition everything we think is relevant to it. (This might be what happened to the author of definition 5.) It takes practice to compress the essential meaning of a term into a brief and easy to memorize definition. It is a challenging but rewarding skill to learn.

25) Rules for Testing Definition (5) Equity

Rule 9: The definiens should bias us only when appropriate. To "bias" someone is to dispose them *for* or *against* something, to bring about a pro-attitude or a con-attitude. This is appropriate in some cases, and inappropriate in others, but it's not always easy to decide.

Ours is a culture of diversity, skepticism, and extreme tolerance. We are often reluctant to pass judgment on the beliefs and lifestyles of others, or to use divisive terms like "right" and "wrong," or "good" and "evil." When it comes to definitions, this mindset translates into a tendency to define things in a *neutral* fashion. To be neutral is to *take no side* in a contest or conflict. When it comes to defining terms, neutrality involves defining a term *without trying to dispose someone for or against* the denotata. The idea, here, is that we should not make people *partial to* something or *prejudiced against* something.

This is a healthy concern, to be sure, but we can get carried away by it. A mother should be concerned for the physical safety of her son, but bubble-wrapping him is not the solution. By neutralizing the way we speak and think, we *bias ourselves to see the world neutrally*. (Is the statement "We should be neutral" a neutral statement?) The world is not a neutral place. There *is* right and wrong, good and evil, virtue and vice, health and sickness, beauty and ugliness, light and darkness. By trying to neutralize the world, we are in fact distorting it.

Neutral definitions (non-evaluative): You know that literary connotation is an idea or feeling we tend to *associate* with the literal meaning of a word. For some of us, the words "dog" or "cat" have a literary connotation, since they evoke an emotional or evaluative reaction. Some think of dogs as man's best friend, or as virtually on par with human children. Others think of them as filthy things that stink up a home and breed allergies. Some think of cats as cute and cozy lap pets, while others think of them as unsociable and manipulative ingrates. But these psychological associations are not part of the *essence* of dogs or cats. The literal meanings of "dog" and "cat" include nothing about *our attitude* toward them. This explains why we should define these creatures in a more or less *neutral* manner.

Evaluative definitions (non-neutral): There are other words whose logical meaning *should* evoke a particular attitude. The words "murder," "rape," "theft," and "cowardice" signify things which, *in their very nature*, are bad. Sins are *sins*. Crimes are *crimes*. To define "cruelty," for example, without conveying that it is *bad*, is to omit part of its essence; it is to fail to define cruelty for what it *is*. Recall what we said about privations like blindness. It is impossible to define "blindness" without identifying the absence of something that *ought* to be present. The same principle applies here: some things cannot be explained without indicating that it is *contrary* to the way things *should* be.

Evaluative terms can be positive or negative. For the sake of clarity, we will call words like "kindness" and "health" *terms of approbation*. ("Approbation" comes from a word meaning "to assent to as good," or "to regard as good."[66]) Words like "cruelty" and "ugliness" and "dishonesty" are *terms of disapprobation*.

Evaluative definitions, then, *indicate that the definiendum is a term of approbation or disapprobation*. By ascribing value or disvalue to something, an evaluative definition disposes one for or against something. Such definitions are not neutral.

Guidelines for evaluative definitions: There are five rules to follow when using evaluative definitions. The first two are framed positively (what to do) and the next three are phrased negatively (what not to do).

First, non-neutral terms should be defined non-neutrally: Terms of approbation must be defined in terms of approval. According to one dictionary, a "hero" is *somebody who commits an act of remarkable bravery or who has shown an admirable quality such as great courage or strength of character*.[67] Terms of disapprobation must be defined in terms of disapproval. The same dictionary defines "murder" as *the crime of killing another person deliberately and not in self-defense or with any other extenuating circumstance recognized by law*.[68]

Secondly, neutral terms should be defined neutrally: The word "city" can evoke positive associations (lively and exciting nightlife) or negative associations (crowded, chaotic, dirty, crime infested). Logically, however, it is best defined neutrally, *as an urban area where a large number of people live and work*.[69]

Thirdly, non-neutral terms should not be defined neutrally: This rule is violated in two ways.

First, the rule is violated when positive value terms are defined neutrally, so as to remove the positive attitude that should be associated with the word. In Christian theology, the "gospel" is literally *good* news, a promise of peace, hope, and joy for those in Christ. There is no way to define it neutrally without omitting its essence. For example, if one defined "gospel" neutrally as *the core of Jesus' teaching*, or as *the central message proclaimed by Jesus*, we would have a true definition (as far as it goes), but no clear understanding of its essential meaning.

---

[66] Online Etymology Dictionary
[67] Encarta 2013
[68] Encarta 2013
[69] Encarta 2013.

Second, the rule is violated when negative value terms are defined neutrally, so as to remove the negative attitude that should be associated with the word. Pro-choice advocates define "abortion" as *the termination of a pregnancy*. This is a neutral definition. In reality, abortion is the act of killing a preborn human being. And since the human being in question is innocent, abortion is not merely killing; it is murder. This is the real definition of "abortion." This is what it essentially is. The definition above—*the termination of a pregnancy*—is a nominal definition in our culture, which blinds us to the true nature of abortion.

It might be objected, that since a neutral definition satisfies many of the rules of definition covered so far, there is really no need to use a non-neutral definition. For example, the neutral definition of "abortion" as *the termination a pregnancy* is probably convertible (not too narrow, not too broad),[70] informative, and positive. The problem is that, though this neutral definition may be true as far as it goes, it does not go far enough. It does not satisfy the essentiality rule. Abortion is literally *killing an innocent preborn human being*. The neutral definition omits this information. By doing so, it fails to bias us properly. Instead, it conditions us into thinking neutrally about a non-neutral act.

Fourthly, neutral terms should not be defined non-neutrally: Suppose one defined "String Theory" as a *pseudo-scientific theory of physics, which conceives of the elementary constituents of matter as string-like loops rather than point-like particles*. The term "*pseudo*-scientific" portrays String Theory in a negative light. The implication is that it's not *really* scientific—it's a wannabe scientific theory; it's a fanciful theory or piece of wild speculation. And yet, many competent scientists think it is a legitimate theory in physics. It's probably best to define it neutrally, by eliminating the word "pseudo."

Fifthly, non-neutral terms should not be inverted. The prophet Isaiah once declared, "Woe to those who call evil "good," and good "evil"; who substitute darkness for light and light for darkness; who substitute bitter for sweet and sweet for bitter!" (5:20). Isaiah is faulting the way the Israelites' *defined* things. They were defining things in a manner opposite of how they should be defined. They were *inverting* their terms of evaluation. To "invert" is to reverse things or change things into their opposite. Inversion happens in two ways.

Sometimes positive value terms are defined negatively. Take the concept of femininity. Basically, "femininity" is the quality, or set of qualities, that is supposed to distinguish the personality of a woman *as a woman* from that of a man. This is not quite a definition, of course, since it does not identify *which* quality, or set of qualities, is supposed to distinguish women from men. But Christians

---

[70] Though this definition would, strictly speaking, include accidental deaths.

historically considered it to be a positive quality. The Apostle Peter's exhorted Christian women with these words: "Your beauty should not come from outward adornment, such as elaborate hairstyles and the wearing of gold jewelry or fine clothes. Rather, it should be that of your inner self, the unfading *beauty of a gentle and quiet spirit, which is of great worth in God's sight*." Whereas Peter assumed that there was something distinctive and good about God-created femininity, many today think the very idea of "femininity" is arbitrary, oppressive, and patriarchal. According to this view, it is a mistake to suppose that there *is* such a quality. They insist that there is no way in which a sexual female's experience ought to differ from that of a sexual male. A female may feel and behave in a way traditionally associated with men, and a male may feel and behave in a way traditionally associated with women. This egalitarian philosophy makes it hard for Christians to talk about femininity or masculinity at all, let alone to stake out a position on exactly what it looks like.

The Nine Rules for Testing Definition

1.	The definiens should denote all that is denoted by the definiendum; it should not be narrow.	Equivalence entails Convertibility
2.	The definiens should denote only what is denoted by the definiendum; it should not be broad.	
3.	The definiens should be informative; it should not be circular (i.e., it should not repeat the definiendum either explicitly or implicitly).	
4.	Do not define the indefinable.	
5.	As a general rule, the definiens should be positive (stating what things) rather than negative (stating what they are not). (Exception to Rule 5: Privations should be defined negatively.)	
6.	The definiens should signify essential attributes, not accidental ones.	
7.	The definiens should be as precise as possible; it should not contain vague, ambiguous, or figurative terms.	
8.	As a general rule, the definiens should be concise.	
9.	The definiens should bias us only when appropriate.	

26) Biconditional Definitions

As noted earlier, the Aristotelian method of definition can be difficult to apply. Sometimes we need to content ourselves with simply listing a *unique set* of characteristics. In the case of seagulls, for example, there doesn't seem to be any one attribute unique to it, no one "specific difference" to distinguish it from other species in its proximum genus (if, in fact, there *is* a definite proximum genus of seagulls). To identify what makes seagulls distinct from non-seagulls, we found it necessary to list the *combination* of characteristics which, taken together, is possessed by seagulls alone. While it may be that *any one* of those characteristics is had by other birds, no other bird has *all* of those and *only* those. Let's say that all seagulls have four characteristics *a, b, c*, and *d*, and that only seagulls have those four. Suppose, moreover, that any one of those four is had by other birds (e.g., the tern has *a* and *b*, as well as *e* and *f*, but not *c* and *d*). What defines a bird as being a seagull, then, is not so much that it has *a* or *b* or *c* or *d*, but that it has *all* of them together and *only* them (it does not share the tern's characteristics *e* and *f*). This approach to defining terms suggests another method to compliment the Aristotelian method. We will call it the "biconditional method."

Three types of conditions—necessary, sufficient, biconditional: Let's begin by listing and explaining three types of conditional statements:

> If x, then y (x is a "sufficient condition")
>
> y only if x (x is a "necessary condition")
>
> y if and only if x (x is a "bicondition")

First, a sufficient conditional statement asserts that one thing being the case is enough (or "sufficient") for another to be the case. For instance, stepping off the ledge of a building is a sufficient condition for falling to the ground. We state this as "If one steps off the ledge, then one will fall."

Secondly, a necessary condition is that without which something cannot be the case. If one cannot see unless one has eyes, we can state this as, "One can see only if one has eyes."

Thirdly, sometimes we find that one thing is both necessary and sufficient for something else to be the case. On the one hand, a person cannot be justified without faith in Christ; faith is thus a necessary condition for being justified. On the other hand, faith in Christ is also enough to justify him; such faith is also a sufficient condition for being justified. Therefore, faith in Christ is necessary and sufficient for being justified. We can state this as the biconditional, "One is justified if and only if one has faith in Christ."

As the name itself states, a biconditional definition is expressed in the form of a biconditional statement:

> Something is a "seagull" *if* and *only if* it has a, b, c, and d.

The three-step method for constructing biconditional definitions: Let's begin with a brief overview of how this works, and then we will go over it again more slowly. Suppose we are trying to define "seagull." We must first list necessary conditions for being a seagull. We might say:

> Something is a "seagull" *only if* it has a and b and c and d.

Secondly, when we think we have enough necessary conditions, we then test this assumption by reformulating all of them as one big sufficient condition.

> If something has a, b, c, and d, then it is a seagull.

Thirdly, if the sufficient conditional is true, we can then put the two statements together to form a biconditional definition:

> Something is a "seagull" *if* and *only if* it has a, b, c, and d.

This biconditional version is the definition. Sometimes authors will use a more formal statement. Letting S = "seagull," they might write:

> For any x whatever, x is an S if and only if x has a, b, c, and d.

Let's work through the three-step method again using a more interesting and complicated example—"marriage."

Step 1: Formulate a set of necessary conditions: We must start by identifying necessary conditions. To do this, it might help to pose the problem as a question: What are the characteristics *without which* we would not call something "marriage"? For instance, would you call something a "marriage" that did not involve a relationship of some sort? Surely not. Therefore, the characteristic of being a relationship is a necessary condition. We could express this fact using the "…only if…" locution:

> x is a "marriage" only if x is a relationship

While the characteristic of being a relationship is a necessary condition, it is not yet a sufficient condition; that is, we could not say:

If x is a relationship, then x is a marriage.

This is false, since there are many types of relationships that are not marriages (e.g., parent-child, employer-employee, friend-friend, etc.). Therefore, more necessary conditions are needed. Here are some of the necessary conditions a former class of mine managed to identify:

- x must be a relationship between persons, so animals cannot be married.
- x must be a relationship between a male and a female, so there cannot be a homosexual marriage.
- x must be a relationship between only two persons, so polygamists cannot be married.
- x must presumably be a permanent, life-long relationship.
- x must also be a sexually exclusive relationship.

We now have six necessary conditions: [a] a relationship; [b] between persons; [c] between males and females; [d] between only one male and only one female; [e] permanent, life-long; [f] sexually exclusive. Using a bracket, we can express all six as one complex necessary condition:

x is a marriage only if { a, b, c, d, e, f }

Notice that, while no *one* of these conditions is enough to constitute a marriage, taken *together* they might be. It's now time to test it.

Step 2: Test the set of necessary conditions by reformulating them as a (complex) sufficient condition: To test our set of necessary conditionals, we can crunch all six characteristics together into a sufficient condition, and then ask whether it is true:

If x is {a, b, c, d, e, f}, then x is a marriage.

We need to ask whether there is anything that has all six characteristics a, b, c, d, e, and f, but which is still not a marriage. If there is, then the definition is false. In fact, all six characteristics *are* had by what are currently called "domestic partnerships," in which a man and a woman pledge to permanently live together in a sexually exclusive relationship, though they are not officially married. Their relationship has not been authorized or sanctioned, whether by God or by the state.

This means we omitted at least one more necessary condition.[71] We must therefore increase the number of necessary conditions to seven. Let "g" = "properly authorized." We can then reformulate the sufficient condition, and ask whether it is true that:

If x is {a, b, c, d, e, f, g}, then x is a marriage.

Is there is anything with all seven characteristics but which is still not a marriage? I cannot think of one.

Step 3: Combine the results into a biconditional definition: For the sake of argument, let's say that all seven characteristics are necessary conditions and that together they are also sufficient. We can then express this by saying:

x is a marriage if and only if x is {a, b, c, d, e, f, g}

Significantly, a biconditional is like a mathematical equation.

marriage = {a, b, c, d, e, f, g}

Recall that every good definition must be convertible, just like a math equation. As you see here, the biconditional definition upholds the equivalence rule.

Converting biconditional definitions into connotative definitions: When the conditions are not too numerous, a biconditional lends itself to being reformulated as a connotative definition, e.g., *a permanent, properly authorized, and sexually exclusive relationship between a man and a woman*.

---

[71] Mustn't we think of marriage as necessarily having a purpose? If so, then what is it—the procreation and rearing of children? But what about those who do not want children? What about those who cannot bear children? There is obviously room for more discussion here! The great thing about the biconditional method is that it allows for a very *precise* debate about how to define terms. The debate will revolve around *whose list* of necessary conditions should be accepted.

Unit III:
The Inferential Side of Argument

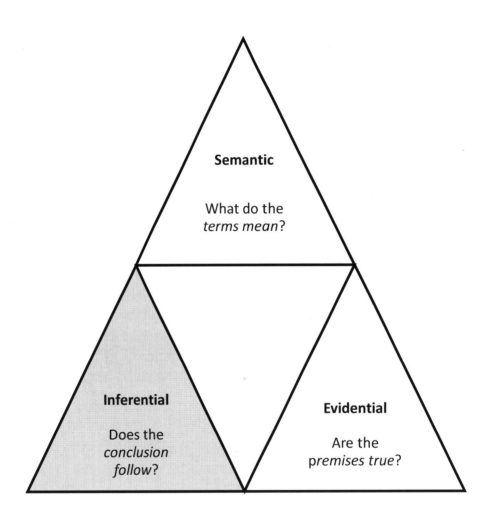

27) Deduction and Induction

The necessary conclusions of deduction and probable conclusions of induction: In this lesson we will contrast two different ways a conclusion can follow a premise: with *necessity* or with *probability*. The first is called "deductive" inference (or deduction), and the second is "inductive" inference (or induction). To see the difference, suppose we are trying to determine if Mr. Nomor robbed the convenient store. Now contrast the following scenarios.

> Scenario 1: The man who robbed the store looked just like Mr. Nomor. However, the robber had an Irish accent, and Mr. Nomor is not Irish. Therefore, Mr. Nomor did not rob the store.

> Scenario 2: The man who robbed the store looked just like Mr. Nomor. However, the robbery occurred at 12:30PM, and Mr. Nomor was positively identified in his home at 12:15PM. But it takes 40 minutes to drive from his home to the store, perhaps 30 if he drove well over the speed limit. Therefore, Mr. Nomor did not rob the store.

> Scenario 3: The man who robbed the store looked just like Mr. Nomor. However, Mr. Nomor died seven years ago in a sensational, nationally televised NASCAR crash. Therefore, Mr. Nomor did not rob the store.

In each of the three scenarios, the conclusion is the same—"Mr. Nomor did not rob the store." Now, let's assume that all the premises are true in each scenario. On that assumption, what do you notice about the different ways in which the conclusion follows in each case? [Try answering this question before reading further.]

The conclusion of S1 is plausible but not compelling, since Mr. Nomor could have faked an Irish accent. The conclusion of S2 is much stronger. Even so, it is still only probable, not quite necessary. This is because there are realistic possibilities (however improbable) that could explain how Mr. Nomor robbed the store. Suppose he has an identical twin brother standing as his alibi. The conclusion of S3, on the other hand, *is necessary*. We know that whoever robbed the convenient store was, well, *alive*.

Characterizing necessary and probable inferences: Contrast the conclusions in the chart below, noticing the ways in which they follow on each side.

Deductive arguments (characterized by *necessary* inference)	**Inductive arguments** (characterized by *probable* inference)
If Bob is a bachelor, Bob is a man.	If Bob is a bachelor, Bob desires to marry.
If road X is the shortest possible distance between points A and B, road X is straight.	If road X is the shortest possible distance between points A and B, road X is the fastest way to get from A to B.
If all Baptists are Christians, some Christians are Baptists.	If all Baptists are Christians, some Baptists know the lyrics to *Amazing Grace*.

The distinction between necessary and probable inference pertains to the *degree of logical force* with which the conclusions follow. In deductive inferences, it is *impossible* for the conclusions not to follow. In inductive inferences, it is *possible* for the conclusions not to follow.

Deductive arguments divide into "valid" and "invalid": We will define a deductive argument as *any argument whose conclusion is intended to follow with necessity*. The word "intended" is an important qualifier. Every deductive argument is meant to show that the conclusion necessarily follows the premises. But this does *not* mean that every deductive argument actually succeeds. The argument on the right is most likely *meant* to be deductive, though it fails in its intention.[72]

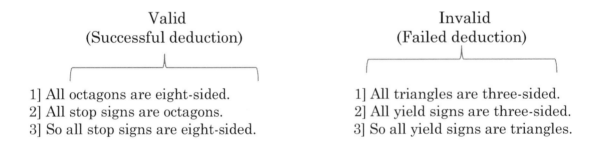

Valid
(Successful deduction)

1] All octagons are eight-sided.
2] All stop signs are octagons.
3] So all stop signs are eight-sided.

Invalid
(Failed deduction)

1] All triangles are three-sided.
2] All yield signs are three-sided.
3] So all yield signs are triangles.

Bear in mind that there are no *degrees* of validity or invalidity. There is no such thing as a "very valid" argument or a "somewhat invalid" argument. The terms "valid" and "invalid" are like "alive" and "dead," or "on" and "off." The conclusion will either follow with necessity or not. If it does, it is "valid." If not, it is "invalid."

---

[72] If we define an invalid argument as any argument whose conclusion does not necessarily follow, then all inductive arguments would be invalid too; but we want to keep "valid" and "invalid" for deductive arguments only.

We might say that "valid" means "successful deduction," and "invalid" means "failed deduction."[73]

It must be stressed that the terms "validity" and "invalidity" pertain *only* to whether a conclusion *follows* its premises. These terms do *not* pertain to whether the conclusion or the premises are *true*. Therefore, as the following arguments illustrate, it is possible to have (1) an invalid argument with a true conclusion, and (2) a valid argument with a false conclusion.

(1) All totalitarians are fascists.
All Nazis are fascists.
Therefore, all Nazis are totalitarians.

(2) All Nazis are egalitarians.
All egalitarians are humanitarians.
Therefore, all Nazis are humanitarians.

Inductive arguments divide into "strong" and "weak": Since inductive conclusions are intended to follow with probability, an inductive argument succeeds when the conclusion probably follows; otherwise it fails. If the conclusion probably follows, it is "strong." If it does not probably follow, it is "weak."

| Strong | Weak |
(probably follows)	(does not probably follow)
1] Over 80% of men weigh over 150lbs.	1] Under 5% of men weigh over 250lbs.
2] Joe is a man.	2] Tim is a man.
3] Therefore, Joe weighs over 150lbs.	3] Therefore, Tim weighs over 250lbs.

Unlike valid and invalid arguments, there is no absolute line separating strong and weak arguments. An inductive argument is either *more* or *less* strong, *more* or *less* weak. There are degrees here. If deduction is black and white, inductive is gray.

Here, too, it's worth emphasizing that the terms "strong" and "weak" pertain *only* to whether a conclusion *follows* its premises. These terms do *not* pertain to whether

---

[73] Do not make the mistake of defining a deductive argument as any an argument whose conclusion necessarily follows. In that case "deductive" and "valid" would *mean the exact same thing*, in which case there would be no room for speaking of "invalid" arguments as deductive.

the conclusion or the premises are *true*. It is possible to have a weak argument with a true conclusion, or a strong argument with a false conclusion.

Though inductive arguments are often easy to identify, determining whether they are strong or weak can be a difficult task. We will address these challenges in Unit 3, Part 2, where we examine three types of probable inference (generalizations, analogical inference, and causal inference), and then again in Unit 4, where we wrestle with abductive arguments and arguments from authority.

Identifying deductive and inductive arguments: Knowing the definitional difference between deduction and induction is only half the battle. We must also learn to identify them in books, articles, papers, journals, speeches, and so on. Here are a few clues for deciding whether an argument is deductive or inductive.

Universal v. particular quantifiers: Deductive arguments (unlike inductive arguments) often involve *universal* propositions, which are propositions about entire classes.

- *All* Christians believe in Jesus.
- *Every* rose is fragrant.
- *No* man is infallible.
- *None* of the social conservatives I know vote pro-choice.
- One should *never* disrespect the deceased at their own funerals.
- Toddlers *always* get themselves in trouble.

The italicized terms are universal quantifiers. In each case, all the members of a class are referred to by the proposition—*all* roses, *all* men, *all* social conservatives, etc. Universal propositions ground necessary inferences.

All Christians believe in Jesus.
Paul is a Christian.
Therefore, Paul believes in Jesus.

No man is infallible.
The Pope is a man.
Therefore, the Pope is not infallible.

Inductive arguments, on the other hand, use *particular* propositions:

- *Some* Christians are Baptists.
- *Sometimes* Independents vote Democratic.
- Little girls *occasionally* play with toy soldiers.

- Little boys *generally* play with toy soldiers.
- *Most* children enjoy candy canes.
- Older people *frequently* complain about their health.
- Americans *commonly* celebrate Independence Day.
- Parents *usually* care for their children.
- The *vast majority* of people oppose theft.
- *Virtually everyone* believes in God.

If we know that most parents care for their children, we can infer, as a matter of probability, that the next parents we meet care for their children. This is not a necessary inference, however, since not all parents care for their children.

Strong expressions like "vast majority of" and "virtually all" are still particular quantifiers. They are an indirect way of saying "not all." Suppose a jar contains 100 marbles, and that 99 of the marbles drawn are white. 99% is still "some." From this "some" we cannot necessarily infer that the last marble will be white, though it's highly probable. This shows why, with rare exceptions,[74] particular propositions do not enable us to draw necessary conclusions.

Modal indicators: The notions of *necessity* and *probability* are "modal" notions.[75] The English language has a variety of words used to indicate the presence of these inferences. Necessary inferences are signaled by expressions such as these:

- It *must* be the case that...
- It is *necessarily* the case that...
- It is *necessary* to infer that...
- The conclusion is *necessitated* by...
- It is *not possible* that...
- We have *no other option* than to conclude that...
- We are *forced* to infer that...
- The conclusion is *inescapable*...
- The conclusion is *unassailable*...
- The conclusion is *irresistible*...
- The conclusion is *irrefragable*...

---

[74] If "Some dogs are Great Danes," then (necessarily) "Some Great Danes are dogs." This is the formal inference of conversion, which you will learn about later. This disproves the idea that arguments using "some" are inductive.

[75] "Necessary" and "probable" link very closely to "deductive" and "inductive." Though these are not synonyms, what they signify often go together. It is arguable, however, that while all deductions are necessary inferences, some necessary inferences may not be best described as deductive (e.g., transcendental arguments). Similarly, while all inductive arguments are probabilistic, some say that not all probabilistic arguments are inductive (e.g., abduction).

Probable inferences are indicated by the following expressions:

- It *might* be the case that...
- It is *plausible* to think that...
- It is *likely* that...
- It is *reasonable* to believe that...

Definitional arguments: In some deductive arguments, the conclusions follow from premises that are "true by definition." In the argument below, the definition of "bachelor" serves as the first premise:

> Bachelors are unmarried adult males.
> Billy is a bachelor.
> Therefore, Billy is a male.

Definitions are *universal* propositions, since definitions are about entire classes (e.g., *all* bachelors are "unmarried adult males"). This is why definitions are often used to construct deductive arguments. Moreover, definitions often inform us about the essential nature of a thing and about the properties it *must* have. For instance, if the capacity for emotion is essential to personhood, then computers cannot be persons.

The particular propositions of inductive arguments are not definitionally true. The proposition "Boys like to dig in the dirt" is only *generally* true. Even if it were universally true, it would not be "true by definition," since the definition of "boy" is not (for example), "A two-legged creature that likes digging in the dirt."

28) Soundness and Cogency

As noted, Unit III is about inference, about deduction and induction. Before we dive into the details of the inferential side of argument, we should briefly note how it differs from the evidential side of argument (the focus of Unit IV). The point of this lesson is to help you see that a correct inference (whether valid or strong) is only *part* of what makes an argument good. It is also necessary for the argument's premises to be *true*.

The study of inference cannot, by itself, tell us whether an argument "proves" its conclusion. Strictly speaking, the term "inference" *only* refers to whether and how a conclusion *follows* its premises. The Inferential Test tells us nothing about the *truth-value* of the premises or the conclusion.

You know that an argument is a set of propositions used to prove a point, and that to prove a point is to show that a *conclusion* is either *true* or *probably true*. This means that no argument with a *false* conclusion can be a "proof." To see why, consider these arguments, one of which is valid and the other strong:

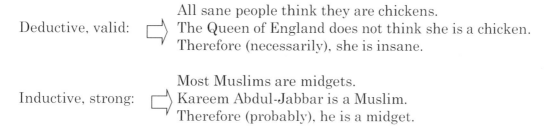

Both arguments pass the Inferential Test. Since both conclusions are false, however, neither argument amounts to a "proof." These examples illustrate that the Inferential Test is incomplete on its own. The goal of an argument is not merely to show that a conclusion *follows* its premises; the ultimate goal is to show that the conclusion itself is *true*. This means that we must also show that the *premises* are true.[76] This is why an argument must also pass the Evidential Test: Are the premises true?

---

[76] You may wonder why we do not ask a fourth question of whether the *conclusion is true*. If one knows the *premises are true* (Evidential Test), and that the *conclusion follows* either necessarily or probably (Inferential Test), then one *also* knows that that the *conclusion* is either necessarily true or probably true. Once we answer these two questions, we automatically have an answer to the fourth question of whether the conclusion is true. Hence, the fourth question is not necessary to ask. It is *assumed* in the other two questions.

Proof involves transmitting the truth of the premises to the conclusion (i.e., "truth-transmission"): For any given argument, the rules of inference enable us to say, "If the premises of this argument are true, the conclusion of this argument is true or probably true." More precisely, for a *valid* argument we can say:

> "If the premises of this argument are true, then the conclusion of this argument is true *necessarily*."

For a *strong* argument we can say:

> "If the premises of this argument are true, then the conclusion of this argument is *probably* true."

But the rules of inference do not enable us to say that the *premises* are true. The rules of inference speak to us in a conditional or hypothetical manner. They say, in effect, "We cannot tell you *whether* the premises are true, but we can tell you that *if* the premises are true, then the conclusion is either true if valid, or probably true if strong." While the rules of inference do not establish the truth of the premises, they do preserve and pass on the truth of the premises to the conclusion whenever the premises are in fact true. There is a way in which inference *transmits the truth of the premises to the conclusion*. We can think of an argument as a *truth-transmitter*.

Since we know there is a difference in the way a conclusion follows (i.e., either necessarily or probably), there will also be a difference in the force or reliability of the truth-transmission. Compare the following arguments, whose premises we will assume to be true:

Deductive truth-transmission:

1. All chronic cigarette smokers ingest nicotine.   ← True
2. <u>Mr. Koff is a chronic cigarette smoker</u>.   ← True
3. Therefore (necessarily), he ingests nicotine.   ← True

Inductive truth-transmission

1. Most chronic cigarette smokers cannot finish marathons.   ← True
2. <u>Mr. Koff is a chronic cigarette smoker</u>.   ← True
3. Therefore (probably), he cannot finish the marathon.   ← True

The first argument is "valid" and all its premises are true. So the conclusion *must be true*. The second argument is "strong" and all its premises are true. So the conclusion is *likely to be true*.

Let's now display, in a more systematic way, how the truth-value of the premises maps onto the two types of inference.

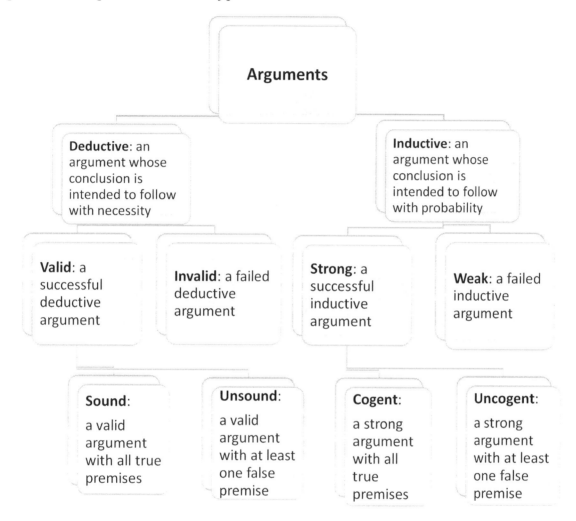

Soundness and unsoundness: An argument is sound if it is valid with all true premises.[77] The word "sound" is an apt one, as it communicates the idea of safety. We say the foundations of a house are "sound," for example, meaning that they are solid and reliable. "Unsound" suggests that there is a flaw, defect, or failing that renders the foundations hazardous. Likewise in the case of argument: if it is sound, it is reliable in every sense of the term—the conclusion necessarily

---

[77]Only "valid" arguments sub-divide in the chart. Since an invalid argument is unacceptable because of its failed conclusion, there is no point asking whether its premises are true. Only the valid argument remains a concern for us. And what we want to know is whether *both* premises are true.

follows and the premises are true. It is therefore completely trustworthy. If it is unsound, it may look solid (it is valid), but it contains a falsehood (a crack, as it were), which throws the whole thing into question. If we suspect that even one of the premises is false, we cannot necessarily infer that the conclusion will be true. Contrast this pair:

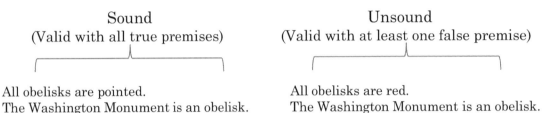

Sound
(Valid with all true premises)

All obelisks are pointed.
The Washington Monument is an obelisk.
So the Washington Monument is pointed.

Unsound
(Valid with at least one false premise)

All obelisks are red.
The Washington Monument is an obelisk.
So the Washington Monument is red.

If all the premises of a valid argument are true, only truth is transmitted to the conclusion (the pointed obelisk). But if even one premise is false, it is *possible* that the conclusion will be false (the red obelisk).[78] A few other points should be kept in mind.

First, an argument can be sound only if it is valid. This means that as soon as we learn that an argument is 'sound,' we automatically know that it is also valid. But to learn that an argument is 'valid' does not yet tell us whether it is sound. Secondly, since a valid argument will have all true premises or not, it follows that a valid argument will be either sound or unsound, with nothing in between. Thirdly, since truth does not come in degrees, there are no degrees of soundness.

Cogency and uncognecy: A "cogent" argument is any *strong* argument with *all true premises*. Notice that what soundness and unsoundness are to validity, cogency and uncogency are to strength. One false premise renders a strong argument uncogent.

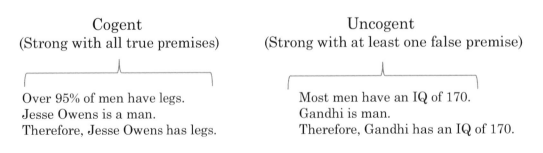

Cogent
(Strong with all true premises)

Over 95% of men have legs.
Jesse Owens is a man.
Therefore, Jesse Owens has legs.

Uncogent
(Strong with at least one false premise)

Most men have an IQ of 170.
Gandhi is man.
Therefore, Gandhi has an IQ of 170.

---

[78]I say "possible" because sometimes an unsound argument can have a true conclusion, e.g.
All obelisks are white.
The Washington Monument is an obelisk.
Therefore, the Washington Monument is white.

Much of what we said about deduction applies to induction. An argument is cogent only if it is strong. So, if an argument is cogent, we know it must be strong. But a strong argument is not necessarily cogent, since it might have one or more false premises. And since either both premises are true or at least one is false, a strong argument must be cogent or uncogent, not more or less cogent.

Here is a chart for review.

	Deductive	Inductive
1st) With what force is the conclusion intended to follow?	With necessity	With probability
2nd) Does it succeed?	If so, it is valid; if not, it is invalid	If so, it is strong; if not, it is weak
3rd) Are all premises true?	If so, it is sound; if not, it is unsound.	If so, it is cogent; if not, it is uncogent.

Part 1: Necessary Inference

Section 1: Categorical Reasoning

29) Introduction to Categorical Inference

Deductive inference divides into "categorical" (also known as "Aristotelian" logic), and "propositional" (also known as "Stoic" logic).[79] We will study each in turn, and then move on to inductive inference in Unit 3, Part 2.

Four types of categorical propositions: Aristotle sought to explain how the human mind reasons about classes or categories of things. He found that we do so using four different types of *categorical proposition*:

>All *x*s are *y*s.   (e.g., All Mormons are missionaries)
>No *x*s are *y*s.   (e.g., No Mormons are Muslims)
>Some *x*s are *y*s.   (e.g., Some Mormons are polygamists)
>Some *x*s are not *y*s.   (e.g., Some Mormons are not polygamists)

In each case, the first term is the *subject*-term, and the second is the *predicate*-term. We can use "S" and "P" to symbolize this:

>All S are P.
>No S are P.
>Some S are P.
>Some S are not P.

Quality of the propositions—affirmative or negative: The subject and predicate terms are related to each other by means of linking verbs ("is" and "are" or "is not" and "are not") called "copulas." The copula determines the *quality* of the proposition, that is, whether the proposition is *affirmative* or *negative*. The proposition "Greeks *are* philosophers" affirms a membership relation between the categories of Greeks and of philosophers. The proposition "No men are apes" negates (or denies) a relation between men and apes.

Quantity of the propositions—universal or affirmative. A categorical proposition will be about *all* the members of a category or only *some* members of a category. The former propositions are called "universal" and the latter are

---

[79] Named, respectively, after the form of reasoning (using categories or propositions), or the philosophers most responsible for developing them (Aristotle and the Stoics).

"particular." As noted in the previous lesson, since the terms "all," "no," and "some" determine the *quantity* of the propositions, they are therefore called "quantifiers."

There are two universal propositions: All S are P and No S are P. Let's consider them in order.

1st, All S are P: The *whole* category of Greeks is *included in* the category of humans. The universal proposition "*All* Greeks are humans" expresses this relation.

2nd, No S are P: The *whole* category of Greeks is *excluded from* the category of apes. It is tempting (but misleading) to express this relation with the proposition "*All* Greeks *are not* apes." But this can mean that at least *some* Greeks *are not* apes.[80] To express the relation of universal exclusion, then, we need the clearer proposition "*No* Greeks are apes." Although the propositions "All Greeks are humans" and "No Greeks are Chinese" differ in *quality* (one is affirmative and one is negative), they are the same with respect to *quantity*, i.e., both are universal. This is why we call them "universal" propositions.

There are two particular propositions—i.e., Some S are P and Some S are not P. While the propositions "Some Greeks are philosophers" and "Some Greeks are not philosophers" differ in *quality* (one is affirmative and one is negative), they are the same in *quantity*.

1st, Some S are P: Suppose we want to relate the category of Greeks to the category of philosophers. Only some Greeks are included in this category (e.g., Socrates, Plato, and Aristotle). Since only a *part* of the category of Greeks is included in the category of philosophers, the extent of membership is said to be "particular" rather than universal.

2nd, Some S are not P: Since some Greeks are *excluded from* the category of philosophers, we express this negative relationship by the proposition "Some Greeks are not philosophers."

Naming categorical propositions: For any categorical proposition, one category will either be included in ("affirmatively") or excluded from ("negatively") another category, either in whole ("universally") or in part ("particularly"). This gives us the four types of categorical propositions. Propositions that are universal in quantity and affirmative in quality are "universal affirmatives." Those that are universal in quantity but negative in quality are "universal negatives." Those that are particular in quantity and affirmative in quality are "particular affirmatives." Those that are particular in quantity and negative in quality are "particular negatives."

---

[80] Here is a more common example of the ambiguity: "All Marylanders are not Democrats." Taken in its most literal fashion, this would mean "No Marylanders are Democrats.' But it is often used to mean 'Some Marylanders are not Democrats.'

| | | QUANTITY ||
		Universal	Particular
QUALITY	Affirmative	"All men are mortal"	"Some men are happy"
	Negative	"No men are immortal"	"Some men are not happy"

Formalizing categorical propositions: In subsequent lessons we will work with formalized versions of categorical propositions. To understand what is meant by "formal," consider the following examples:

(1) All S are P	*(2) No S are P*	*(3) Some S are P*	*(4) Some S are not P*
All men **are** mortal	**No** dogs **are** cats	**Some** birds **are** flyers	**Some** cars **are not** fast
All women **are** females	**No** balls **are** square	**Some** foods **are** healthy	**Some** cats **are not** friendly
All fish **are** swimmers	**No** jewels **are** cheap	**Some** men **are** liars	**Some** bugs **are not** pests

The categorical terms give a categorical proposition its *content*. In (1), the proposition is about men, the next is about women, and the last is about fish. Since each of these three propositions involves different categories, they differ in *content*. But note that all three propositions have the same "All...are" form or structure. Regardless of the *varying content* of the propositions, their form remains the same in each case.

Symbolizing categorical propositions with A E I O: From the Latin word *affirmo* ("I affirm"), we can take the letters "A" and "I" to represent a universal affirmative and a particular affirmative, respectively. From the word *nego* ("I deny") we can take "E" and "O" to represent a universal negative and a particular negative, respectively. The following graph may help you memorize the classification.

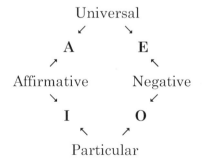

30) Immediate Inference (1) Compatibility

If all Mormons are missionaries, does it follow that all missionaries are Mormons? Or, if some Mormons are not polygamists, could we infer that some Mormons are polygamists? These questions exemplify a larger set of questions you will learn to answer in this lesson. They all pertain to logical relationships among the four types of categorical propositions. Each of the four stands in a certain logical relation to the other three. As the following diagram demonstrates, we will need to consider 12 relationships.

The overarching question we will ask is this: If we assume that one of the four propositions is true (or false), what can we infer about the truth-value of the other three? Will they be true, or false, or perhaps indeterminable? There are 24 specific versions of the question:

"If true..." inferences		"If false..." inferences	
1) If A is true, E is ?	7) If I is true, A is ?	13) If A is false, E is ?	19) If I is false, A is ?
2) If A is true, I is ?	8) If I is true, E is ?	14) If A is false, I is ?	20) If I is false, E is ?
3) If A is true, O is ?	9) If I is true, O is ?	15) If A is false, O is ?	21) If I is false, O is ?
4) If E is true, A is ?	10) If O is true, A is ?	16) If E is false, A is ?	22) If O is false, A is ?
5) If E is true, I is ?	11) If O is true, E is ?	17) If E is false, I is ?	23) If O is false, E is ?
6) If E is true, O is ?	12) If O is true, I is ?	18) If E is false, O is ?	24) If O is false, I is ?

Before we cover the rules, see if you can fill in the following lines with "T" (for true) or "F" (for false) or "U" (for undetermined). At this point you must rely on logical intuition.

If it is **true** that (A) *all men are creatures bearing God's image*, then...

…it is _____ that (E) no men are creatures bearing God's image.
…it is _____ that (I) some men are creatures bearing God's image.
…it is _____ that (O) some men are not creatures bearing God's image.

If it is **true** that (E) *no men are the glory of women*, then...

…it is _____ that (A) all men are the glory of women.
…it is _____ that (I) some men are the glory of women.
…it is _____ that (O) some men are not the glory of women.

If it is **true** that (I) *some church elders are to be able to teach*, then...

…it is _____ that (A) all church elders are to be able to teach
…it is _____ that (E) no church elders are to be able to teach
…it is _____ that (O) some church elders are not to be able to teach

If it is **true** that (O) *some Christians are not socialists*, then...

…it is _____ that (A) all Christians are socialists.
…it is _____ that (E) no Christians are socialists.
…it is _____ that (I) some Christians are socialists.

If it is **false** that (A) *all schools are classical*, then...

…it is _____ that (E) no schools are classical
…it is _____ that (I) some schools are classical
…it is _____ that (O) some schools are not classical

If it is **false** that (E) *no lawyers are liars*, then...

…it is _____ that (A) all lawyers are liars
…it is _____ that (I) some lawyers are liars
…it is _____ that (O) some lawyers are not liars

If it is **false** that (I) *some television shows are effective means of quality education*, then...

…it is _____ that (A) all television shows are effective means of quality education
…it is _____ that (E) no television shows are effective means of quality education
…it is _____ that (O) some television shows are not effective means of quality education

If it is **false** that (O) *some theologians are not unskilled thinkers*, then...

…it is _____ that (A) all theologians are unskilled thinkers
…it is _____ that (E) no theologians are unskilled thinkers
…it is _____ that (I) some theologians are unskilled thinkers

THE SQUARE OF OPPOSITION

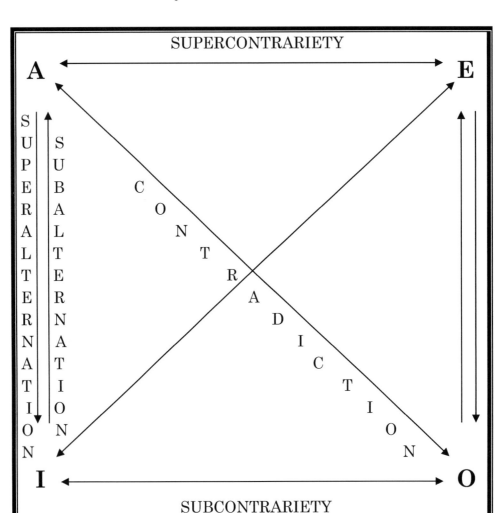

Contradiction (between A ↔ O and E ↔ I): The diagonal relations on the square represent the relation of contradiction. A contradiction occurs between propositions that *cannot both be true* and that *cannot both be false*. Propositions A and O are contradictories, as are E and I.

Let's first consider the contradictories A and O. We will take the following two propositions as examples: "All feminists are angry women" and "Some feminists are not angry women." It is logically impossible for both to be true. The first asserts that *all* feminists are *in* the category of angry women. The second asserts that *some* women are *outside* that category. But it is also impossible for both to be false. To deny the proposition "All feminists are angry women" is to affirm the proposition "Some feminists are not angry women." Likewise, to deny the proposition "Some feminists are not angry women" is to affirm the proposition "All feminists are angry women." In other words, the falsity of one proposition necessarily entails the truthfulness of the other, and the truthfulness of one proposition necessarily entails the falsity of the other. So contradictories *cannot both be true* and *cannot both be false*. This means that, for any pair of contradictory propositions, *one must be true* and *one must be false*.

Consider the pair of E and I propositions: "No marines are effeminate men" and "Some marines are effeminate men." One must be true and one must be false. If it is true that "No marines are effeminate men," it is false that "Some marines are effeminate men." If it is false that "No marines are effeminate men," it is true that "Some marines are effeminate men."

Alternation (A ↔ I and E ↔ O): When considered in relation to each other, A and I propositions are called "alterns," as are E and O propositions. The relationship between those in each pair is called "alternation." Whereas the inference of contradiction moves diagonally across the Square, the inferences of alternation move vertically. We can move from the top to the bottom or from bottom to top. We must distinguish the two directions using the pre-fixes "super" and "sub." The inference that moves from top to bottom—from A to I, or from E to O—is "*super*alternation." The inference from bottom to top—from I to A, or from O to E—is "*sub*alternation."

Superalternation (A→ I and E→ O): May both propositions in each pair be *true*? Yes. It is logically possible to affirm both A and I, and it is logically possible to affirm both E and O. May both propositions in each pair be *false*? Yes. It is logically possible to deny both A and I, or to deny E and O. Note, however, that if A is true, then I is true by necessity. If *all* terrorists are menaces to society, then *some* terrorists are menaces to society. But if A is false, we cannot infer anything about I. Likewise, if E is true, O is true by necessity. If *no* Mustangs are slow, then *some* Mustangs are *not* slow. But if E is false, we cannot infer anything about O.

Subalternation (I → A and O → E): If I is true, we cannot infer anything about A, since we cannot move from what is true about some members of a class to what is true about all members of a class. However, if I is false, we can infer that A is false. For if it is false that *some* terrorists are menaces to society, then it is certainly false that *all* terrorists are menaces to society. If O is true, we cannot determine anything about E. However, if O is false, we can infer that E is false. For if it is false that *some* Mustangs are *not* slow, it is certainly false that *no* Mustangs are slow.

Contrariety (A ↔ E and I ↔ O): We now come to the horizontal relationships on the Square. When considered in relation to each other, A and E are called "contraries," as are I and O. The relationship between those in each pair is called "contrariety." Since we already used the pre-fixes "super" and "sub" in the case of alternation, we will use them again for the sake of consistency. The top horizontal relation is "*super*contrariety," and the bottom is "*sub*contrariety." So we can call A and E "supercontraries," and I and O "subcontraries."

May both *super*contraries be *true*? No. If one of them is true, the other must be false. May both be *false*? Yes. What about subcontraries? May both *sub*contraries be *true*? Yes. But may both be false? No.

Supercontrariety (A → E and E → A): If A is true, E must be false. But if A is false, the truth-value of E is left undetermined. If E is true, then A must be false. But if E is false, the truth-value of A is left undetermined.

Subcontrariety (I → O and O → I): If I is true, the truth-value of O is left undetermined. But if I is false, O must be true. If O is true, the truth-value of I is left undetermined. But if O is false, I must be true.

PROPOSITIONS CONCERNING COMPATIBILITY			
Alternatives and subcontraries: *can* both be *true*	Alternatives and supercontraries: *can* both be *false*	Contradictories and subcontraries: *cannot* both be *true*	Contradictories and supercontraries: *cannot* both be *false*
A ↔ I	A ↔ I	A ↔ E	A ↔ O
E ↔ O	E ↔ O	A ↔ O	E ↔ I
I ↔ O	A ↔ E	E ↔ I	I ↔ O

31) Immediate Inference (2) Equivalence

An inference of equivalence is *a logical operation whereby we move validly from one type of categorical proposition to a logically equivalent type of categorical proposition*. There are three such operations: (1) *conversion*, (2) *obversion*, and (3) *contraposition*.

Conversion: Propositions are converted by simply switching their subject and predicate terms. Only E and I propositions may be converted.
Here is an argument using an E proposition:

   [E] No men are alien imposters (converts to ⇒) No alien imposters are men

Here is an example of an argument using an I proposition:

   [I] Some dogs are fast animals (converts to ⇒) Some fast animals are dogs

To see why we cannot convert A and O propositions, consider these:

   [A] All chickens are birds. Therefore, all birds are chickens.

   [O] Some birds are not chickens. Therefore, some chickens are not birds.

Either one of these two is called the "fallacy of illicit conversion."

Obversion: This is a two-step process. Propositions are obverted by (1st) *changing their quality* and (2nd) *negating their predicate term*. For example, the proposition "all men are mortal" may be obverted to "no men are non-mortal" by the following step-by-step process:

"All men are mortal"
↓
(1st, change quality to...)
↓
"No men are mortal"
↓
(2nd, negate predicate to...)
↓
"No men are non-mortal"

All four categorical propositions may be obverted.

[A] All birds are flying animals. Therefore, **no** birds are **non**-flying animals.
[E] No fish are flying animals. Therefore, **all** fish are **non**-flying animals.
[I] Some cars are fast vehicles. Therefore, some cars **are not non**-fast vehicles.
[O] Some cars are not fast vehicles. Therefore, some cars **are non**-fast vehicles.

Contraposition: This third immediate inference uses both conversion and obversion. To contrapose a proposition (and *only* A and O propositions may be contraposed), we take three steps: (1st) obvert, (2nd) convert, and (3rd) obvert again. The A proposition is on the left and the O proposition is on the right.

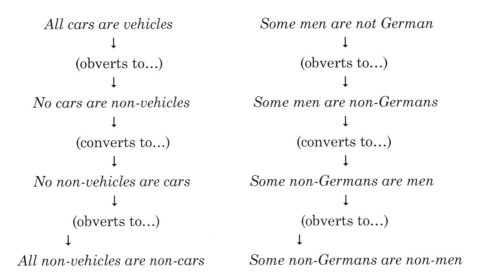

There is a shortcut. As the above schemas show, in the left column we move from "A are B" to "All non-B are non-A." In the right column we move from "Some A are not B" to "Some non-B are non-A." In both cases, then, we find that the contraposed proposition (which is the final proposition in each case) has changed from its original form in two respects. First, the subject and predicate have switched positions. Secondly, each term has been negated into its term complement (signified by "non"). So, to contrapose "All A are B" we need only switch the terms and negate them—"All non-B are non-A." This is also true of O propositions.

Let's see why we cannot contrapose E and I propositions, starting with the E proposition. We know all four categorical propositions can be obverted, including E propositions. So "No A are B" would become "All A are non-B." We have thus completed the first step successfully. The problem arises at the second step of conversion, since an A proposition may not be converted. This explains why you cannot contrapose an E proposition. Likewise with an I proposition. Any attempt at contraposing an E or an I proposition commits the formal "fallacy of *illicit contraposition.*"

STEPS FOR EQUIVALENT TRANSFORMATIONS	
To convert...	Switch the subject and predicate terms
To obvert...	Change the quality and negate the predicate
To contrapose...	Switch the subject and predicate and then negate them (obvert, convert, obvert)

VALID INFERENCES OF EQUIVALENCE			
	Conversion	Obversion	Contraposition
All A are B		Valid	Valid
No A are B	Valid	Valid	
Some A are B	Valid	Valid	
Some A are not B		Valid	Valid

INFERENCES OF EQUIVALENCE

All A are B
↓
obvert
↓
No A are non-B
↓
convert
↓
No non-B are A
↓
obvert
↓
All non-B are non-A

No A are B
↙　　　↘
convert　　*obvert*
↓　　　　↓
No B are A　　All A are non-B
↓
obvert
↓
All B are non-A

Some A are B
↙　　　↘
convert　　*obvert*
↓　　　　↓
Some B are A　　Some A are not non-B
↓
obvert
↓
Some B are not non-A

Some A are not B
↓
obvert
↓
Some A are non-B
↓
convert
↓
Some non-B are A
↓
obvert
↓
Some non-B are not non-A

32) Mediate Inference (i.e. Syllogisms)

Aristotelian logic involves two types of inferences: mediate and immediate. In the previous two lessons we studied the immediate inferences of compatibility and equivalence. They are "immediate" because they move *directly* from one premise to a conclusion, without the need for a second, mediating premise.

No need for mediating premise ⇒
All men are rational.
↓
Therefore, some men are rational.

We will now turn to the study of mediate inference, which always involves at least two premises. Notice how the following inference differs from the one above:

Need for mediating premise ⇒
All men are rational.
↓
Therefore, some Aussies are rational.

Here the conclusion does not follow the lone premise. If the argument appears reasonable, that is only because we *took for granted* the *missing premise* that "Some Aussies are men." But the argument does not *state* this. The missing premise is needed to *mediate* the inference from the premise to the conclusion.

Definition of a syllogism: By "categorical syllogism" is meant: *an orderly grouping of three categorical propositions that relate one category (found in one premise) to another category (found in another premise) by means of a third category (found in both premises).* Here is an example:

All men are mortals.
<u>All Greeks are men</u>.
Therefore, all Greeks are mortals.

The conclusion expresses a relationship between the two categories "Greeks" and "mortals." This relationship is based on their mutual relationship to the category of "men." Because all men are in the category of mortals, and because all Greeks are in the category of men, it follows that all Greeks are in the category of mortals.

Components: There are three categorical propositions in each syllogism. Each proposition contains two categorical terms, a *subject term* and a *predicate term*. By doing the math 2 + 2 + 2, we might be led to conclude that we're dealing with six terms. Actually, we are only dealing with three different terms ("men," "mortal," "Greeks"), each of which is used twice.

When used in a syllogism, the subject and predicate terms of each proposition have technical names: "major," "minor," and "middle." The predicate of the conclusion is the *major term*. The subject of the conclusion is the *minor term*. The major and the minor terms will each show up once more in the premises. The remaining term, the *middle term*, appears once in each premise. Here they are:

All men [*middle*] are mortals [*major*]
All Greeks [*minor*] are men [*middle*]
Therefore, all Greeks [*minor*] are mortals [*major*]

For any given syllogism, its three terms will be arranged in one of the following four ways:

Major Premise →	Mid	Maj	Maj	Mid	Mid	Maj	Maj	Mid
Minor Premise →	Min	Mid	Min	Mid	Mid	Min	Mid	Min
Conclusion →	*Min*	*Maj*	*Min*	*Maj*	*Min*	*Maj*	*Min*	*Maj*

Note that the minor and major in the conclusion retain their position throughout—minor first, major second. But each one moves around in the premises. To ease our discussion of a syllogism, it is customary to put the major term in the first premise and minor term in the second premise (though writers do not always do this). Hence we call the first premise the "major premise," by virtue of it containing the major term, and the second the "minor premise," since it contains the minor term. Lastly, notice that while the middle term can also move around in the premises, it is never in the conclusion.

Form: Every syllogism has a certain "form" or "structure." Its form is determined by two characteristics: *mood* and *figure*. We can think of it as an equation: Form = [Mood + Figure].

The mood of a syllogism consists of the *types* of propositions involved (A or E or I or O) and the *order* in which they are used. Here, too, an equation is helpful: Mood = [Type of Propositions + Order of Propositions].

Suppose we have a syllogism consisting of an A, E, and O proposition. We can order these three propositions in six different ways:

Original Syllogism	Five Other Possible Orderings of those Propositions				
A) All S are P	E ...	O ...	E ...	O ...	A ...
E) No S are P	A ...	E ...	O ...	A ...	O ...
O) Some S are not P	O ...	A ...	A ...	E ...	E ...

The figure of a syllogism is determined by the *position of the middle term* within that syllogism. Since the middle term occurs once in each premise, and as either the subject or the predicate, there will be four possible figures:

1st	*2nd*	*3rd*	*4th*
M are P	P are **M**	**M** are P	P are **M**
<u>S are **M**</u>	<u>S are **M**</u>	<u>**M** are S</u>	<u>**M** are S</u>
S are P	S are P	S are P	S are P

Since the form of the syllogism consists of its mood and its figure, we state its form by listing its proposition types in their order followed by its figure. For example, we can use "EAE-1" to represent the form of this syllogism:

- No events occur without a cause.
- All explosions are events.
- Therefore, no explosions occur without a cause.

The first premise is an E proposition. The second premise is an A proposition. The conclusion is also an E proposition. The *mood* of the syllogism is therefore "EAE." What is the *figure*? Since "events" is the middle term, and it occupies the first figure, we represent this by placing "1" after the letters of the mood. This gives us the symbolized form of EAE-1.

Other examples are in the box to the right. Try determining the form of this more complicated argument:

1. No syllogisms with two negative premises are valid arguments.
2. Some valid arguments are syllogisms with only one affirmative premise.
3. Therefore, some syllogisms with only one affirmative premise are not syllogisms with two negative premises.

All *men* are mortals <u>All Greeks are *men*</u> All Greeks are mortals	AAA-1
No dogs are *cats* <u>Some *cats* are leopards</u> Some leopards are not dogs	EIO-4
Some *sons* are obedient kids <u>Some *sons* are soccer players</u> Some soccer players are obedient kids	III-3
All nationalists are *patriotic citizens* <u>Some Americans are not *patriotic citizens*</u> Some Americans are not nationalists	AOO-2

33) Proving Invalidity by Counter Examples

In this lesson we will learn how to expose invalid syllogisms by means of "counter examples." To appreciate how this works, recall that if the premises of a valid argument are true, the conclusion is necessarily true. This means that it is *impossible* for the conclusion of a valid argument to be false if *both its premises are true*. Therefore (and this is the main point), an argument with obviously true premises and an obviously false conclusion must be *invalid*. For example:

> All cheetahs are fast land animals.
> All greyhounds are fast land animals.
> Therefore, all greyhounds are cheetahs.

Even the most simple-minded reader will recognize that something is wrong with this argument. But some invalid arguments are not so obviously invalid:

> All soldiers are government employees.
> No soldiers are civilians.
> Therefore, some civilians are not government employees.

This argument is not so obviously incorrect. Is there any way to *prove* that it is incorrect? Yes there is.

Formal analogies: Recall that every syllogism exhibits a "form" (mood + figure). Let's formalize the previous argument, an AEO-3:

> All S are GE
> No S are C
> Some C are not GE

Now, *if* this argument is invalid, it follows that *any argument exhibiting the same form must also be invalid*. (Remember, validity pertains to an argument's form or structure, not to its content.) Therefore, if we can find another AEO-3 with obviously true premises and an obviously false conclusion, we can show that the original (and not so obvious) argument must also be invalid. Consider the following:

All fathers are male.	=	All F are M
<u>No fathers are three-year-old boys.</u>	=	<u>No F are 3YB</u>
Some three-year-old boys are not males.	=	Some 3YB are not M

The forms of the two syllogisms below are identical:

1st Syllogism
All S are GE
<u>No S are C</u>
Some C are not GE

2nd Syllogism
All F are M
<u>No F are 3YB</u>
Some 3YB are not M

Now, because the second argument has the same form as the first, the second is called a "logical analogy" of it. Because the second one is *obviously* invalid, we can refute the first one by simply setting it next to the second. This is called "refutation by logical analogy." In extended form, the refutation might go like this:

"You have argued that some civilians are not government employees, since all soldiers are government employees, and no soldiers are civilians. But if this reasoning is correct, it would also be correct to infer that some three-year-old boys are not males, since all fathers are males, and no fathers are three-year-old boys. But this is obviously incorrect. Therefore, something is wrong with your argument."

Limits of the method: Counter-examples are a powerful means of exposing an invalid argument. But their power is limited. They cannot tell us whether an argument is *valid*. The mere fact that we cannot come up with a counter-example does not *necessarily* imply that the argument is valid. For what if the argument is invalid, and we simply aren't creative enough to devise a counterexample? Clearly something more is needed. Hence our next lessons on the rules of inference.

34) Distribution of Terms

The concept of term-distribution is essential for understanding the rules of validity, since two of those rules employ this concept. A term in a categorical proposition is said to be "distributed by the proposition" *when the proposition refers to **all** the members of the category represented by that term*. The meaning of this will become clear as we examine the four types of categorical propositions.

The universal affirmative (All A are B): This proposition refers to every member of the category represented by the subject term. In the proposition "All mustangs are horses," every member of the category of mustangs is in view. So A propositions distribute their subject term. But A propositions do not distribute their predicate term. This is why it would be incorrect to convert the proposition into "All horses are mustangs."

The universal negative (No A are B): E propositions distribute their subjects and their predicates. The proposition "No men are women" refers to all men and to all women. If no men are included in the category of women, then *all* men are *excluded* from that category. Likewise, *all* women are excluded from the category of men.

The particular affirmative (Some A are B): I propositions do not distribute their subjects or their predicates. The proposition "Some dogs are black animals" refers to only some dogs. And since only some members of the subject category are members of the predicate category, the most we may infer is that some members of the predicate category are members of the subject category. (Recall that I propositions may in fact be converted. Hence "Some dogs are black animals" becomes "Some black animals are dogs".)

The particular negative (Some A are not B): O propositions distribute their predicates but not their subjects. Like the I proposition, the O proposition "Some men are not Americans" obviously does not distribute its subject term. Why does it distribute its predicate? Recall why the predicate term of an E proposition is distributed: since no members of the subject category are members of the predicate category, we inferred that no members of the predicate category are members of the subject category. This same principle affects the distribution of predicate terms in O propositions. Though we are dealing with only some men in the proposition "Some men are not Americans," we know that with respect to *these members* it is the case that *none of them* are Americans. But if no Americans are members of this particular sub-group in the overall category of men, it follows that *all* Americans are excluded from *that* particular sub-group. Therefore, the proposition distributes its predicate term.

There are two ways of remembering which propositions distribute which terms. You can memorize the following paradigm, in which the distributed terms are marked:

$$A = \text{All } \underline{A} \text{ are B}$$
$$E = \text{No } \underline{A} \text{ are } \underline{B}$$
$$I = \text{Some A are B}$$
$$O = \text{Some A are not } \underline{B}$$

Or you may memorize the following two principles as represented in the chart below.

Principle #1: *universal* propositions (A and E) distribute their *subjects*,

Principle #2: *negative* propositions (E and O) distribute their *predicates*:

	Subjects Distributed		
Predicates Undistributed	All A are B	No A are B	**Predicates Distributed**
	Some A are B	Some A are not B	
	Subjects Undistributed		

35) Rules for Testing Syllogisms

As was explained in a previous lesson, a categorical proposition relates two categories (represented by the subject and predicate terms) to each other in one of four possible ways: as either *belonging* or *not belonging* in either *whole* or in *part*. Whether the members of one category belong to another category is indicated by the *quality* of the proposition; that is, by whether the proposition is *affirmative* ("is") or *negative* ("is not"). Whether the members belong in whole or in part is determined by the *quantity* of the proposition; that is, by whether the proposition is *universal* ("all" and "no") or *particular* ("some"). By keeping these points in mind, you should be able to grasp the rationale behind each of the rules below.

Rule #1) The middle term must be distributed at least once:
The following syllogism shows how an undistributed middle term prevents a valid connection between the major and minor terms:

> Some animals **(middle)** are Collies (major).
> Some dogs (minor) are animals **(middle)**.
> Therefore, some dogs (minor) are Collies (major).

The middle term, "animals," is undistributed in both instances. Can you see the problem? The second premise states that some dogs are animals. Yet some animals are not dogs. It is possible that Collies are members of that part of the category of animals, i.e., the part of non-dogs. In this case, Collies would have no relation to the category of dogs. Remember: the conclusion of a categorical syllogism asserts a membership relation between the minor and major terms. This relationship is determined by means of their respective relationships to the middle term: the middle term will either link them or sever them. These linkages and severances must be *complete*; that is, one of the major or minor terms must be included in or excluded from the *whole* of the middle term. The rationale behind this rule is this: If we assume that the major term is only partially included in (or excluded from) the middle term, and that the minor term is only partially included in (or excluded from) the middle term, then these two terms—the major and the minor—might be included in (or excluded from) *different parts* of the middle. In conclusion, in order to determine the relation between the major and minor term (which is always discovered by means of the middle term) one of them must be included in (or excluded from) the *whole* of the middle. So the middle term must be distributed at least once. The violation of this rule is called the "fallacy of undistributed middle."

Rule #2) A term distributed in the conclusion must be distributed in the premise. The rationale behind this rule is simple: the information supplied in the conclusion cannot go beyond what is provided in the premises. Consider this example:

All Collies are animals
Some dogs are animals
All dogs are Collies

The minor term "dogs" is distributed in the conclusion, but it is not distributed in the respective premise. We cannot validly draw information about *all* dogs from a proposition regarding *only some* dogs. The inference is invalid. In short, if either the minor or major term is undistributed in the premises, it cannot be distributed in the conclusion. The violation of this rule is called the "fallacy of illicit minor or major."

Keep something in mind: rule #2 does *not* state that a term in the conclusion *must* be distributed. It states only that *if* there is one, that same term must also be distributed by one of the premises. Bear in mind, as well, that if *both* terms in the conclusion are distributed, then *both* of them must also be in the premises.

If this seems confusing, don't worry, you can still apply the rules. You only need the ability to pick out which terms in a syllogism are distributed and undistributed. There is a difference between the ability to find distributed terms and the ability to explain why they must be distributed. The former is essential, the latter is not.

Rule #3) A negative conclusion must have one and only one negative premise: Technically, rule 3 is a combination of two rules: (i) a negative conclusion must have *one* negative premise, and (ii) a negative conclusion must have *only one* premise. However, it is easier to remember these two rules as the one stated above—"one and only one." Why the rule? Let's consider two examples:

EXAMPLE 1	EXAMPLE 2
No dogs are frogs	All dogs are animals
No frogs are cats	Some chimps are animals
No cats are dogs	Some chimps are not dogs

In both examples we find a negative conclusion. Example 1 has two negative premises. Example 2 has two affirmative premises. According to rule 3, both are fallacious arguments. As you can see in both examples, a negative conclusion asserts a relation of exclusion between the minor and major terms. Now, to validly infer that relation from the premises, the two terms must be related to each other by virtue of their relations to the middle. That is, one of the terms in the conclusion must be *included in* the middle and one must be *excluded from* the middle. So Example 1 is fallacious. For when neither the minor nor the major term is included in the middle, as is the case when both premises are negative, then their exclusion from each other (as stated in the conclusion) is actually left undetermined. Therefore, *a negative conclusion cannot be derived from two negative premises*. Example 2 is also fallacious. For if neither the minor nor the major terms are excluded from the middle (i.e., if both are included in the middle), as is the case when both premises are affirmative, then there is no relationship of exclusion being asserted. If the minor and major terms are in no way excluded from each other in the premises, we cannot assert a relation of exclusion between them in the conclusion. Therefore, *a negative conclusion cannot be derived from two affirmative premises*.

Hence we may state these two principles as the following rule: *a negative conclusion must have one and only one negative premise*.

Rule #4) An affirmative conclusion must have two affirmative premises: The logic of affirmative conclusions should be easier to grasp now. Since in this case a relation of inclusion is asserted between the minor and major (in the conclusion), it is necessary that the relation of both terms to the middle (as found in the premises) is also one of inclusion. Hence, *an affirmative conclusion requires two affirmative premises*. In other words, an affirmative conclusion cannot be drawn from a negative premise.

Rule #5) The syllogism must contain three and only three terms: This last rule may strike you as too obvious to mention. It follows from the very *definition* of a syllogism, which is an orderly grouping of three categorical propositions that serve to relate one category (found in one premise) to another category (found in another premise) by means of a third category (found in both premises). So a syllogism *just is* an argument with three and only three terms.

Even so, it is easy to make the mistake of constructing syllogisms with four terms, or sometimes with only two. It is helpful to keep the three-term rule in mind. Consider this argument:

1. Whoever supports terrorism is immoral.
2. The Koran supports terrorists.
3. Therefore, the Koran is immoral.

Looking to the conclusion first, we find that "the Koran" is the minor term. But what is the major? It just says "immoral." But an immoral *what*? To answer that, we must consider what kind of thing the minor term is said to be. In this case, it is obviously a book. Therefore, the major term is more specifically "immoral book." Now, since books, as such, cannot literally be immoral, the real meaning must rather be: "a book that teaches immoral behavior." The full conclusion, then, is: "The Koran is a book that teaches immoral behavior." We are now set to go back into the premises to find the minor and major terms. The minor term ("the Koran") is the subject of the second premise. But where is the major? It's not there. Don't be fooled by the predicate of the first premise (i.e., "immoral"). In that proposition, "immoral" modifies the subject, which is "whoever supports terrorism." The subject category is a group of *people*, namely, those who support terrorism. Let's make the number of terms more explicit:

- [People who support terrorism] are [people who are immoral].
- [The Koran] is [a book that supports terrorism].
- [The Koran] is [a book that teaches immoral behavior].

To make the number of terms more explicit still, we can formalize the argument using letters taken from the syllogism:

- [PST] are [PI].
- [K] is [BST].
- [K] is [BTI].

We have two distinct terms in first premise, two different ones in the second premise, and a fifth different term in the conclusion. There is no need to call it the "five-term fallacy," though; any more than three is sufficient to call it the "four-term fallacy." It is also possible, though not as likely, to construct a syllogism with only *two* terms. Consider this one:

1. People who watch too much TV often have a difficult time concentrating.
2. Those whose minds tend to wander also watch too much TV.
3. Therefore, some people whose minds tend to wander also have a difficult time concentrating.

In this syllogism, the middle term is people-who-watch-too-much-TV. The minor term is "people whose minds tend to wander." The major term is "people who have a difficult time concentrating." There appears to be three terms. But are the major and minor terms really two different things? What exactly is the difference between "a mind that struggles to concentrate" and "a mind that tends to wander"? There might be a difference, at least in the author's mind, but maybe not. If it turns out that the major and minor terms are really synonymous, the syllogism commits what we can call the "two-term fallacy." Let's suppose that, in this example, the major and minor terms are just synonyms. We could then simplify the syllogism this way:

- [Too-much-TV-watchers] are [poor concentrators].
- [Poor concentrators] are [too-much-TV-watchers].
- Therefore, [poor concentrators] are [poor concentrators].

This revised argument shows that we are only dealing with two terms. To summarize Rule #5, a syllogism must have three terms (in order to avoid the two-term fallacy) and only three terms (to avoid the four-term fallacy).

How many rules are there…really? It is worth noting that logic texts include different numbers of rules. I have seen as few as four and as many as eleven. This does not mean that logicians cannot reach agreement on the matter. Nor does it imply that we might be missing something with only five rules. Why the discrepancy? First, some texts aim to make everything as explicit as possible. In this text, for example, we gave two rules about the conclusion: that an affirmative must have all affirmative premises, and that a negative must have one and only one negative premise. These two rules *imply* what other texts make explicit, namely, that for every valid syllogism, *there must be at least one affirmative premise*. Authors aiming to make everything explicit will list more rules. Secondly, some texts combine two rules into one. In this text, rules 3 and 5 each combine two rules. Our rule 3 ("one and only one") is actually two rules; likewise in the case of rule 5. Thirdly, some authors make the definitions of a syllogism serve as rules. For instance, one text makes it a rule that *every syllogism must contain three categorical propositions*. Finally, some texts include as rules what they call "corollaries" from "axioms." Axioms are unproved (or improvable) propositions. Corollaries are propositions that can be proved from axioms. So if we make it an axiom that *one premise must be affirmative*, it would then follow (as a corollary) that *there cannot be two negative premises*.

36) Non-Standard Syllogisms (1) Enthymemes

Definition of: You know that a standard form syllogism has three propositions: a major premise, a minor premise, and a conclusion. Yet it is not uncommon to find a syllogism missing one of these propositions. This is called an enthymeme.

Forms of (1st, 2nd, 3rd): A syllogism missing its major premise is called a "first order" enthymeme; a syllogism missing its minor premise is a "second order" enthymeme; a syllogism missing its conclusion is a "third order" enthymeme. The word "enthymeme" is a Greek term meaning "in the mind." The name is appropriate. In each of the three orders, one proposition is left unstated because it is already *in your mind*. The one using the enthymeme assumes that the missing premise or conclusion is obvious to you; hence it is unnecessary to state. Here is a standard syllogism in its three enthymematic forms:

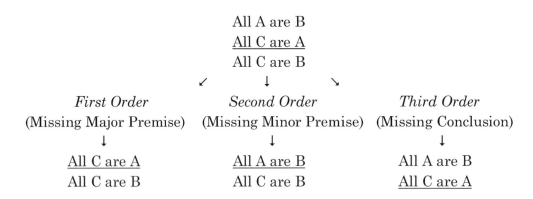

In order to put some meat on these bones, let's consider each of the above forms in the context of natural language.

1st Order
Socrates is a man.
Therefore, Socrates is mortal.

2nd Order
All men are mortal.
Therefore, Socrates is mortal.

3rd Order
All men are mortal.
Socrates is a man.

The first two orders *assume* that an (unstated) premise is true: the first order enthymeme assumes that "All men are mortal." The second order enthymeme assumes that "Socrates is a man." The third order enthymeme assumes that you will draw the conclusion yourself.

Enthymemes are rhetorically effective. They force the reader to think more about the argument and make the reader feel like they are part of the process. Moreover, by spelling out the entire syllogism, you run the risk of boring your readers, insulting their intelligence, or appearing pedantic.

To determine if an enthymeme is valid or not, you will need to fill in the missing proposition. In a third order enthymeme, you must ask yourself what the most obviously intended conclusion is, add it to the premises, and then test it according to the five rules. But when the conclusion is present, how do you determine whether it is a first or second order enthymeme? The answer lies in the conclusion. Remember, the major and minor premises take their name from the conclusion; the major premise contains the major term (the predicate of the conclusion), and the minor premise contains the minor term (the subject of the conclusion). So if the lone premise contains the minor term, you know it is the minor premise, and that the argument is therefore missing its major premise; in which case you are dealing with a 1st order enthymeme. But if the lone premise contains the major term, it must be the major premise; the missing premise, consequently, is the minor premise, and the argument is therefore a 2nd order enthymeme.

37) Non-Standard Syllogisms (2) Sorites

Nature of: Some arguments pile up standard syllogisms into larger super-syllogisms called "sorites." The name comes from the Greek word *soros*, or "heap," which conveys the idea of syllogisms getting stacked together. Contrast these two:

There are several contrasts to note. First, the sorites has at least three premises, though it can have more. Secondly, like the standard syllogism, the sorites has one minor and one major term; but unlike the standard syllogism, the sorites has at least two (or more) middle terms; in this case, B and C. The heaping up of propositions increases the number of middle terms. Thirdly, while the

Standard	Sorites
All A are B All B are C All A are C	All A are B All B are C All C are D All A are D

conclusion of the standard syllogism is reached by means of only one link, the conclusion of a sorites is reached by two (or more) links. It is this longer chain-like structure that distinguishes sorites from simple three-term syllogisms.

Method of evaluating: To determine whether a sorites is valid, the basic guideline is to ensure that each link in the chain is valid. A chain is only as strong as its weakest link. To evaluate a sorites, then, consider each link in turn. Let's think through the following example:

1. Whatever has mass has size.
2. Whatever has size has shape.
3. Whatever has shape can be studied by geometers.
4. Whatever can be studied by geometers is orderly.
   Therefore, whatever has mass is orderly.

You should intuitively see that it is valid, though it is not valid *as stated*. It is actually an enthymeme. In fact, all sorites are enthymemes. To understand why, let's take the first step of formalizing the argument:

1. All M are SI
2. All SI are SH
3. All SH are SG
4. All SG are O
   All M are O

There are five terms. The minor and major terms, M and O, are related in the conclusion by means of a three-link chain—SI, SH, and SG. To evaluate each link, the trick is to make explicit the entire heap of syllogisms involved in the argument. To do this, we must *state the unexpressed conclusion of each simple syllogism* in the sorites. In the following analysis, each of the component syllogisms is marked off with vertical lines, each of the original premises is numbered, and each unstated conclusion is made explicit in bold.

	|	1. All M are SI	
1st Syllogism	|	2. All SI are SH	
	|	**All M are SH**	|
		3. All SH are SG	| 2nd Syllogism
	|	**All M are SG**	|
3rd Syllogism	|	4. All SG are O	
	|	**All M are O**	

The 1st syllogism proves All M are SH. This conclusion is then used as a premise in the 2nd syllogism, which proves All M are SG. This conclusion becomes, in turn, a premise for the 3rd syllogism, which proves the conclusion of the entire sorites, All M are O.

38) Non-Standard Syllogisms (3) Natural Language

You will now learn about some of the irregularities that characterize syllogisms in real life argumentation. To understand what is meant by "non-standard," compare these syllogisms:

Whatever began to exist had a cause.	All [things that began to exist] are [things that had a cause].
The universe began to exist.	All [the universe] is [a thing that began to exist].
The universe had a cause.	Therefore, all [the universe] is [a thing that had a cause].

There is no difference in the *meaning* of these two syllogisms. But there is obviously a difference in their *form*. Only the argument on the right is in standard form, since it uses standard form categorical propositions. Because the other argument is in non-standard form, it is not immediately obvious that it too is an AAA-1 syllogism. Yet which of these two arguments is more natural to write? Which is easier and more pleasant to read? From a rhetorical standpoint, the non-standard argument is clearly superior.

Negative terms: Standard form categorical syllogisms require three terms and only three terms—major, minor, and middle. So what are we to make of the following syllogism?

> All photographers are non-writers.
> Some editors are writers.
> Therefore, some non-photographers are not non-editors.

This argument really has six terms: (1) photographers, (2) non-writers, (3) editors, (4) writers, (5) non-photographers, and (6) non-editors. Do you see the problems? First of all, the minor and major terms are not even in the premises. Secondly, it seems we have two middle terms. Yet we can reduce these six terms to only three. We dealt with negated propositions before, when we learned about the principles of conversion, obversion, and contraposition. We can use them here to standardize the above syllogism. As a rule of thumb, we will start with the conclusion. Knowing that A and O propositions can be contraposed, we can contrapose this O proposition into "Some editors are not photographers." This leaves us with uniform minor and major terms. But we are still left with different middle terms. We can reduce the two middle terms to one without altering uniformity of the major and minor terms. Knowing that every categorical proposition can be obverted, we can obvert the major premise to "No photographers are writers," which gives us the valid EIO-2:

No photographers are writers
Some editors are writers.
Therefore, some editors are not photographers.

Synonymous terms: Sometimes syllogisms use more than three different *terms* to designate what are really only three *concepts*. For example:

No wealthy persons are vagrants.
All lawyers are rich people.
Therefore, no attorneys are homeless.

Here we have six different *terms*: (1) wealthy persons, (2) vagrants, (3) lawyers, (4) rich people, (5) attorneys, and (6) homeless. However, we only have three different *concepts*. For we have three pairs of synonyms, i.e., different words having the same meaning. If we represent 3 and 5 with the letter *S*, 2 and 6 with the letter *P*, and 1 and 4 with the letter *M*, we then have the following syllogism:

No M are P
<u>All S are M</u>
No S are P

The above example is extreme. In most cases there will only be one pair of synonyms at most.

Singular propositions: Since the subject in the proposition "Socrates is a man" denotes a *singular* object, we call it a "singular term." Singular terms stand in contrast to class terms ("man"). Even so, there is a sense in which we can identify a singular object as its own class. Since Socrates is the only member in his class, he constitutes *all* the members of his class. So we can treat the singular "Socrates" as a *universal* term, and translate "Socrates is a man" into the standard form "All Socrates is a man." Likewise, we can translate "Socrates is not a woman" as "No Socrates is a woman." We can translate singular propositions using "parameters." For example, "Socrates is mortal" translates into:

[*All persons identical to*] Socrates [*are persons who*] are mortal.

We used "All *persons*..." for the obvious reason that Socrates is a person; but we must adjust the parameters to the given subject matter. Here are some examples:

"...*places* identical to...are places where..."
"...*things* identical to...are things that..."
"...*cases* identical to...are cases which..."
"...*times* identical to...are times when..."

Indefinite propositions (i.e., unexpressed quantifiers): Many categorical propositions have unexpressed quantifiers, e.g., "Those who believe in Jesus are forgiven." Theologically speaking, it is likely that *all* men are in view. So the universal quantifier is *implicit*. Sometimes it is not so obvious, e.g., "Girls just want to have fun." Does the proposition have all girls in view or only some? Since we cannot tell, the proposition is said to be indefinite. What makes a categorical proposition indefinite is not only the lack of a quantifier ("all" or "no" or "some") but also a lack of context for deciding. In some cases we do not need a context. For example, the proposition "Bachelors are unmarried men" is referring to *all* bachelors by definition.

Non-standard quantifiers: The following propositions have non-standard quantifiers:

1. *All* men *are not* mortal.
2. *Not every* dog is an animal with pointed ears.
3. *Not a single* cat is an animal that can fly.
4. Girls *are all* the same.
5. *Not one* man is able to save himself.
6. *A few* good lessons are better than many poor ones.
7. *Many* teachers are full time students.
8. *Most* people are frightened by spiders.

You can decipher the quantity of some of these propositions rather easily. The first one is the most difficult. Logically, it might mean either "No men are mortal" or "Some men are not mortal." We need a context to determine the intended meaning. The meaning of the second proposition is fairly obvious, i.e., "Some dogs do not have pointed ears." The third proposition means "No cats can fly." The fourth proposition means "All girls are the same." The fifth means "No man can save himself." The sixth means "Some good lessons are better than many poor ones." We should read the last two in the same way: in Aristotelian logic, "most" and "many" logically mean "some."

Predicate adjectives: Roughly speaking, *nouns* (e.g., "roses") denote things, and *adjectives* (e.g., "red") denote the *attributes* of things. Since all categorical propositions assert a relation between two nouns, we need to have some form of noun in both the subject *and the predicate* position. Yet some propositions omit the noun-predicate, e.g., "All roses are *red*." Red is not a noun but rather an attribute or a property of a noun. So we must translate "All roses are red" into "All roses are red flowers."

Non-standard verbs: Categorical propositions will often lack the standard form verbs of "is/are" and "is not/are not." Non-standard propositions such as "All birds fly" and "Some men will be glorified" must be translated into "All birds *are* flying animals" and "Some men *are* persons who will be glorified."

Section 2: Propositional Reasoning

39) Introduction to Propositional Inference

Contrasting categorical and propositional arguments: You learned that Aristotle developed a method for arguing about *categories*. Shortly after him, the Stoics refined his methods for arguing about *propositions*. Compare the bracketed components of the following arguments:

Categorical	Propositional
All [men] are [mortal].	If [all men are mortal], then [Socrates is a man].
[Socrates] is a [man].	[All men are mortal].
Therefore, [Socrates] is [mortal].	Therefore, [Socrates is a man].

The bracketed terms on the left are *categories*; those on the right are *propositions*. In Section 2 we will study the basic[81] forms of propositional inference, displayed in the following box:

Names	Forms	Examples
Sufficient Conditional	If p, then q	If life begins at conception, then abortion is murder.
Necessary Conditional	p only if q	Argument is possible only if there are laws of thought.
Biconditional	p if and only if q	The Bible is infallible if and only if it is totally inspired.
Disjunctive	p or q	You are for Christ or you are against Him.

To mark the difference, we use *p*s and *q*s to represent entire propositions, rather than the *A*s and *B*s that stood for categories.[82]

Like Aristotelian arguments, the validity of Stoic arguments depends on their *form*. The ten valid forms below are easily memorized.

---

[81] Unlike categorical logic, which was virtually completed in Aristotle's day, the development of propositional logic carried on into the 20th century, when it became known as the "propositional calculus." The latter uses a formalized system of technical symbols. Perhaps you've seen them before, e.g., (~p v q) ≡ [(r ⊃ s) · (t v u)]. The study of propositional calculus has great value for computer engineers, logicians, and professional philosophers, but not so much for our more general purposes.

[82] The variable *p* (*r*, *s*, *t*) was introduced by Russell and Whitehead in their *Principia Mathematica* (1910).

\	Principal Valid Forms of Stoic Logic			
Sufficient Conditionals	If p, then q p q		If p, then q Not q Not p	
Necessary Conditionals	p only if q p q		p only if q Not q Not p	
Biconditionals	p if and only if q p q	p if and only if q q p	p if and only if q Not p Not q	p if and only if q Not q Not p
Disjunctives	p or q Not p q		p or q Not q p	

The three kinds of conditions: The next few lessons explain the three *conditional* propositions and their patterns of inference. (Disjunctive inference will be treated separately.) Let's begin by examining the *meaning* of conditional propositions. (Some of this will be a review of the lesson on biconditional definitions.)

Sufficient conditions: When one proposition is enough for inferring another proposition, the former is a "sufficient condition" for the latter. The truth of "Joe trusted in Christ" is sufficient to infer that "Joe is justified before God."

Necessary conditions: A necessary condition is that without which something cannot be the case. Without legs one cannot walk; without ears, one cannot hear; without a nose, one cannot smell. Therefore, legs are a "necessary condition" for walking, eyes for seeing, ears for hearing, and a nose for smelling. If x cannot be the case unless y is also the case, then y is a *necessary condition* for x.

Biconditionals (or, "necessary and sufficient conditions"): Sometimes y is both a necessary and sufficient for x to be the case. For example, it is true that one cannot be justified without faith in Christ, so faith is a necessary condition for being justified. It is also true that faith in Christ is enough to justify them (such faith is a sufficient condition for being justified).

Some facts are neither necessary nor sufficient conditions for other facts. Attending a school is neither necessary nor sufficient for being educated. It is not necessary because it is possible to be educated at home. It is not sufficient because one might attend school and yet refuse to learn.

The three forms: Where "p" is a sufficient condition, we express this with "If p, then q" (e.g., "If one believes in Christ, then one will be saved"). Where "p" is a necessary condition for q, we express this with "q only if p" (e.g., "One will be saved only if one believes in Christ"). Where "p" is both a necessary and sufficient condition for q, we use the biconditional "q if and only if p" (e.g., "One will be saved if and only if one believes in Christ").[83]

---

[83] For biconditionals, technical writers use the abbreviation *iff* for 'if and only if.' Hence "p if and only if q" would be "p *iff* q." This abbreviation should only be used for audiences versed in logic.

40) Inferences Using Sufficient Conditionals

Antecedents and consequents: The proposition "If p, then q" has two elements: p is the *antecedent* and q is the *consequent*. The antecedent is always the first element of the proposition and the consequent is always the second.

Sufficient conditionals are also called "hypothetical" propositions. The proposition "If the Universe is infinite, then the Universe is God" does *not* affirm that the Universe *is* infinite. It proposes the claim as a hypothetical. Nor, then, does it affirm that "the Universe is God." The truth-value of both the antecedent and the consequent are left undetermined. To infer anything from a conditional proposition, one of the two components must be either *affirmed* to be true or *denied* being true.

The rules of inference for sufficient conditionals: There are four easy rules to learn. Two of them are positive, telling us what we *may* do, and two of them are negative, telling us what we *may not* do. The two positive rules state that we may either (1) *affirm the antecedent* or (2) *deny the consequent*. The two negative rules state that we may not (3) *affirm the consequent* or (4) *deny the antecedent*. Following rules 1 and 2 yields valid inferences. To break rule 3 or 4 yields invalid inferences. Here are all four inferences, both the valid and invalid:

	Valid	Invalid	
Affirmed → Antecedent	If p, then q *p* q	If p, then q *Not p* ?	Denied ← Antecedent
Denied → Consequent	If p, then q *Not q* Not p	If p, then q *q* ?	Affirmed ← Consequent

Affirming the antecedent is known as *modus ponens* (lit. "way of affirmation"). Denying the consequent is known as *modus tollens* (lit. 'way of denial'). The question marks in the invalid column reveal that no conclusion can be drawn from the premises.

The rationale for these rules: The logic of modus ponens needs no explanation; its validity is self-evident. But why is it invalid to deny the antecedent? Consider an example:

> If Joe is a Republican, then Joe admires Ronald Reagan.
> Joe is not a Republican.
> Therefore, Joe does not admire Ronald Reagan.

The first premise is only concerned with what would be the case if Joe *were* a Republican; it says *nothing* about what would be the case if Joe were *not* a Republican. That is why the inference is fallacious.

The logic of modus tollens is not as obvious as modus ponens. Consider this example:

> If Bob is an American, then Bob likes apple pie.
> Bob does not like apple pie.
> Therefore, Bob is not an American.

The first premise is saying, in effect, that one cannot be an American and *not* like apple pie. So Bob's dislike of apple pies implies that Bob is not an American. The first premise asserts that if the antecedent is true, the consequent is *also* true. If the consequent is not true, then, we can make a "backward" inference to the conclusion that the antecedent is not true either.

The fallacy of affirmed consequent makes a simple mistake. Consider this example:

> If Joe voted for Obama, then Joe is a Democrat.
> Joe is a Democrat.
> Therefore, Joe voted for Obama.

The first premise is not asserting anything about what would be the case if Joe were a *Democrat*. It only addresses what would be the case if he voted for Obama, namely, that he would be a Democrat. But whether Joe's being a Democrat would cause him to vote for Obama is not clear *from this argument*. If we think it is valid, this is because we already know that Obama is a Democrat, and we naturally assume that being a Democrat is a sufficient reason to vote for a Democratic candidate. We are allowing the *meaning* of the argument's *words* to blind us to the *invalidity* of the argument's *form*. The tendency to rely on the fallacy of affirmed consequent is more common than we may think. One of the more outstanding examples occurs in science. Scientists regularly reason this way:

> If hypothesis *x* is true, then effect E will occur when we run experiment *y*.
> Effect E *does* occur when we run experiment *y*.
> Therefore, hypothesis *x* is true.

The first premise says nothing about what will be the case if effect E occurs. It only addresses what will be the case if the hypothesis is true. So when the second premise affirms the consequent (i.e., that effect E occurs when experiment *y* is performed), this entails nothing about the truth of the hypothesis.

Refutation by counter examples: You learned about this principle in lesson 33. A valid argument is any argument in which it is impossible for the premises to be true and the conclusion false. So any argument with true premises and a *false* conclusion is necessarily *in*valid. So we can expose the invalidity of an argument by giving a counter argument of the *same form* as the original, but which, unlike the original, has true premises and a false conclusion.

The Original Invalid Argument	Refutation by Counter Example
If Joe is a Republican, then Joe admires Ronald Reagan. Joe is not a Republican. Therefore, Joe does not admire Ronald Reagan.	If cats are mice, then cats are animals. Cats are not mice. Therefore, cats are not animals.
If Joe voted for Obama, then Joe is a Democrat. Joe is a Democrat. Therefore, Joe voted for Obama.	If cats are mice, then cats are animals. Cats are animals. Therefore, cats are mice.

The variety of "If...Then" connections: The strength or weakness of the connection between the antecedent and the consequent will vary with the content of the premise. The following chart shows some of the more common connections used in everyday discourse:

Kinds of "If...Then" Connections	
Logical (formal)	If all men are mortal, then no men are immortal.
Definitional	If Joe is a bachelor, then Joe is an unmarried male.
Causal	If the leaves are set on fire, then they will smoke.
Intentional	If I go to school tomorrow, then I will try to behave.
Associational	If Julia studied Roman history, then she must have learned about Caesar.
Analogical	If Sam thought N.Y.C. was a great place to visit, then I'm sure Sue will also.
Rhetorical	If aliens exist, then chimps can play Beethoven's Fifth Symphony.

The proposition "If all men are mortal, then no men are immortal" is an instance of the valid inference of obversion (see lesson 31). The connection here is necessarily true, but the connection is purely formal: "If all A is B, then no A is non-

B." The connection does not depend on the meaning of the words; it relies solely on the form of the proposition.

The proposition "If Joe is a bachelor, then Joe is an unmarried male" is likewise unassailable; it's true because of the meaning of the words, not the form of the proposition. The word 'bachelor' *means* 'unmarried male.' The connection is true by definition.

Unlike the previous two, the connection expressed by the proposition "If the dry leaves are set on fire, then they will smoke" is not certain in the same sense. It is not true by definition. It is true by virtue of the cause-effect relationship between fire and smoke. (Some would argue that it's not even a certain truth, since God could perform a miracle of preventing burning leaves from smoking.)

The proposition "If I go to school tomorrow, I will try to behave" expresses an entirely different sort of connection, which depends on the will of man. The individual might not choose to behave once he gets to school.

The truthfulness of the proposition "If Julia studied Roman history, then she must have learned about Caesar" is only probable. Since Julius Caesar is a major figure in Roman history, we assume that anyone who studies Roman history has learned something about him. The inference rests on our belief that these two things are closely associated.

The proposition "If Sam thought N.Y.C a great place to visit, then Sue will also" rests on a perceived likeness (or analogy) between two people. Presumably, Sue is very much like Sam. Given this similarity, we make this (merely) probable inference.

The proposition "If aliens exist, then chimps can play Beethoven's Fifth Symphony" is purely rhetorical. There is no connection between the antecedent and the consequent. Note that the argument is really an enthymematic way of using modus tollens. Standardized, it reads:

> If aliens exist, then chimps can play Beethoven's Fifth Symphony.
> Chimps cannot play Beethoven's Fifth Symphony.
> Therefore, aliens do not exist.

The argument assumes that everyone knows that Chimps, smart as they are, cannot play orchestral instruments. So we will *automatically deny the consequent*, and therefore the antecedent.

So why call the condition "sufficient"? It's easy to see why some conditions should be called sufficient. The antecedent of the statement "If Fuji is a type of apple, then Fuji is a type of fruit" gives us *enough* information to infer the consequent. But this is not the case with other "If p, then q" statements. Take the statement "If the store sells apples, then it sells Fuji apples." Knowing that a store sells apples is *not* enough to infer that it sells Fuji apples. So why call it a "sufficient" condition? When people use the "If p, then q" statement, they generally *intend* to express that p is sufficient for inferring q. That's the point of the statement. The fact that some antecedents are not truly sufficient conditions means that some sufficient conditionals are subject to criticism. But this does not change the fact that "If...then" statements function to express sufficient conditions.

Complex sufficient conditionals: We can use sufficient conditionals to construct more complex arguments such as these:

Extended use of Modus Ponens	*Extended use of Modus Tollens*
If p, then q	If p, then q
If q, then r	If q, then r
If r, then s	If r, then s
p	Not s
s	Not p

There is no limit to the number of premises one may use; as long as they are properly linked, the argument will be valid.

41) Inferences Using Necessary Conditionals

Necessary conditionals follow the same rules: In the sufficient conditional proposition, "If p, then q," p is the antecedent and q is the consequent. In the necessary conditional proposition, "p only if q," we will continue referring to p as the antecedent and q as the consequent. In both propositions below, the *first* component is the antecedent and the *second* component is the consequent.

    If [antecedent], **then** [consequent]   [Antecedent] **only if** [consequent]

The rules governing the necessary conditional are the *same* as those governing the sufficient conditional: we may (1) affirm the antecedent or (2) deny the consequent, and we may not (3) deny the antecedent or (4) affirm the consequent. [84]

	Valid	Invalid	
Affirmed → Antecedent	p only if q *p* q	p only if q *Not p* ?	Denied ← Antecedent
Denied → Consequent	p only if q *Not q* Not p	p only if q *q* ?	Affirmed ← Consequent

The valid forms: Recall that "p only if q" asserts that p cannot be the case unless q is also the case. So if p is true, q must be true.

        p only if q
        p
        q

On the other hand, if p cannot be the case without q, it follows that if q is not the case, p cannot be the case either. Hence we have the other valid form:

        p only if q
        Not q
        Not p

---

[84] Do not use the terms 'modus ponens' and 'modus tollens' when speaking of necessary conditionals. These terms have a universally accepted meaning, applying only to sufficient conditional arguments.

Take the proposition "Moral absolutes exist only if God exists." On the one hand, this asserts that moral absolutes cannot exist without God. So if moral absolutes exist, God must also exist. We can standardize this as:

>Moral absolutes exist only if God exists.
>Moral absolutes exist.
>Therefore, God exists.

Or we can reason in the other direction by saying that if God does not exist, moral absolutes cannot exist either. In standard form:

>Moral absolutes exist only if God exists.
>God does not exist.
>Therefore, moral absolutes do not exist.

The invalid forms: To understand why the invalid forms are invalid, recall what necessary conditionals are *not* asserting. Take the proposition "Christ rose from the dead only if miracles occur." This says nothing about what would be the case if Christ did *not* rise from the dead. It is therefore invalid to deny the antecedent:

>Christ rose from the dead only if miracles occur.
>Christ did not rise from the dead.
>Therefore, miracles do not occur.

Nor does the first premise say anything about what would be the case if miracles *do* occur. So it is also invalid to affirm the consequent.

>Christ rose from the dead only if miracles occur
>Miracles do occur.
>Therefore, Christ rose from the dead.

How the *content* of a necessary conditional blinds us to the logical meaning of its form: Think about the following propositions:

1. Coach to athlete: "You will become a pro only if you practice."
2. Doctor to cancer patient: "You will survive only if you get chemotherapy."
3. Lottery player to friend: "I will give you one million dollars only if I win."
4. Captain of boat to person who falls overboard: "I will throw you a life-preserver only if I find it."

In the case of 1, it's understood that practicing is necessary for going pro but not sufficient. Even if you practice and fail to become a pro, the coach's claim will not be falsified.

In case 2, the doctor only means that chemo is a necessary condition for surviving, not a sufficient one. Therefore, if one were on his death bed in spite of chemo treatment, he could not accuse the doctor of lying.

What about 3 and 4? Here we may feel misled. This is because we're allowing the content of the propositions to blind us to their form. We understand that when a person makes a promise like *that*, his intention is to act when the conditions are satisfied. If he does not act, we think he's failed to do what he said. Strictly speaking, however, the conditions in question (i.e., him winning the lottery or finding the preserver) are *only necessary* conditions, not sufficient. If he said "I will give you one million dollars *if* I win" or "I will throw you a life-preserver *if* I find it," we could scold him (logically, anyway). But that's not what he literally said. Perhaps he *meant* to say it (and the context and common sense suggest that he did mean it that way); but that is not what he said.

Contrasting necessary and sufficient conditionals: The previous examples show that 'sufficient condition' and 'necessary condition' do not mean the same thing. Contrast these two:

1. **If** <u>Jones is the President of the U.S.A</u>, then Jones is a citizen of the U.S.A.
2. Jones is a citizen of the U.S.A. **only if** <u>Jones is the President of the U.S.A</u>.

The underlined statement "Jones is the President of the U.S.A" acts as a sufficient condition in 1 and as a necessary condition in 2. As these propositions show, to say that x is a sufficient condition for y does not mean that x is a necessary condition for y (and vice versa). The first proposition is true and the second is false. Moreover, it is possible for something to be *both* necessary and sufficient (e.g., "Jones is the President of the U.S.A if and only if he holds the highest office in the land.") This presupposes a distinction in the *meaning* of the two conditions.

Why do some people think these propositions mean the same thing? It's probably due to the fact that these propositions *entail* one another. For example:

1. If [this bowl is made of crystal], then [this bowl is fragile].

2. [This bowl is made of crystal] only if [this bowl is fragile].

Proposition 1 asserts that if the antecedent is true, the consequent is also true—i.e., if p, then q. In other words, the antecedent *p* cannot be true *unless* the consequent *q* is *also* true. We can therefore state this using the necessary conditional "p only if q." This makes the following compound proposition true:

>If [*if p, then q*], then [*p only if q*]

Now take it in the reverse order. If I know that p is the case *only if* q is the case, then p being the case *entails* that q is the case—i.e., if p, then q. Therefore:

>If [p *only if q*], then [*if p, then q*]

The fact that one entails the other has led some authors to say that the two propositions are "equivalent." But this should only mean that they entail one another.

Complex necessary conditionals: As with sufficient conditionals, we can use necessary conditionals to construct complex arguments.

p only if q	p only if q
q only if r	q only if r
r only if s	r only if s
p	Not s
s	Not p

42) Inferences Using Biconditionals

The structure of biconditionals: The proposition "p if and only if q" is a combination of a necessary conditional and a sufficient conditional. We can break it into two propositions:

"**p if** and only if **q**" ↓ **p if q**	"p if and **only if q**" ↓ **p only if q**

In each case 'q' the biconditional statement, since it serves as *both* a necessary condition and a sufficient condition. In the proposition on the left, q is a *sufficient* condition. (Remember, the proposition "p if q" is a non-standard way of expressing "If q, then p".) In the proposition on the right, q is a *necessary* condition.

The rules and their rationale: The following chart contains all four valid biconditional arguments.

The Valid Argument Forms of Biconditionals			
1	**2**	**3**	**4**
p if and only if q	p if and only if q	p if and only if q	p if and only if q
p	q	Not p	Not q
q	p	Not q	Not p

Since "p if and only if q" is a combination of "p if q" and "p only if q," we can view "p if and only if b" *from either one of two perspectives*. We can view it as proposition containing "p if q" or as a proposition containing "p only if q." Therefore:

Form **1** is valid because it contains the component "p only if q"; we may thus affirm p. (If we focused only on the component "p if q," it would appear invalid to affirm 'p.'

Form **2** is valid because it contains the component "p if q"; we may thus affirm q. (Again, if we focused only on the component "p only if q," it would appear invalid to affirm 'q.')

Form **3** is valid because it contains the component "p if q"; we may thus deny p. This time, were we to focus only the component "p only if q," we would find it invalid to deny 'p.'

Form **4** is valid because it contains the component "p only if q"; we may thus deny q. If we focused only on the component "p if q," we would find it invalid to deny 'p.')

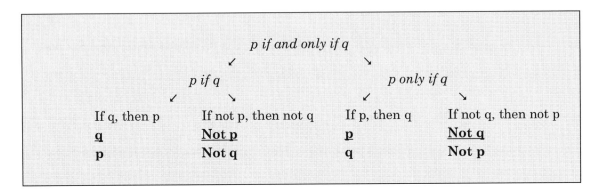

The rules governing biconditionals can be reduced to simply this: We may affirm or deny the antecedent and we may affirm or deny the consequent; but if we *affirm* one, we must *affirm* the other; and if we *deny* one, we must *deny* the other.

The use of biconditionals: What gives God the right to command men? One philosopher, Jean Burlamaqui, argued that God's sovereignty was based on His having three attributes: (1) power, (2) wisdom and (3) goodness. Burlamaqui said that omnipotence *by itself* did not give God the right to command; nor did omniscience *by itself*; nor did omni-benevolence *by itself*. As Burlamaqui argued, power and wisdom without goodness can be used maliciously; power and goodness without wisdom can be used recklessly; and wisdom and goodness without power is ineffectual. In none of these cases would God be fit to command men. However, when all three attributes are united, they explain God's right to command. We can express Burlamaqui's reasoning using the biconditional proposition. To understand how, let 'S' = sovereign, 'P' = omnipotent, 'S' = omniscient, and 'B' = omnibenevolent. We then have:

God is S if and only if God is P and S and B.

This proposition asserts that P and S and B are necessary conditions for God to be S. And since they are *all* the necessary conditions needed, they *together form a sufficient condition* for God to be S.

Complex structures: You may construct syllogistic arguments using biconditionals. Since you already understand the principle, we will not bother with any further discussion. Here is an example:

>p if and only if q
>q if and only if r
>p
>r

43) Non-Standard Formulations of Conditionals

In Aristotelian logic we learned that standard form propositions are often expressed in non-standard form; this is true in Stoic logic as well.

Alternative ways of expressing sufficient conditions: There are several ways of conveying the proposition "If Mt. Vesuvius sustains a major eruption, then the city of Pompeii will be affected."

- "The city of Pompeii will be affected if Mt. Vesuvius sustains a major eruption."
- "Should Mt. Vesuvius sustain a major eruption, the city of Pompeii will be affected."
- "A major eruption of Mt. Vesuvius would result in Pompeii being affected."

The terms "entails that," "entailed by," "implies that," "implied by" are non-standard ways of expressing the "If…then" locution. Here are some examples:

- "The fact that John is breathing *entails that* John is alive"
- "The fact that John is breathing *implies that* John is alive"
- "The fact that John is alive is *entailed by* the fact that John is breathing."
- "The fact that John is alive is *implied by* the fact that John is breathing."

All of these propositions assert the same point, and so all can be restated as the sufficient conditional, "*If* John is breathing, *then* John is alive."

Alternative ways of expressing necessary conditions: As with sufficient conditionals, necessary conditionals are often stated in non-standard form. Here are some examples:

- "Cats are pleasant pets only when they are raised in a calm and sociable environment."
- "Only on the supposition that God exists would it follow that atheists are fools."
- "Faith is that without which men cannot be saved."
- "The sign reads: 'In the absence of water, please do not dive into the pool.'"
- "True happiness cannot be attained but by obeying God's will."

The proposition "Cats are pleasant pets only when they are raised in a calm and sociable environment" can be standardized by replacing "only when" with "only if" ("Cats are pleasant pets *only if* they are raised in a calm and sociable environment." The proposition "Only on the supposition that God exists would it follow that atheists are fools" can be standardized as "Atheists are fools *only if* God exists." The proposition "Faith is that without which men cannot be saved" can be standardized as "Men can be saved *only if* they exercise faith." The proposition "In the absence of water, please do not dive into the pool" can be standardized as "Dive in the pool *only if* there is water in it." The proposition "True happiness cannot be attained but by obeying God's will" can be standardized as "True happiness can be attained *only if* one obeys God's will."

The use of 'unless': The term 'unless' means 'if not.' This raises a problem: Does 'unless' express a necessary condition or a sufficient condition?

The sufficient conditional "*If* Jones does *not* go to school, *then* Jones will not be educated" is logically equivalent to "Jones will not be educated *unless* he goes to school" which, in turn, is logically equivalent to the necessary conditional "Jones will be educated *only if* he goes to school." We thus have:

Jones will not be educated **unless** he goes to school
↙ ↘
Jones will be educated **only if** he goes to school.   **If** Jones does **not** go to school, he will not be educated

The diagram shows that either of the bottom propositions is logically equivalent to the top. We may formalize an 'unless' proposition as either a necessary or a sufficient conditional.

Using negative conditionals: Sufficient conditionals are often formulated with negative terms. It is important that you learn how to apply the rules of inference correctly when reading these propositions.

1	2	3
If not p, then q	If p, then not q	If not p, then not q
Not q	q	Not p
p	Not p	Not q

In **1** we find that the antecedent, 'Not p,' is a negative proposition. Using modus tollens, we may apply premise 'Not q' to the premise 'If not p, then q.' By denying the consequent we must deny the antecedent. But what would that look like? The antecedent is already in a negative form. Okay, fine, so we'll just negate it again. As you know, two negatives equals a positive. Therefore, to deny 'Not p' is to affirm 'p,' and that is our conclusion. So the argument is valid.

In **2** we find that the consequent is in a negative form. So, using modus tollens, we may use 'q' to deny 'not q.' We may therefore deny the antecedent so as to obtain 'Not p.'

In **3** we find that both the antecedent and the consequent are in negative forms. Be careful here (this is where some students get a bit confused). This argument is actually a case of modus ponens. Do you see why? The second premise, 'Not p,' is identical to the antecedent 'Not p.' Therefore, we may use the negative proposition in the second premise to *affirm* the negative antecedent in the first premise.

Negative necessary conditionals: The potential confusion we mentioned in connection with sufficient conditionals is also present in the case of necessary conditionals that use negative terms.

1	2	3
Not p only if q	p only if not q	Not p only if q
Not p	q	Not q
q	Not p	p

Though we're now dealing with necessary conditionals, nothing else has changed; the principles are still the same. Example 1 affirms the antecedent and thus affirms the consequent. Example 2 denies the consequent and thus denies the antecedent. Example 3 also denies the consequent and thus denies the antecedent.

3) Biconditionals: The above remarks apply here as well. By now you get the point.

1	2	3
Not p if and only if q	p if and only if not q	Not p if and only if not q
Not q	Not p	Not p
p	q	Not q

Again, there's no difference here either; the same principles apply. In example 1, 'Not q' denies 'q' (thus rendering it 'Not q') which denies 'Not p' (thus rendering it 'p'). In example 2, 'Not p' denies 'p' (rendering it 'Not p' and thus denies 'not q' (rendering it 'q'). Finally, in example 3 'Not p' affirms 'Not p' which, in turn, obliges us to affirm 'Not q.'

44) Disjunctive Inferences

Disjunctive propositions: Every disjunctive argument contains a *disjunctive proposition*, "p or q," otherwise known as a *disjunction*. In the disjunctive proposition "Jesus is the Christ or Jesus is a liar," the component propositions—"Jesus is the Christ" and "Jesus is a liar"—are called *disjuncts*.

The valid and invalid forms/rules: The rules are simple: one is positive, stating that you *may deny* a disjunct, and the other negative, stating that you *may not affirm* a disjunct. Here are the valid and invalid forms.

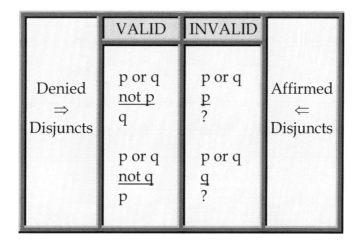

The twofold meaning of 'or': To see why 'or' is ambiguous, contrast these two statements:

[1] I could get married or remain unmarried.
[2] I could eat a burger or some fries.

We know that the states of being married and unmarried are mutually exclusive (i.e., there is no middle ground) and jointly exhaustive (i.e., there is no third option). So [1] means that one is *either* married *or* unmarried but *not both*. This is appropriately called the *exclusive* sense of "or." But we often use "or" in the *inclusive* sense of [2], when we do not mean to preclude the truth of both disjuncts ("I could eat a burger, or some fries, or both.")

In short, the strong "or" *excludes* the possibility that both disjuncts are true, while the weak "or" *includes* that possibility.

> 'Or' in the *exclusive* (or "strong") sense = "p or q but *not both*" (either\or)
>
> 'Or' in the *inclusive* (or "weak") sense = "p or q but *maybe both*" (and\or)

Unlike English, Latin avoids the ambiguity by using two different words: *vel* has the exclusive sense, and *aut* has the inclusive sense. English speakers must detect the intended meaning of "or" by its context, which is often easy enough to do. It is obvious, for example, that death and life are mutually exclusive states of existence, so we automatically understand that "Joe is dead or alive" is a strong disjunction. Likewise, since we know it is possible to be an American and a Californian, we readily understand that "Joe is an American or a Californian" is a weak disjunction.[85]

How the twofold meaning of 'or' affects the logic of a disjunctive inference: The rules for disjunctive inference depend on the postulate, that in the context of such reasoning, "or" is always to be understood in the *inclusive* sense. Let's see why.

If the strong sense of "or" were the only sense, the rules stated above would not apply, since then we could *affirm* a disjunct. The following strong disjunction illustrates why:

>Joe is thirsty or Joe is hungry (but not both)
>Joe is thirsty
>Therefore, Joe is not hungry

By using the strong sense of "or," the first premise tells us that at least one of the disjuncts is false. Since the second premise asserts that the first disjunct is true, we can infer that the second disjunct is false. Read this way, the argument is valid. But now read it as a weak disjunction.

>Joe is thirsty or Joe is hungry (but maybe both)
>Joe is thirsty
>Therefore, Joe is not hungry

---

[85] It is possible that a given speaker will use (unthinkingly) a weak sense of "or" in a strong sense. For example, one might intend the statement "One is religious or agnostic" to convey either/or when, *in fact*, these are not two mutually exclusive, since some agnostics (like Immanuel Kant) are religious.

The second premise asserts the truth of the first disjunct. But since the first premise allows for the truth of *both* disjuncts, we cannot infer anything about the second disjunct; it may be true, it may be false.

As the chart below reveals, there are some cases in which it is invalid to affirm a disjunct, but there are *no* cases in which it is invalid to *deny* one. This is why we should *presume* that every disjunctive argument uses "or" in the weak sense.

	If 'or' is *strong* or exclusive, then...	**If** 'or' is *weak* or inclusive, then...	
Valid	p or q not p q	p or q not p q	Valid
Valid	p or q not q p	p or q not q p	Valid
Valid[86]	p or q p not q	p or q p ?	**Invalid**
Valid	p or q q not p	p or q q ?	**Invalid**

---

[86] That is, *definitionally* valid, but *not formally* valid. This is true of the one below it as well.

45) Complex Arguments

You now know how to work with the four types of propositional statements and their patterns of inference. Any one of them may be combined with the other three to form complex structures.

1	2	3
If p, then q	p or q	p if and only if q
q only if r	if p, then r	q only if r
<u>p</u>	if q, then s	not r or s
r	<u>not s</u>	<u>not s</u>
	r	not p

4	5	6
p only if q	p or q or r	p only if q
If q, then r	r only if s	If q, then r
r if and only if s	If s, then t	r if and only if s
If s, then t	If t, then q	s only if t
<u>Not t</u>	<u>Not q</u>	<u>p</u>
Not p	p	t

7	8	9
If not p, then q	Not p or not q	p if and only if not q
If q, then not r	Not p if and only if r	Not r or s
Not r only if s	If r, then not s	If s, then not t
<u>Not s</u>	<u>s</u>	If not t, then u
p	Not q	u only if p
		If v, then r
		<u>v</u>
		Not q

Every argument here is valid and you can prove it. Note that in every argument there is only one premise (the underlined one) stating that something is actually the case. You must begin with that underlined premise. Try using it to prove another premise (whichever one has the same proposition in it). Once you have proven the second premise, keep moving step by step through the chain until you prove the conclusion (below the line).

46) The Process of Elimination

The process of elimination is a powerful form of reasoning used by scientists, philosophers, and detectives. Its basic form is:

> 1] p or q or r.
> 2] Not r.
> 3] Therefore, p or q.
> 4] Not q.
> 5] Therefore, p.

This is an extended version of the disjunctive argument, differing only in the number of disjuncts in the premises. Any number of disjuncts may be used. The basic form above will remain the same except for the addition of premises.

Let's consider an argument from Christian apologetics. A historian named Frank Morison sought to disprove the resurrection of Jesus. Morison trusted the gospel accounts that Jesus was actually buried and that His body actually disappeared. But did that prove he was resurrected? Not according to Morison, who proposed that Jesus' body was simply stolen. But this hypothesis required an explanation of its own. Who stole the body? Morison set out to answer this question. He assumed there were only four candidates: the Christians, the Jews, the Romans, or (as the scriptures teach) the angels. By the process of elimination, Morison came to the conclusion that the angels moved it. We can formalize his reasoning thus:

1) The Christians or the Jews or the Romans or the angels moved the stone.
2) *The Christians did not move the stone*, because...
3) Therefore, the Jews or the Romans or the angels moved the stone.
4) *The Jews did not move the stone*, because...
5) Therefore, the Romans or the angels moved the stone.
6) *The Romans did not move the stone*, because...
7) Therefore, the angels moved the stone.

The key premises are italicized. (Technically, you do not need to state the sub-conclusion 3; it's obvious.)

A general reason for each of the premises is the fact that the Roman soldiers who guarded the tomb were well disciplined and liable to severe punishment (even death) for dereliction of duty. This casts doubt on the suggestion of skeptics, that the guards were bribed or deceived.

Why not the Christians? Had the Christians stole the body, they would have known the Gospel was a lie. They would have no basis for zealously living out their faith and even dying for it. (It is one thing for *later* Christians to die for what they *believe to be true*, and another for the *Apostles* to die for what they *knew to be false*.)

Why not the Jews? By stealing the body, they would have provided Christians with grounds for inferring that Jesus had indeed rose, which is the last thing they would have wished.

Why not the Romans? The Romans desired to maintain social concord in Palestine. They did not want to encourage a religious sect that was sure to bring about discord.

In light of these considerations, Morison concluded that none of the three candidates had a sufficient motive for stealing the body. To the contrary, all of them had a sufficient motive *not* to steal it. He therefore inferred that the angels moved the stone.

Morison's reasoning is perfectly valid, which is only to say that the conclusion necessarily follows from the premises. But are the premises true? That is a separate question. Can *you* identify any problems with it?

Keep two rules in mind when constructing a process of elimination argument. First, ensure the disjuncts are *jointly exhaustive*; that is, make sure there is no other option in addition to the ones you state. The following argument is *not* jointly exhaustive:

> One is either a Buddhist or a Muslim or a Christian.
> Joe is not a Buddhist.
> Joe is not a Muslim.
> Therefore, Joe is a Christian.

Joe might be a Hindu or a Confucian or a Zoroastrian or some other religious adherent. Or Joe might just be an atheist. In any case, notice that the argument is actually valid. But the first premise is not true, since it does not "exhaust" all the options.

Secondly, ensure the disjuncts are *mutually exclusive*; that is, make sure the stated options do not overlap or blur into each other in any way, as they do in the following:

> Tom drives a Ford or a Mustang or a blue car.

These disjuncts are not mutually exclusive, since Mustangs are Fords and many Mustangs/Fords are blue. You should also avoid options that are blurry or fuzzy. For example,

> Joe is nice or decent or unfriendly or mean.

These terms are vague. What exactly is the distinction between 'nice' and 'decent,' or between 'unfriendly' and 'mean'? This makes the task of eliminating options virtually impossible. How will we prove that Joe is not "nice" if we do not know what the term means?

47) The Dilemma

The nature of a dilemma: One of the most effective ways of challenging an opposing view is to impale it on the horns of a *dilemma*. According to Matthew (21:23-27), a group of hostile religious leaders asked Jesus where he derived the authority to act and speak as He did. Jesus replied: "I will ask one thing of you, which if you tell Me, I will also tell you by what authority I do these things." He then posed this question: "The baptism of John was from what source, from heaven or from men?" The leaders quickly turned to consult with one another on how best to answer Him: "And they began reasoning among themselves, saying, 'If we say 'From heaven,' He will say to us, 'Then why did you not believe Him?' But if we say, 'From men,' we fear the multitude; for they all hold John to be a prophet.' Realizing they had been trapped by a dilemma, the men replied simply "We do not know." To which Jesus responded: "Then neither will I tell you by what authority I do these things."

Dilemmas are obviously powerful. Here is an example of a dilemma debated by theologians:

      1) Either Jesus could sin or Jesus could not sin.
      2) If Jesus could sin, then Jesus was not divine.
      3) If Jesus could not sin, then Jesus was not human.
      4) Therefore, Jesus was not divine or Jesus was not human.

The creator of a dilemma is seeking to impale his opponent upon the "horns" of the dilemma, which are the two conditional propositions (premises 2 and 3 above).

What makes for an effective dilemma? If we reflect on the preceding dilemma, we find there are at least three features that make it a problem worth solving: (1) the opponent accepts both antecedents of the conditionals; (2) the opponent does not accept either consequent; and (3) the consequents appear to follow their antecedents.

Concerning condition (1), an opponent who does not accept an argument's antecedents need not fear the argument's consequents. The consequents might be completely unacceptable, but if they are not rooted in acceptable antecedents, there is no threat of impalement. Here's an example with antecedents italicized:

1) If *God did not know that Adam would sin*, then God is ignorant.
2) If *God forced Adam to sin*, then God is unjust.
3) Therefore, God is either ignorant or unjust.

Since neither antecedent is true, there is no real dilemma here. The consequents are unacceptable, but we need not bother refuting them.

Concerning condition (2), it goes without saying that acceptable consequents are (no pun intended) pointless. Such an argument may be likened to a hornless bull. Here's an example with the consequents italicized:

1) One is either a man or a woman.
2) If one is a man, *then one is a son.*
3) If one is a woman, *then one is a daughter.*
4) Therefore, one is either a son or a daughter.

Though this has the form of a dilemma, there is nothing controversial about the consequents.

Concerning condition (3), an argument might have acceptable antecedents and unacceptable consequents, and yet still fail to be a dilemma *if* the consequents *do not follow* from the antecedents. Here's an example:

1) Either Abe Lincoln was a Republican or Hitler was a Nazi.
2) If Abe was a Republican, then Cicero was a poor public speaker.
3) If Hitler was a Nazi, then Aristotle was a dunce.

We would accept both antecedents and reject both consequents. Yet the consequents do not follow by a long shot.

But now consider, once again, the *genuine* dilemma about Christ's ability to sin:

1) Either Jesus could sin or Jesus could not sin.
2) If Jesus could sin, then Jesus was not divine.
3) If Jesus could not sin, then Jesus was not human.
4) Therefore, either Jesus was not divine or Jesus was not human.

All three conditions appear to be satisfied. The first premise is irrefutable. Some people accept the first antecedent ("Jesus could sin") and others accept the second ("Jesus could not sin"). But the former group does not to accept the first consequent ("Jesus was not divine"), and the latter group does not accept the second consequent ("Jesus was not a man"). Both groups reject both consequents. And yet, both consequents *appear* to follow. All of this accounts for why this is such a powerful dilemma.

A dilemma is intended to impale an opponent upon the horns. So how can we keep from being impaled?

Escape route #1: going between the horns: Every dilemma is designed to force an opponent to accept one or both of two unacceptable consequents. These consequents, in turn, are supposed to flow from what are assumed to be only two alternatives. To go "between the horns" of a dilemma is to find a *third* alternative.

a) A student will either love logic or they will hate it.
b) If they love logic, they will not need motivation from the teacher.
c) If they hate logic, motivation from the teacher will be of no help.
d) Therefore, in either case the teacher needn't try motivating logic students.

We are not impaled on the horns of (d) if we can find a third alternative, such as a student being faintly interested in logic. (As we will see next, we could also challenge premises b and c, especially c.)

Escape route #2: grabbing the bull by the horns: It is not always possible to go between the horns. Let's revisit the dilemma mentioned earlier.

a) Either Jesus could sin or Jesus could not sin.
b) If Jesus could sin, then Jesus was not God.
c) If Jesus could not sin, then Jesus was not a man.
d) Therefore, either Jesus was not divine or Jesus was not human.

Premise (a) has the form "p or not p." There is no third alternative here. By the principle of contradiction, one disjunct must be true and one must be false. Without a third alternative, we cannot go between the horns.

But we can try "grabbing the horns" of the dilemma by *rejecting one of the conditional premises*. This involves explaining why at least one of the consequents does not follow from its antecedent. In this particular case, the first horn is obviously true: if Jesus could sin, then Jesus was not God. Some would argue that the second horn, however, is not obviously true. There is no logical reason why being human *necessarily* involves the ability to sin. In fact, Christian theology holds that, in heaven, humans will no longer be able to sin. They will lose their "peccability" (i.e., their ability to sin) but not their humanity.

Here's another dilemma used to deny that God can be both loving and omnipotent (all-powerful).

    a) Either God is loving or God is omnipotent.
    b) If God is loving, then He would save everyone.
    c) If God is omnipotent, then He could save everyone.
    d) Not all are saved.
    e) Therefore, God is either unloving or impotent.

Clearly there are other options besides the two mentioned in the disjunct, e.g., God is also holy and God is also spirit, etc. However, the fact remains that God *is both* loving and omnipotent, so there is no point in going between the horns. We must try to grab a horn. The third horn (c) seems obviously true: if God is omnipotent, He could save everyone. But the second horn (b) is not obviously true; in fact, it is false. God's love is not at all compromised by His decision to punish sinners *worthy* of death.

"Escape route" #3: counter-dilemma: The third way of replying to a dilemma is by means of a counter-dilemma. This involves a dilemma that uses the same disjuncts and/or antecedents, but with contrary consequents. The idea is to turn the dilemma back on the opponent. Here's an example:

DILEMMA: If you say what is just, then men will hate you. If you say what is unjust, then the gods will hate you. One must say what is just or unjust. Therefore, you will be hated by men or by gods.

COUNTER-DILEMMA: If I say what is just, the gods will love me. If I say what is unjust, then men will love me. One must say what is just or what is unjust. So I will be loved by the gods or by men.

The counter-dilemma employs the same antecedents and the same disjunctive as the original dilemma. The counter-dilemma states *contrary consequents*. This may be a rhetorically effective reply to a dilemma, but it does not really refute the consequents of the original dilemma. In this respect, a counter-dilemma bears similarity to a red-herring.

Part 2: Probable Inference

48] Introduction to General Induction

Lesson 27 introduced you to the Inferential Question of whether a conclusion follows its premises. There you learned that a conclusion is meant to follow a premise with necessity or with probability. The former inference is "deductive" and the latter is "inductive." Successful deductions are "valid" (otherwise they are invalid). Successful inductions are "strong" (otherwise they are weak). In addition to the chart below, it will help to review other distinctions discussed in lesson 26.

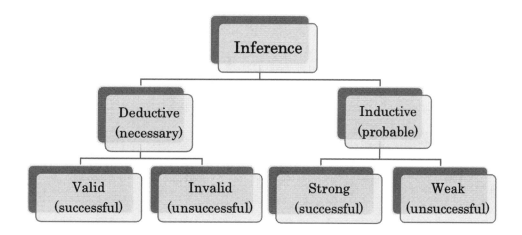

Recall that in categorical logic anything less than *all* means *some*. In a jar of one-hundred marbles, ninety-nine are still only *some* of the *all*. Suppose an opaque jar is filled with 100 marbles. You begin pulling out marbles one by one until you go through ninety-nine of them. All ninety-nine are white. Would it *necessarily* follow that the last one is white? No, that would be a deductive fallacy. But it would be a *very* strong inductive inference.

There are numerous forms of inductive inference. We will focus on inferences using (1) classes, (2) analogies, and (3) causality. We will start with inferences using classes, which we can call "general induction" (from *genus*, which literally means a "kind" or "sort" or "class" of things).

Generalizing and applying generalizations: We often draw conclusions about a class of things on the basis of what we know about its sample members. If all of one's Korean friends eat kimchi, one might be inclined to infer that Koreans in general eat kimchi. This is called a "generalization," which we can define as *an inference from a premise about some members of a class to a conclusion about most (or all) members of that class*. A generalization moves from what is true of some members of a class (the Koreans one knows) to what is (presumably) true of most members of the class. But we can also reason in the other direction, by making inferences from what is generally true of a class to what is (presumably) true of one of its members. For example, if one knows that most Koreans eat kimchi, one might then infer that the next Korean one meets eats kimchi.

We can distinguish these two directions of inference this way: in one case we move *to* general truths, and in the other case we move *from* general truths. In the first case we *make* a generalization, and in the other we *apply* a generalization.

Inferences *to* general truths (*Making* generalizations)	Inferences *from* general truths (*Applying* generalizations)
• Premise: "These few *x*s are *y*s." • Conclusion: "Therefore, most *x*s are *y*s."	• Premise: "Most *x*s are *y*s." • Conclusion: "Therefore, this *x* is a *y*."

To make a generalization is simply to generalize. To apply a generalization is to infer something about a particular case on the basis of a general rule (i.e., a previously formed generalization). The following chart illustrates the difference:

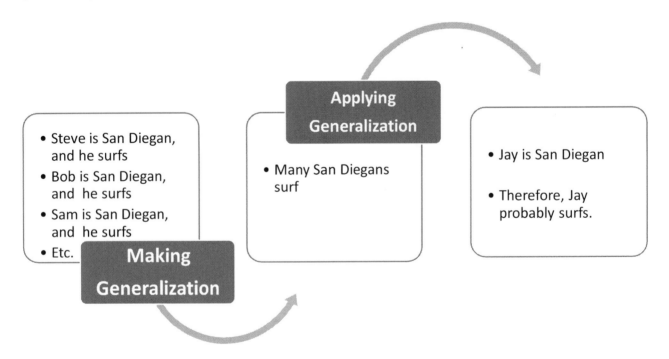

Closed classes and open classes: A class is *closed* if all of its members are known. A class is *open* if all of its members are not known. See the following chart for examples.

Closed Classes	Open Classes
o The class of planets in our solar system o The class of U.S. Presidents o The class of sub-classes of North American bears (e.g., Grizzlies, Black Bears, Polar Bears, etc.) o The class of eggs in my fridge o The class of the Apostle Paul's New Testament writings	o The class of planets in the Universe o The class of ancient rulers o The class of sub-classes of animals, including those now extinct o The class of eggs in the world o The class of the Apostle Paul's writings, including those that were lost

Complete induction: It is possible to *inspect all* the members of a closed class. This means we can make confident judgments about the entire class, e.g., "All U.S. Presidents are men."[87] These judgments, known as "complete inductions," are not (properly speaking) inferences. They are simple exercises in arithmetic. One need only *count* the individuals in the class (U.S. presidents), note what they have in common (e.g., being male), and then make a pronouncement, "All U.S. Presidents are men."

> The first U.S. president was a man.
> The second U.S. president was a man.
> The third…
> The fourth….
> Etc.
> The current U.S. president is a man.
>   — Premises
>
> Therefore, all U.S. presidents are men.

Though there is a stated conclusion (signified by "therefore"), this is not so much an inference to a conclusion as it is an observation; it is only a statement of the results acquired by counting. While on this point, it's worth noting that complete inductions are prone to the fallacy of circular reasoning. For example:

> *P1*: All U.S. Presidents are men.
> *P2*: Ulysses Grant is the sixteenth U.S. President.
> *C*: Therefore, Ulysses Grant is a man.

---

[87] Note that "closed" does not mean "fixed." If a woman became president, it would no longer be true that "All U.S. Presidents are men." But the class would still be closed, since we would still know all of its members.

To know that all U.S. presidents are men, one must inspect all forty-five of them. But this includes the eighteenth president (Ulysses Grant). Therefore, the major premise already assumes the truth of the conclusion. In this respect, the conclusion is not so much *inferred from* the premises as it is *assumed in* the premises.

Incomplete induction: We said that a class is "open" if all its members are not known. Some classes are open only because we have not tried closing them (e.g., the class of flowers in my flower bed). Other classes are open because we *cannot* close them no matter how hard we try. It is impossible to know the number of chicken eggs that have existed throughout history. When scientists draw conclusions about stars, molecules, or biological systems, they are making incomplete inductions. Scientists cannot inspect all the members of these classes. In many cases, one cannot even inspect the majority of them. According to one source, there are a septillion stars in the universe (100,000,000,000,000,000,000,000,000). We can only see about 9,000 of them with the naked eye, and somewhere between several hundred thousand to a few million with the aid of a telescope.[88] This means scientists are inferring the size of the entire class from an incredibly small sample of its members.[89]

It is possible to make incomplete inductions about closed classes. Suppose a student in an American history class studies twenty presidents from across U.S. history, noting that all of them are men. If she were to conclude that all forty-five presidents were men, this would be an incomplete induction *for her*. The class is technically closed, of course, but *this student* does not know that all the presidents are male. Until she personally inspects the closed class, she must rely on an inference instead.

In other cases a closed class might be *beyond our powers of personal inspection*. For example, the class of Wal-Mart stores is closed, practically speaking. (One source states that there are 11,230 stores spread out over 27 countries.) Now suppose that, of the fifteen stores I visited, all have the same distinct smell. I might then be tempted to infer that all of them have this smell. But it's practically impossible *for me* to inspect all of them; that would require an impossible sacrifice of time and money. Nor can I simply pick up a book to find my answer. (I'm pretty sure this information has not been documented!) There is no realistic way *for me* to verify my hunch that all of them have the same scent. This example shows that we

---

[88] http://www.universetoday.com/102630/how-many-stars-are-there-in-the-universe/
[89] It is worth noting that, in inferences like these, we are not merely inferring a property or characteristic of the entire class; we are actually trying to infer the *number of members* in the class. (One cannot help but wonder if this is even possible!)

must not assume that incomplete inductions always relate to open classes, though most incomplete inductions probably do.

An incomplete induction, then, could occur in any one of the following three cases: (1) as an inference moving from some members of an *open* class to most or all of its members, e.g., the number of stars in the universe; (2) as an inference moving from some members of a *technically closed but practically open* class to most or all of its members, e.g., the smell of Wal-Mart stores worldwide; and (3) as an inference moving from a closed (and easily closable) class to most or all of its members, e.g., e.g., the gender of U.S. presidents.

Incomplete induction can be made about *general* truths or *universal* truths: In lesson 2, where we addressed the concept of absolute truth, we distinguished between universal and general propositions. Here again is the chart.

Universal Truths	General Truths
Triangles have three sides.	Convicted criminals are guilty of crimes.
Ants are insects.	Pastors preach from the Bible.
Water is hydrogen and oxygen.	Maryland winters bring snowfall.
Men cannot hold their breath for an hour.	Canadians enjoy ice hockey.

Universal truths are about *all* members of a class, and general truths are about *most* members of a class. Though none of the statements in the box have quantifiers (lesson 27), universal truths have implied *All*s and *No*s, and general truths have implied *Most*s.

Generalizing and universalizing: To infer a universal truth is to draw a conclusion about every member of a class. It is to *universalize*. For example: "All the chicken eggs we have experienced break. Therefore, all chicken eggs break." To infer a general truth is to draw a conclusion about most members of a class. It is to *generalize*. For example: "Most of the chicken eggs we have experienced are white. Therefore, most chicken eggs are white."

We sometimes think it is appropriate to generalize rather than universalize, and at others times to universalize rather than generalize. It is reasonable to infer that most (but not all) people in the world wear shoes. It would seem strange, however, to infer that most eggs (but not all) are breakable. Whether we universalize or generalize will depend on a variety of factors we will consider later.

49] The Uniformity of Nature

In this lesson we will explore what it is about the world that enables us to generalize. Consider, first, whether this proposition is true.

"If I drop this egg from a 100-foot rooftop onto the paved street below, this egg will break when it hits the street."

Most of us would say that we "know" this to be true. But on what basis do we think we know this? How could we prove this assumption? What argument could we give? Consider this one:

1] All eggs will break under such conditions.
2] This is an egg.
3] Therefore, this egg will break under such conditions.

The argument is valid but do you see the problem? To know that *all* eggs will break under this condition, one must *already know* that *this* egg will break. After all, this egg is itself one of the "all eggs" in premise 1. The argument therefore commits the fallacy of circular reasoning, in which we assume as true the very thing we are supposed to prove. The conclusion is already smuggled into the premise.

It would seem, then, that until we drop this egg, we cannot verify that it too will break. There is at least one egg in the category of eggs, then, about which we are still ignorant—namely, this egg. So we do not really know (from experience, anyway) that "*All* eggs are such as will break under this condition."

If the deductive argument above is bad (because it's circular), perhaps we can use an inductive argument instead. Let's change the first premise from "All" to "Most."

1] Most eggs will break under such conditions.
2] This is an egg.
3] Therefore, this egg will break under such conditions.

The conclusion is no longer valid (it's an IAA-1 syllogism). But that's okay, since we're now engaged in inductive reasoning. This seems to be a strong argument. Its conclusion seems likely to follow. But just *how* likely? Our answer depends on the meaning of "most." How many eggs are we talking about? According to one source, American farmers alone produce almost 90 billion eggs per year. This means that the total number of chicken eggs that have existed is astronomically high. But what percentage of chicken eggs have we (or all humans combined) actually *experienced*, let alone dropped off a roof? Compared to the total number of eggs that have *existed*, the number we have experienced is extremely small. Even so, let's be generous and say that humans have experienced one out of every ten eggs produced in history (which, again, is not even close to the truth). We can them plug this number into the above argument. This means we must revise the first premise:

1] At least 10% of eggs break under such conditions.
2] This is an egg.
3] Therefore, this egg will break under such conditions.

This is a more realistic argument, to be sure, but it now appears to be weakened to the point of being *improbable*. It's similar to inferring that we will probably draw a white marble from a jar containing 9 black marbles and 1 white marble. That's a bad bet.

One might object that 10% of all the eggs we have experienced is still a *huge* number of eggs. If mankind has experienced trillions of eggs, including millions of dropped and broken eggs, isn't that enough to *know* that the next dropped egg will break? Well, as long as we don't know that *all* eggs break under such conditions, it seems possible that this egg will not break; the most we can say, it seems, is that this egg might also break. But surely we want to say something stronger than this. It seems absurd to say that the egg might *not* break!

The uniformity of Nature: The considerations above are meant to provoke a more fundamental question: On what basis are we convinced that the egg will break when it hits the street? The answer is not to be found *merely* in our experience of *eggs*. Our conviction is founded, rather, on a deeper belief in the *uniformity of Nature*. Put very simply, by the "uniformity of Nature" is meant that Nature *always operates in the same way*. Nature operates uniformly across *space* (eggs break in China the same way they break in America) and across *time* (eggs broke in 2000 B.C. as they break today).

Whether the breaking of eggs, the rising and setting of the sun, the downward flow of water, or the upward movement of smoke, we find that Nature behaves in a regular and predictable way. Nature, in other words, is *patterned*.

What does it mean to say that Nature is patterned? It means that the world is populated with individual objects (atoms, molecules, eggs, cats, trees, volcanoes, planets, galaxies, etc.) that are *instances* of what are variously called "kinds," "categories," "classes," "types," "sorts," "sets," etc. Traditionally, philosophers called the individuals "particulars" and the classes "universals." As a *member* of a class, an egg is a particular. As a member of a *class*, the egg shares a common nature with every other member in the class; this common nature is the universal. The universals are what philosophers have in mind by the "uniformity of Nature."

At some level, all the things we encounter in the world are particular instances of universal patterns. Nature is characterized by uniformities. There are universal [1] *attributes* or *properties* of things (all eggs have fragile shells, all bats use echolocation); [2] *processes* (all oak leaves turn color; all cells divide; all carbon decays; all acorns grow into oak trees, at least under the right condition); [3] *locomotions* (all falling objects accelerate at a uniform rate; light travels at 186,282 miles per second); [4] *causes and effects* (all eggs crack when dropped onto streets; all fire causes smoke; all poison causes sickness or death); and so on.

Sometimes these universals are referred to as "laws of Nature," e.g., laws of motion, of chemical reaction, or biological reproduction, etc. The uniformity of Nature inspires confidence that there is a *sufficient reason* for eggs to break under similar conditions. The uniformity of Nature means that things don't "just happen"; nothing occurs in a literally causeless way. To put it in metaphorical terms, there are "laws of Nature" according to which things behave as they do; there is an underlying cause of the patterns we find in Nature. This is why we don't feel the need to keep piling up egg-breaking experiences to increase our confidence that the next egg will break. At some point we just recognize that this is how Nature operates when it comes to eggs. When we say that it is "likely" or "probable" that the next egg will break, we're assuming that the way Nature has operated in the past is the way that Nature will *continue* to operate. This is how the uniformity of Nature explains our inference about the next dropped egg.

Intuitive induction: Since the world is populated with individual members of classes, this means that *each member has within itself the power of representing its entire class*. To some extent, the chicken egg in my fridge represents all the chicken eggs that have ever existed. Imagine that you know nothing about eggs. You have never seen one, touched one, or learned about them from others. You then encounter your first white chicken egg. You see its shape and color, and you feel its texture and weight. Supposing you later encounter a second white chicken egg, what would you learn from the second that you did not already learn from the first? The answer is, not much! What if you saw a third egg, and a fourth, and a fifth? You still wouldn't discover anything essentially different. The reason is that the first egg indicates something about the entire class. All the other eggs are basically identical to the first. Since each one has the power to represent the entire class, each one provides us (to some degree) an understanding of them all. This example shows that the nature of an entire class can be discovered in any one of its members. This is called "intuitive induction." Put in more philosophical terms, intuitive induction involves the discovery of the *universal in the particular*; that is to say, by intuitive induction we see the essential nature that is common to all the individuals within the class.[90]

Experimental induction: To the extent that an individual *x* represents the entire class of *x*s, we do not need to inspect numerous *x*s to infer something about the class of *x*s. If cracking one egg represents what will happen to all eggs under similar conditions, we do not need to crack numerous eggs in order to know that all eggs can be cracked. There is a sense in which *one* cracked egg is sufficient.[91]

The problem, of course, is to determine which features of a sample truly are representative. Intuitive induction does not tell us exactly *which* attributes are shared. This is where we run up against the limits of assuming the uniformity of Nature, and where mistaken generalizations begin to occur. Though Nature is uniform, it is not *absolutely* uniform. For example, suppose the very first egg we inspect happens to be rotten and to smell foul. Should we infer that all eggs smell foul? Of course not. This shows that intuitive induction is not, by itself, a reliable guide to understanding a class. It may happen that our first sample of a thing does not perfectly represent the entire class to which it belongs.[92] Therefore, by moving from one example to conclusions about its entire class, there always lurks the possibility of a *mistaken* inference. While intuitive induction is a natural, fruitful, and legitimate way of gaining understanding, it can also get us in trouble.

Hence the need for experimental induction.[93] As the name suggests, this involves testing the reliability of our intuitive inductions by further experience of particular samples. Instead of inferring, from one rotten egg, that all eggs stink, we should inspect other eggs.

In some cases experimental induction still does not solve the problem. To use a well-known example, it is said that Europeans believed (for hundreds of years)

---

[90] Intuitive induction involves two beliefs: (1) that natural classes exist, and (2) that the members of these classes *share* a set of *essential* attributes. Concerning (1), it is obvious that the world is ordered according to kinds; so we assume that each of the things we encounter is a member of a real class. For example, if we saw one lone flower in the woods, a flower we had never seen before, we should automatically infer that there are *others like it*, which is to say, we infer that there is a natural class of which this flower is a member. Concerning (2), we assume that the members, while they may differ in some respects, will nevertheless share basic similarities, or what we call "essential" attributes.

[91] We'll discuss the limits and problems of this "from-one-to-all" inference subsequently.

[92] Notice that, in a way, it still represents an entire class, namely, the sub-class of all Rotten Eggs.

[93] I refrain from calling this "scientific" induction since this is not the same as the scientific method. Nor is it the same as Mill's "Methods" of reasoning about causes and effects.

that all swans are white. By exploring Australasia, it was later discovered that some swans are black. Now, suppose you were a European living hundreds of years before this discovery. You see your first white swan. By intuitive induction you conclude that this bird is a member of a class which it therefore represents. Knowing that an animal's coloration is an attribute that can vary among members of its class, you cautiously reserve judgment until you can inspect other members. You inspect thousands of swans across Europe, interview people who have seen swans, read books about swans, and so forth. Everything suggests that being white is essential to being a swan. After years of researching, you eventually conclude that all swans are white. Your intuitive induction now seems *confirmed* by experimental induction. Or so it seems.

The black swan case shows that, in spite of our best efforts, sometimes we simply *cannot* verify (i.e., "know") the *extent* to which a member represents an entire class.

But this doesn't mean that we cannot know *anything* about the extent to which an individual represents its class. For example, seeing one swan with a head is enough (I hope!) to know that all swans have heads. Even so, the swan example shows that some inductive inferences (both intuitive and experimental) can never go beyond *probable* conclusions.

The theological foundations of inductive inference: Generalizing is not merely necessary for us as human beings. It is natural and appropriate to our rational nature as God's image bearers. God designed our minds to generalize. It is one of the means by which we expand our understanding of the world. God designed the world to be understood by us in terms of categories. In Genesis we read that God created the world "according to kinds." The world is filled with natural classes of things, of animals, plants, rocks, minerals, etc. It is because the world consists of kinds (lit. *genera*) that we can *general*ize about the world. But it is also because God designed our minds to think in terms of classes or categories that we can recognize and speak about these natural kinds. There is a God-intended "fit" between the (objective) structure of the world and the (subjective) power of our minds to think about the world. God designed our minds to "map" the structure of reality.

50] Making Generalizations

Evaluating generalizations for degrees of probability (strength) and improbability (weakness): Suppose there is a restaurant chain called "Burgerdom." You eat at ten different stores and find that the service is consistently poor. You then make the generalization that most Burgerdoms have poor service. If "most" = 51% or more, then the conclusion is either true or false: either most Burgerdoms have poor service or not. Strictly speaking, you cannot *know* whether it is true without complete induction, i.e., without investigating all the stores. This is why you are forced to make an inference from the stores you have sampled (i.e., incomplete induction).

Note that, in incomplete induction, your aim cannot be to determine whether the conclusion *is* true, but whether it is *likely* to be true. Without complete induction, you cannot know if you are *right*; the real question is whether you're being *reasonable*.[94] This is because the conclusions of incomplete induction *always go beyond the evidence*. You assume that the few stores you experienced enable you to conclude something about the stores you have *not* experienced. What justifies your thinking that you've gone beyond the evidence *in a reasonable way*? (This is particularly puzzling when the stores you have not inspected far outnumber the stores you have inspected.) This is the conundrum of induction, and it is by no means easy to solve.

As stated in the previous lesson, the problem is to determine whether, and to what extent, the inspected members of a class *represent* the uninspected members. For any open class, how does one know whether one has studied *enough* of its members to generalize about the class? Scientists teach us that Blue Whales spend most of their lives alone. How do they know this? *Can* they know it? They've inferred it on the basis of a small sampling of whales. But no one knows how many Blue Whales are alive today. It's impossible to say. The vast size of the ocean makes this difficult, and their habits only compound the problem (e.g., Blue Whales can dive to six-thousand feet and stay under water for two hours). Moreover, their population was presumably reduced by whaling. This means that scientists are forced to make inferences about the species using a very small sample set.

At the foundation of the scientists' inference is the assumption that the class-members we have experienced *represent* the class-members we have not experienced. Indeed, all of our generalizations assume that the members of a class

---

[94] We will later find that these two terms are not exact synonyms. There may be beliefs that are reasonable though improbable, or probable though unreasonable.

have something in common (e.g., buildings have foundations, dogs wag their tails, women have a nurturing instinct, Jehovah's Witnesses oppose blood transfusion, etc.). If most (or all) members of a class *y* share an attribute *x*, then any one member of *y* would represent most (or all) of the other members in that class. The problem, of course, comes in *our determining whether* this attribute *x is in fact shared* by the remainder of the class.

Rules for generalizing: Unlike the formal inferences of Aristotelian and Stoic logic, we cannot test inductive inferences with black or white rules. The rules for testing these inferences are more like *guidelines*. Since inductive inferences are more complex than deductive inferences, we must be more thoughtful when evaluating them. There is no mechanical method to follow here.

Violations of these rules typically result in the "the fallacy of hasty generalization." The word "hasty" suggests that the mistake results from not taking time to carefully think through the grounds of our inference.

The subsequent rules involve what is known as a *ceteris paribus* clause, which means "all other things being equal" or "all other things being held the same." For example, we could say that, *ceteris paribus*, people who fall off buildings die. We recognize that it is not a necessary or universal truth that people who fall off buildings die. There may be exceptional circumstances; one might land in a pool, hay truck, or canopy. In view of extenuating circumstances like these, we may qualify our claim with the *ceteris paribus* clause by saying, "*All other things being equal*, people who fall off buildings die." The *ceteris paribus* clause is saying, in effect, that *as long as exceptional circumstances are not factored into our thinking* (e.g., pools at the bottom of the building), such and such will likely be the case. As we will see, inductive inferences regularly *assume* a *ceteris paribus* qualification.

***Ceteris paribus*, generalizations about Nature, are more reliable than generalizations about Man; or, put negatively, generalizations about Man are less reliable than those about Nature**. Suppose you had to answer the following questions:

1. What will happen to this egg if you drop it on the ground?
2. What will happen to this teenage boy if you give him keys to a Lamborghini?

We know the egg will break. We do not know the boy will crash, but we do suspect it! What makes the difference here? Unlike eggs, humans are *free agents*, who are capable of determining themselves to contrary courses of action.[95] This makes human behavior more variable and unpredictable than that of natural phenomena. It is one thing for us to predict a missile's trajectory, or a hurricane's path, and another to predict how people will spend their money. Or again, it is one thing to study the chemical reactions of iron and oxygen, and another to study the personal interactions of employers and employees. Chemicals exhibit patterns of behavior that are definite, unchanging, mathematically measurable, and uniform the world over. What is true of H_2O in fifth century Africa is true of H_2O in twenty-first century Alaska. Employers and employees, on the other hand, interact in different ways depending on their *unique personalities* operating in unique contexts. When we think about the bewildering variety of people's beliefs, attitudes, interests, abilities, careers, and lifestyles, we realize that human behavior is variable and unpredictable because it is *free*.

It is difficult (if not impossible) to know exactly how someone will act at a given time. Think of a toddler playing in a toy room. Will he pick up the red block or the blue car or neither? Think of adults conversing around a dinner table: who will speak next, and about what topic, and with what choice of words? We know that all baby beavers will grow up to build dams, but can a father know whether his son will be a doctor or a soldier, or a plumber, teacher, painter, mayor, rock star, etc.?

This is why it is customary to distinguish the sciences into the "hard" and "soft" sciences. The hard sciences of physics, chemistry, and biology study natural phenomena that are far more constant and predictable. Objects like atoms, molecules, cells, and organs do not change from country to country, or from century to century. The soft sciences, on the other hand, study human behavior and interactions. These include psychology, sociology, history, politics, and economics, all of which have a far greater degree of diversity and unpredictability.

How does all of this relate to induction? It means that reliable generalizations about people are more difficult to make than generalizations about sub-human classes. This is a significant fact when we realize that most of the really crucial controversies revolve around the soft sciences, which use generalizations such as the following:

- Women are more nurturing than men.
- Children who play violent video games are more prone to violence.
- Atheists have poor relationships with their fathers.
- Protestantism inspires a strong work ethic.

---

[95]Interestingly, philosophers who more closely associate men with animals (e.g., Thomas Hobbes) tend to portray men as more mechanical and predictable than those who emphasize man's freedom (e.g., Jean-Jacques Rousseau).

o   Soldiers subject to extreme combat undergo post-traumatic stress syndrome.
o   Korean students are highly disciplined.
o   Stage actors live unconventional lifestyles.

Yes, people will dispute these claims, but that is the point. Generalizing about people is necessary and doable, but also difficult and dangerous.

The fact that we *can* generalize about human behavior means that patterns exist to be discovered. For example, economists generalize that people are prone to look after their own money more than that of their neighbors. Military commanders and master chess players have a strong sense of how their opponents are likely to move. Parents have more confidence than others about how their children will react when told "No." Husbands and wives often predict how the other will act in a given situation.

It's easy to get in trouble when generalizing about people. Here too we assume that a sample member has some representative quality, but how do we know which one? For example, suppose an Asian child experiences his first three Caucasians, all of whom are rude and mean-spirited. How is the child to know whether these three represent Caucasians in general? Hopefully the child will learn that race is a poor indicator of behavior. As Martin Luther King said, we should not judge people according to the color of their skin but the content of their character.

Ceteris paribus, larger sample sets are more reliable than smaller ones: Experiencing poor service at one Burgerdom is an inadequate basis for generalizing about the restaurant chain. Poor service at four of them is a stronger basis, and poor service at ten of them is stronger still. The reason for this rule is simple. Recall that we are trying to determine if the sampled members represent the class as a whole. It makes sense that, *ceteris paribus*, the more numerous the samples, the more likely it is that our samples represent the entire class.

The number of sample members one has experienced does not, by itself, tell us the strength of the inference; one must also have some idea of the *size of the class*. Suppose one has experienced poor service at ten Burgerdoms. If there are only twenty Burgerdoms in existence, ten of them would be 50% of the class. This provides a reasonable basis for generalizing that Burgerdoms provide poor service. But what if there are ten thousand Burgerdoms? Ten of them would constitute only 1% of the class. This would make the generalization far less reliable. Therefore, the larger the class about which we are generalizing, the more numerous our sample should be.

If the number of sampled members must be compared to the size of the class, what do we do when we cannot determine the size of the class? Suppose we want to learn something about the lives of illegal immigrants in America. Since many of them are trying to *conceal their identity* in order to avoid deportation, there is no reliable way to know how many are living in the U.S. This means that, for any sample set of illegals we interview—say, 1,000—we cannot determine *what percent* of the class they represent. The federal government has tried to overcome this problem by *estimating* the number of illegal aliens. This can be a very complicated form of reasoning, especially in the current case. According to some sources, the current (2013) estimate of illegals living in the U.S. is twelve million. We can treat reliable estimates as a sort of unofficial "closing" of a class. Since estimates are more liable to error, however, we cannot always be confident that the "closed" class has been accurately measured.

***Ceteris paribus*, varied sample sets are more reliable than unvaried sample sets.** Suppose one has sampled a large number of Burgerdoms, but that they all happen to be located in notoriously rude and unfriendly counties. This odd circumstance could explain the poor service. It also suggests that poor service at Burgerdom might not be the rule after all. This shows that we must consider the possibility of an exceptional circumstance that makes our samples (even larger samples) non-representative of the class. Consider other examples. If the truck xs I have experienced tend to break down fast, this might be due to the irresponsible driving habits of my friends who drive them, rather than to the trucks themselves. I should not (on this basis alone) infer that truck xs are unreliable. If the kids I have experienced in the day care center are disrespectful, this may be due to the parents and/or day care workers, rather than to the nature of kids per se, so I should not (on this basis alone) infer that children as a class are disrespectful. If the Christians I know believe that gambling is not a sin, this might be due to their cultural context (say, living in Las Vegas), rather than to their Christian belief, so I should not (on this basis alone) infer that Christians as a class believe that gambling is permissible.

These observations illustrate the importance of trying to *diversify* one's sample set. Suppose the ten inspected Burgerdoms (all of which have poor service) are located in ten different states, including some from the western, eastern, northern, and southern regions of the country; and that they're located in different social and economic areas. Given the diversity of these locations, we can no longer explain the poor service in terms of location. This suggests that the problem is with the restaurant chain itself. Likewise, to determine whether truck x is reliable, I should inspect trucks owned by more responsible drivers as well. And so on with other such examples.

Returning to the example of illegal aliens in the U.S., we cannot know how they are faring *in general* by inspecting only a sub-class of them, even if it's a large sub-class. We would need to interview illegals from different states, backgrounds, ages, and so on.

Sometimes even closed classes are so large and diverse in their membership that it becomes very difficult to generalize. This problem becomes tricky when taking polls about people's beliefs or practices. Suppose we want to know whether African Americans believe that racism in hiring has diminished in the United States. According to a 2010 census, there were 37,131,771 African Americans living in the U.S.. Since there is no way to interview them all (which would be a complete induction), we must select samples from cross-sections of the populous. If we only polled affluent African Americans, this might result in an affirmative answer to our question. But if we only polled poorer African Americans, this might result in a negative answer.

Statistical fallacies: The first fallacy is that of *non-representative sampling*. Suppose you encounter a statistical claim that, of 10,000 Christians polled, 99% of them believe that it's morally permissible to fight in war. You later learn, however, that all the Christians polled were also Marines. This is a biased sampling. Even though numerous Christians were polled, the sample set does not represent the mixed composition of Christians. The fallacy here is to base the statistical generalization on an unvaried and non-representative sample set. Again, suppose a massive poll suggests that 89% of Americans polled believe that college loans should be larger and easier to get. But you later learn that the Americans polled were college students. The sub-class does not represent the much larger and more diverse super class. To detect this fallacy, we need to know who was polled.

The second is the fallacy of *misleading percentages*. This fallacy involves a bit of mathematical magic. Suppose we interview only 10 Americans about their confidence in the strength of the U.S. economy, and that 8 of them express little to no confidence. One might then report these (insignificant!) results with the (very impressive!) claim that "*80%* of Americans interviewed" have little to no confidence in the strength of the economy. By specifying "80% of Americans *interviewed*," the statement is technically true. The problem, of course, is that the public will *assume* that far more than 10 Americans were interviewed. Given this background assumption, the figure of 80% is grossly misleading. The problem, in a nutshell, is that the standard phrase "Of the people polled..." does not tell us how *many* people were polled.

51] Applying Generalizations

In the previous lesson we focused on inferences from what is true of a few members of a class to what is presumably true of most or all members of the class. We noted that we can also reason in the other direction, by making inferences from what is generally true of a class to what is presumably true of an individual instance. For example, if most Americans know about Elvis Presley, the chances are that the next American we meet will know about him. We distinguished the two directions of inference by saying that in one case we move *to* general truths, and in the other case we move *from* general truths. It may be helpful to review the chart from that lesson.

To illustrate the difference between making and applying generalizations, let's contrast a forensic scientist and a forensic detective. The scientist is in the business of *making* generalizations. He studies particular cases in order to discover patterns. For example, a forensic scientist examines blood splattering and decomposing bodies in order to formulate general truths (e.g., "Blood splatters in manner x when the person is scared and in manner y when he is sleeping," or "Bodies decompose at rate x under conditions y"). These general truths are put into a textbook for forensic investigators to understand and apply in their job. The investigator reads the book, learns the general truths, and then applies them to a crime scene. He sees a body and infers that the person was killed three weeks earlier. The investigator is in the business of *applying* generalizations.

The strength or weakness of an applied generalization does not depend on the truth of the premises. Consider this argument:

> *P1*: The vast majority of women are gossips.
> *P2*: Susie is a woman.
> *C*: Susie is a gossip.

We would fault this argument on the truth-value of the first premise, not the strength of its conclusion. In fact, even reasonable applications of general truths do not always result in true conclusions. For example, in most single income families, the husband works while the wife stays at home. This is a general truth. Now, suppose we meet a man named Mr. Madre, who informs us that he and his family live on a single income. Given the generalization above, we would reasonably infer that Mr. Madre (rather than his wife) is the family breadwinner. But suppose we later learn that his wife brings home the check and that he stays home to raise the children. Would this new information make our initial inference unreasonable? Not at all. Remember: inductive logic pertains to what is usually the case, not to what is always and everywhere the case.

The problem with "general rule" language: The phrase "general rule" is vague. How *general* is "general"? When dealing with closed classes, it is easier to put numbers on a general rule. If we know there are one-hundred children in a daycare center, and that seventy-five of them come from dual-income homes, we get a general truth in the form of a specific number (75%). This enables us to reasonably infer that the next child interviewed will be from a dual-income home.

When dealing with large open classes, however, it becomes much harder to know what "general" means. Suppose we poll a thousand Christians in America and that 75% of them say they believe that the book of Genesis teaches a literal six-day creation. Should this be accepted as a generalization about the class "American Christians"? Since there are *tens of millions* of Christians in America, a thousand is only a very small slice of the class.

Another problem arises here. Suppose we are dealing with a closed class y, and that 51% of the ys inspected have attribute x. Strictly speaking, we could say that "most" (or the "majority") of the ys inspected have attribute x. But clearly 51% is much weaker than 70%, which is much weaker than 95%. The words "most" and "majority" do not communicate these differences. Likewise, the words "general," "generally," "general rule," etc., do not give a definite idea of how extensive the generalization might be. Consider the difference this makes when considering an argument of this form:

> Generally speaking, xs are ys.
> This is an x.
> Therefore, this is probably a y.

The inference seems strong. But what if "generally speaking..." *really* means 51% of xs are ys? This should make us pause before applying a general rule. Even so, we can still formulate some rules or guidelines to follow when applying generalizations.

***Ceteris paribus*, the more general the rule, the more probable the inference to the particular case**: This rule needs little explanation. If one knows that 80% of xs are ys, one will have more confidence (*ceteris paribus*) that the next x will be y than one would have if only 60% of xs are ys.

Determine if there is anything about the particular case that makes it an exception to the general truth. While the first rule pertains to the general truth being applied, this second rule relates to the *particular case* to which the general truth is applied. If the majority of husbands in single income families are the breadwinners for their families, this would lead us to infer (*ceteris paribus*) that Mr. Madre makes the money and that his wife stays at home. But in real life *particular cases are not always equal*. Suppose we know that Mr. Madre does not have a high-school diploma. This decreases the probability of him being the income earner for his home. Suppose we also know that his wife has a PhD in engineering. The probability of our conclusion would then decrease even further, perhaps to the point that it might seem more reasonable to infer *he* stays at home while she brings home the bacon.

Determine if there are [1] confirming generalizations to strengthen the inference or [2] disconfirming generalizations to weaken it: Let's start with confirming generalizations. Confirming generalizations are general truths which *converge to strengthen one's inference* about a particular instance. One summer my family and I visited a popular shell-collecting beach in Hilton Head, South Carolina. At low tide, the water recedes a quarter of a mile from the beachhead, leaving huge swaths of shells and sea creatures exposed for explorers. We set our beach bag down, kicked off our sandals, and ventured off to find shells. After an hour or so we drifted half a mile around the bend from where we left the bag, which was now well out of sight. It was then that my wife turned to me and asked, "Did you get your wallet out of the beach bag?" Immediately my heart fluttered in mild panic. I left my wallet, filled with cash and credit cards. As I turned back to get it, I found myself engaged in a fairly standard form of inductive reasoning, in which, by applying numerous general rules to the situation, I concluded that my wallet was probably *not* stolen.

My reasoning was more or less as follows: First, people are generally not so unthinking as to leave their wallets or other valuables in unattended beach bags. A thief would likely realize this and so be less tempted to search it. Secondly, the low-class style of the bag made it less of a target. It was a large, straw bag, rather than a fancy, stylish satchel. This made it less likely to standout out as something containing valuables. Third, the bag was loaded with beach toys. People do not usually mix valuables with toys. Fourthly, the time of day (we arrived at low tide, around 8:45 AM) suggested that the only people on the beach were there to find shells, walk their dogs, and so on. Fifthly, the significance of the time connected with the day (Sunday) suggested that the sketchier types of people—the ones more likely to steal—were probably still in bed after a Saturday night of partying. Sixthly, the location itself held significance. The beach is located in an out of the way suburban area, not a Spring-break, wild party destination. Many of the residents were retired elderly folks or wealthy businessmen. Many of the tourists were hardworking, law-abiding family types on vacation. There were no poor areas, no slums, and no homeless people. In sum, those present were least likely to engage in petty theft, and those most likely to engage in petty theft were absent. Finally, there were many other shell seekers out that morning, who would have been a deterrent to anyone considering theft, since they could have served as eyewitnesses.

The conclusion of my reasoning—i.e., the wallet was not stolen—was reached by an application of numerous generalizations to one particular case. Note that none of these generalizations could, by itself, provide a solid basis for the conclusion. Taken together, however, they rendered the conclusion far stronger. As it turned out, my wallet was still in the bag.

Even so, it is possible to use some of these same generalizations *against* my conclusion. One could argue that career thieves use reverse psychology, by targeting locations where people are least suspecting. Places like the one described above!

Let's now consider disconfirming generalizations. These are general truths which *converge to weaken one's inference* about a particular instance. It is not enough to find confirming generalizations; one must also look for disconfirming generalizations that threaten to undermine the inference. Consider again the case of Mr. Madre. The general truth that fathers in single income homes make the money suggests that Mr. Madre makes the money. But we began to question this inference in light of the other general truths that people without high-school diplomas have a harder time getting jobs needed to support an entire family, or that people with PhDs in engineering have an easier time of it. These additional generalizations have the effect of outweighing or offsetting the application of the first generalizations.

This sort of reasoning can go back and forth. This is because the more we learn about the particular case, the greater the number of generalizations we can bring to bear on it. If we learned that Mr. Madre is far more patient than his wife, this might tilt the scale back to thinking that he stays at home. For we could apply the new generalization that more patient parents are better suited to staying home with children all day. But if we also learn that Mr. Madre is confined to a wheelchair, and that he has three small children, the inference might swing back the other direction. The new generalizations—that small children generally require more hands-on care, and that people in wheelchairs generally cannot provide such care—results in tipping the scales back.

In sum, all of this shows that the strength or weakness of applying a generalization is determined by reference to other generalizations.

"The fallacy of misapplied generalization": This fallacy pertains to the application of a general rule to a particular case. But what exactly is the fallacy? We need to be careful in how we define it. It is tempting to oversimplify the nature of this fallacy. It is not merely the application of a general truth to a case it does not in fact cover. This is a bad definition, since that would include many *probable* inferences as well. For example, if the vast majority of NBA players are over 6' tall, it is probable that the next NBA player one meets will be over 6' tall. The reality, however, is that some of them have been under 6'. The fact that my inference might not apply to the next particular case does not, by itself, make it fallacious. The fallacy must consist, rather, in a *weak* or *unreasonable* move from the general claim to the particular claim. This will be determined by the extent to which one follows the rules above. The fallacy occurs, in other words, when the general rule is not general enough to reliably apply, or when the particular case admits of more or less obvious exceptions, or when the generalization is not adequately reinforced by other true generalizations.

52] Introduction to Analogical Argument

Analogical arguments are the second type of probable inference we will study. It is one of the most common, most fascinating, and yet most poorly understood of the inferences we will examine.

How analogical inferences differ from making/applying generalizations: In the previous lessons we focused on making and applying generalizations.

Making generalizations	*Applying generalizations*
• All the poodles we have experienced wag their tails. • Therefore, most poodles wag their tails.	• Most poodles wag their tails. • Therefore, my neighbor's poodle wags its tail.

Notice that whether we move *to* a general truth about poodles or *from* a general truth about poodles, in either case we are dealing with *only one* class of things—poodles. Such inferences are *confined within* a class.

Analogical arguments, on the other hand, involve inferences *across* different classes on the basis of a similarity between them.

Analogical inference
1. Humans play chess, and this is a sign of intelligence. 2. Computers play chess. 3. Therefore, computers are intelligent.

Here we are moving from a truth about one class (humans) to a conclusion about a *different* class (computers) on the basis of a similarity between them (chess playing). It is one thing to compare humans with humans (or computers with computers), and another to compare humans with computers, where the differences outweigh the similarities. And yet there *are* similarities. The question is whether the similarities warrant the conclusion.

We may define an analogical argument as *an inference about one class (A) on the basis of its similarity to a different class (B)*. The word "analogy" means *likeness* or *similarity*. An analogical argument is also called an "argument by analogy."

How analogical reasoning extends our understanding of the world: Generalizing is how we increase our knowledge *within* classes, as when we make inferences from what is true about some Siberian tigers to what is true about most or all Siberian tigers. But we can also increase our knowledge *across* classes, as when we make inferences about tigers based on their *similarities* with *different* classes, such as polar bears. Siberians tigers are solitary land predators on top of their food chain. Polar bears are solitary land predators on the top of their food chain. Noting this similarity, we could reason from what it true of one to what might be true of the other. We know, for example, that adult male polar bears kill young males in order to retain dominance. By analogical reasoning, we might surmise (rightly or wrongly) that adult male Siberian tigers do the same.

The theistic basis of analogical argument: God created individual creatures "according to their kinds" (see Genesis 1-2). In spite of their differences, everything in the world originates from the *same* Creator, who structured the world according to a common design-plan. This means there will be sameness *and* difference, unity *and* diversity. The unity is most obvious *within* classes, when we compare members of the same class with one another (e.g., Siberian tigers with Siberian tigers, or Siberian tigers with Bengal tigers). But there is also unity *in* the diversity. Tigers, lizards, and Venus flytrap are different classes, but all are designed to catch prey. The similarities among different classes make analogical inference possible.

Deciding when an argument is analogical: It is not always easy to determine whether an argument is analogical. An argument comparing people and computers is clearly analogical, since the differences between them are fundamental. An argument comparing Siberian tigers in one region of Russia to Siberian tigers in another region of Russia is not analogical. The difference here (the tigers being in different locations separated by a few hundred miles) is superficial. In the following list of comparisons, note how the differences grow increasingly significant:

- If we compare Siberian tigers in one region of Russia to Siberian tigers in another region of Russia…
- Or Siberian tigers in the wild to Siberian tigers in a zoo
- Or Siberian tigers to Bengal tigers
- Or Siberian tigers to lions
- Or Siberian tigers to polar bears
- Or (to make a jump!) Siberian tigers to amoebas.

In deciding whether an argument is analogical, the word "different" is the key. It is the differences between the things compared that make the similarity interesting and controversial. *Ceteris paribus*, the greater the differences between any two classes, the more questionable will be the analogical link between them.

To determine if the argument is analogical, a rule of thumb is to ask whether the differences between the things compared are significant enough to *cast doubt* on the inference. Suppose two men are debating whether they can teach a toddler to play chess. One of them reasons:

- My fifteen-year-old son can understand rules, and he can play chess.[97]
- My two-year-old son can understand rules (e.g., "No running in the house").
- Therefore, my two-year-old son can play chess.

Though the comparison is between two members of the same class in one sense (the category of humans), they are members of different classes in another sense (the category of age). Should this be considered an analogical argument? Yes, since the difference in age is significant enough to cast doubt on the inference. Such a sizable difference in age involves an essential difference in aptitude. Though both sons are humans, this is not a straightforward case of comparing apples to apples; it's a bit more like comparing apples to oranges.

Strict analogies v. loose analogies: Some analogical arguments use "strict" analogies and others use "loose" analogies.

- Strict analogy = a literal similarity
- Loose analogy = a non-literal similarity

All the similarities we considered above are strict analogies, meaning that their similarities are *literally the same*. But sometimes we argue from less literal (or perhaps non-literal) similarities. The word "leech" literally denotes *a bloodsucking worm*. Now, imagine a man who makes his way through life by borrowing, begging, and otherwise relying on the charity of others. Though he is able to work, he would rather take advantage of others by eating their food, sleeping under their roofs, and so forth. Such a person might be likened to a "leech." This is a loose analogy. Shockingly, Adolph Hitler called Jews "parasites" and "bloodsuckers." He held that they were draining the physical and cultural blood of the German

---

[97] Make sure to clarify that this is not a syllogism. It may seem that the first premise is really "whoever can understand rules can play chess." But this is not what is occurring.

people, sucking out their economic and ethnic vitality. He then used this idea as a *justification* for killing them. For him, there was something really similar between Jews and these lower organisms.

As this example shows, loose analogies are borderline similes. A simile is a figurative expression used to compare one thing to another. ("Life is like a box of chocolates: you never know what you're gonna get.") Similes are not usually used to prove a claim as much as to illustrate or explain a claim. When my son was five years old, he likened "sin" to a chaotic cobweb and righteousness to a beautifully symmetric orb web. He associated sin with an ugly, disordered soul, and righteousness with an orderly one. The two types of web illustrated the two types of lives.

Unlike similes, analogical inferences are used to *prove* something about A *because of* its similarity to B. In Hitler's eyes, the supposed similarity between Jews and parasites was *close enough* to prove a conclusion.

> P1: Parasites thrive at the expense of the host, so we destroy them.
> P2: Jews thrive at the expense of the German host.
> C: Therefore, destroy them.

Legal precedent as a form of analogical argument: Analogical arguments are used in theology, science, history, ethics, and every other major field of debate. They are extremely common in our American legal system, which depends on "argument from precedent." Lawyers argue that a court ruling should be accepted or rejected because of its similarities to a prior ruling that was accepted or rejected.

Our country legalized the abortion of preborn children in the infamous 1973 Supreme Court decision *Roe v. Wade.*. The Court based its decision on a woman's "right to privacy," said to be found in "penumbras" emanating from the Fourteenth Amendment to the U.S. Constitution. Boiled down to its simplest form, the argument is essentially this: what a woman does with her own body is a personal, private matter, and the life within her womb is part of her body. Therefore, what she wishes to do with that life (i.e., to preserve it or to terminate it) should be her decision, not the State's. The argument assumes an essential *similarity* between the child in a woman's womb and any other part of the woman's body.

In 1998, Hawaii and Alaska become the first two states to declare the ban on same-sex marriage "unconstitutional." Over the following decade, a growing number of states legalized gay marriage. In 2015 the Supreme Court declared that same-sex marriage was constitutional. One of their arguments appealed to the legalization of inter-racial marriages: if blacks and whites should be allowed to intermarry, why not two men or two women?

In 2012, Colorado and Washington became the first states to legalize the possession and sale of marijuana. The main argument was that there is no substantial difference between marijuana and alcohol: if the latter is legal, why not the former? All three cases above—abortion, gay marriage, and marijuana use—were momentous legal decisions rooted in arguments by analogy.

53] Evaluating Analogical Arguments

The basic structure of an analogical argument: Though there are various ways of formulating analogical arguments, we will stick with one pattern throughout this lesson.[98]

> 1. A and B have attributes *a*, *b*, and *c*.
> 2. A also has attribute *d*.
> 3. Therefore, B probably has attribute *d*.

[1] The first premise gives us *analogates* and their *analogies*. A and B are called "analogates." Though they are different things (e.g., tigers and polar bears), they are assumed to share similar attributes (e.g., both are large, solitary, land predators at the top of their respective food chains). The similar attributes *a*, *b*, and *c* are the "analogies" that make A and B analogates. A is the "primary analogate," and B is the "secondary analogate."

[2] The second premise ascribes an additional attribute *d* to the primary analogate A, which is information not given to us regarding the secondary analogate B.

[3] The conclusion states (by way of inference) that the secondary analogate has the same additional attribute *d* as the primary one. Attribute *d* is therefore the focal point of the argument. The inference assumes that there is a connection between A's having *a*, *b*, and *c*, and A's having *d*. In other words, *d* depends upon *a*, *b*, and *c* in such a way that the presence of the latter explains, or indicates, the presence of the former. We can therefore call attributes *a*, *b*, and *c* the "basing attributes" and *d* the "based attribute."

The whole point of the analogical argument is to move from what is true of the primary analogate to what is presumably true of the secondary analogate.

---

[98] Another pattern commonly used is:

1. A has attributes *a*, *b*, *c*, and also *d*.
2. B has attributes *a*, *b*, and *c*.
3. Therefore, B probably has attribute *d* also.

Evaluating analogical arguments: The rules for evaluating the strength of analogical inferences are simple. We will introduce them in relation to the following example.

1. Ed and Lonnie are from Southside.
2. Ed is in a gang.
3. Therefore, Lonnie is probably in a gang.

Ed and Lonnie are analogates (Ed is the primary analogate, and Lonnie the secondary analogate). Here there is only one analogy between them—their place of residence. Take a moment to think about the force of the inference. Do you agree with it?

Rule 1: There should be a logically relevant connection between the basing attribute and the based attribute. In the case above, we need to determine if there is a solid connection between living in Southside and being in a gang. If we happen to know that gangs are popular in Southside, the connection would at least be plausible. Yet a more relevant basing attribute would be, for example, special tattoos marking one out as a gang member.

Rule 2: It is better to have more logically relevant analogies than less. *Ceteris paribus*, the more two analogates have in common, the more likely it is that what is true of one will be true of the other. For example:

1. Both Ed and Lonnie are from Southside, drive low-riders, have the same unique tattoo on their left shoulder, have incarcerated dads, drug addicted mothers, and brothers in gangs.
2. Ed is in a gang.
3. Therefore, Lonnie is in a gang.

By increasing the analogies, we have greatly strengthened the inference. But notice the qualification in this second rule—"*logically relevant* analogies." The rule is *not* that it is better to have more analogies than less, since it is possible to have a large number of totally irrelevant analogies:

1. Both Ed and Lonnie are 6'1", like oatmeal for breakfast, and have a freckle on their ring finger.
2. Ed is in a gang.
3. Therefore, Lonnie is in a gang.

This shows that one logically relevant analogy outweighs any number of irrelevant ones. When evaluating analogical inference, always remember that the *quality* of the analogies is more important than *quantity* of analogies.

Rule 3: The logically relevant disanalogies must not override the analogies. Since we are relating different things, there is always the risk that the (unstated) differences are more significant than the (stated) similarities.

Among the disanalogies between Ed and Lonnie, some will be irrelevant to the question (e.g., bodyweight and sports interests), while others will be very significant. Suppose that Ed is seventeen years old and that Lonnie is forty-three. This is a logically relevant disanalogy, since most inner-city gang members are on the younger end of the spectrum. Suppose Ed is a high school dropout and that Lonnie graduated from high school with a 4.0 GPA, and then went to college to secure a degree in social work. This does not fit the profile of a gang member. Finally, suppose that Ed has never been to church and that Lonnie is a faithful churchgoer. This might suggest that, even if Lonnie used to be gang member, he has since changed his ways.

When applying the rules, it may be helpful to use a chart to facilitate comparisons.

	More Relevant:	Less Relevant:
Analogies	<ul><li>Have the same unique tattoo on their left shoulder</li><li>Brothers in gangs</li></ul>	<ul><li>Style of car (drive low-riders)</li><li>Both like pit bulls.</li></ul>
Disanalogies	<ul><li>Drop out v. college graduate</li><li>Involved in church and not involved in church</li></ul>	<ul><li>Age 17 v. 43</li></ul>

Sometimes disanalogies can become difficult to determine. Consider the following ethical example. In some countries men eat primates (e.g., monkeys, chimpanzees, gorillas). Critics of this practice use the following analogical argument:

1. Both humans and primates are intelligent, emotional, social, and communicative.
2. Humans should not eat humans.
3. Therefore, humans should not eat primates.

Humans and primates are analogates. The analogies are intelligence, sociability, and emotional experience. These three attributes "base" the attribute of moral immunity from being eaten.

In evaluating this argument, rules 1 and 3 will be the most critical to uphold (we can assume that rule 2 is more or less upheld here).

As for rule 1, the connection between the based attribute (moral immunity) and the three basing attributes seems plausible. We perceive more humanlike intelligence and emotion in primates than we do in cabbage, crabs, or cattle. The lack of these attributes may explain why we do not hesitate to eat the latter.

If this argument violates any of the rules, it is certainly rule 3. Only men are made in the image of God. It is our status as God's image bearers that gives our lives sanctity (or sacredness) that no other creatures on earth share. This is what makes murder such a heinous sin (see Genesis 9).

The present analogical argument provides a great example of how similarities can be exaggerated. In one very broad sense of the terms, it is true that both humans and primates are "intelligent," "social," and "emotional." But then again, so are pigs and geese, which we eat without thinking twice. The problem, you see, is that these words—"intelligent," "social," "emotional"—are too general and abstract. As such, they *hide* the fact that the *differences are far greater* than the similarities. The difference between the intelligence of a human and a primate is not one of degree (as Darwin claimed) but of kind (as the scriptures teach). It is one thing for a chimp to use a stick to extract termites from the ground; it is entirely something else for men to use a rocket to land men on the moon. We play chess, write works of poetry, history, and philosophy; we formulate algebra, calculus, and equations in physics; we invent nuclear weapons, the Internet, smartphones; we send rovers to Mars and decode our own genome. It is inconceivable how primates could make the slightest move toward such things. It is humans who tame primates and try teaching them a primitive form of sign language to "prove" that they are just like us. Primates might be able to identify the reflection of their bodies in a mirror, but only humans can reflect on their *souls*—on their memories, their beliefs, their theories, their motives, their character, as well as their destinies and the origin and purpose of their existence. This explains the famous Greek oracle of Delphi, who enjoined man to "know thyself." The differences between human and primate intelligence are beyond any real standard of comparison. As for emotion, it is one thing for primates to exhibit a type of attachment to their young, or hostility to their rivals, and altogether another for men to experience moral indignation at evil, guilt and remorse for their sin, joy at a wedding, or sorrow over a tragic opera, laughter from a well-timed punch line in a comedy routine, or depression from a sense of a wasted life. These emotional differences are radically different from primate emotions. Likewise, while primates certainly have some ability to move themselves—they are not robots—humans have the ability to plan, to deliberate, to think through possible options, and to change their minds. Men can change themselves and improve themselves; primates cannot. Men can sculpt marbles (Michelangelo's *David*) and paint murals on ceilings (the Sistine Chapel), and compose symphonies. The list of disanalogies goes on and on. It is remarkable that anyone should think the difference between humans and primates is only one of degree and not also of kind.

Because men and primates have the same designer, we should not be surprised that there are similarities in our respective designs. However, as God's image bearers, we should expect that there are significant differences as well. If we are created in the image of the One who created the Universe, we should expect to have attributes and powers beyond anything in the sub-human realm. This is exactly what we find.

Rule 4: The analogy must not prove too much: The above argument suggests another rule for evaluating analogical arguments—the premises must not prove more than what one is ready to accept. If intelligence, sociability, and emotion are sufficient reasons for not eating primates, *even though they have a far lesser degree of these qualities* than humans, it follows that we should not eat pigs, cattle, fowl, rabbits, deer, or virtually anything other than plants. (It is precisely this inference that leads some to "ethical vegetarianism.") Rule 4 can be applied in the form of *modus tollens*:

- If your analogy proves x, then it also proves y.
- But y is absurd.
- Therefore, your analogy does not prove x.

The complexity of analogical arguments: Analogical arguments can be very challenging to evaluate. In our own day, the debate over legalizing marijuana is based, in part, on numerous analogies between marijuana (still illegal in many states) with alcohol and tobacco (currently legal in every state). The argument is essentially this:

> *P1*] Taken together, alcohol and tobacco have attributes a, b, c, etc., and they are legal.
> *P2*] Marijuana has attributes a, b, c, etc.
> *C*] Therefore, Marijuana should be legal too.

In this argument, there is no need to apply Rule 1, since we are already granting the connection of the based attribute (the lawfulness of alcohol and tobacco) to the basing attributes.

Rule 2 is easily satisfied, since there are many analogies between the primary analogates (alcohol and tobacco) and the secondary analogate (marijuana). The following is a partial list of analogies:

More Relevant:	Less Relevant:
• Morally objectionable to many in society • Addictive • Mood altering • Impairs judgment when used in excess • Impairs motor skills when used in excess • Physically harmful (e.g., damages organs) • Indirectly causes social harms when used in excess (driving accidents, job loss, broken relationships, crime, etc.) • Does not cause physical and social harms when used in moderation • Even when outlawed, people will continue to produce, sell, and buy these substances (but now illegally), which will result in more arrests, court cases, and overall diversion of law enforcement resources.	• Made from natural substance • Medicinal value

These numerous relevant analogies suggest that marijuana should be legalized too, especially in light of the fact that many of the reasons for *not* legalizing marijuana (addiction, bad health, social harms) apply to alcohol and tobacco. If we are going to insist on outlawing the former, it seems we must also (for the sake of consistency) outlaw the latter. If these reasons do not seem strong enough to outlaw alcohol and tobacco, why would they suddenly be strong enough for outlawing marijuana?

It remains to apply Rule 3. If the argument fails, it must be on account of significant disanalogies. Here are some of the disanalogies noted by an opponent of legalizing marijuana.[99]

---

[99] Charles D. Stimson, "Legalizing Marijuana: Why Citizens Should Just Say No," in *Legal Memorandum*, September, 2010 (pub. by The Heritage Foundation)

More Relevant:	Less Relevant:
• Statistically, marijuana users are more prone to use it in excess than they are alcohol and tobacco • Statistically, marijuana users are more likely to "graduate" to harder drugs like cocaine. • Statistically, youth are more prone to abuse marijuana • Marijuana does more damage to the intellect (e.g., memory loss, slowness of thought, reduction of logical reasoning) • Marijuana results in more emotional disorders (withdraw, compulsive behavior) • Marijuana weakens immune system • Marijuana contains more toxins (ammonia, hydrogen cyanide)	• Some forms of alcohol (wine) have health benefits when consumed in moderation (e.g., heart); but not so for marijuana • Marijuana is more of a "taboo" than alcohol and tobacco

If we assume all these disanalogies are true, would they outweigh the analogies? Well, they are serious enough to make one at least *challenge* the legalization of marijuana. They seem to offer good reasons for erring on the side of caution.

The main point of this example, however, is to illustrate how *complicated* analogical arguments can become. To do this argument justice, one would have to research the exact details of *dozens* of analogies and disanalogies, and then weigh each one and calculate their overall force. There are no other quick or effortless ways of resolving arguments like this.

54] Causal Arguments

Causal inference (not *casual* inference) is the third type of probable inference we will study. We reason about cause-and-effect relationships every day. For example, all these questions require causal inference to answer them:

- *In the kitchen*: Why does the milk taste sour?

- *In the doctor's office*: What is the source of my fatigue and back pain?

- *In the courtroom*: Did the defendant shoot the victim?

- *In the physical sciences*: How did the universe form? Why does sunlight tan the skin? Why do organisms appear designed? Why did this species die out? How did the bubonic plague spread throughout Europe?

- *In history and the social or behavioral sciences*: Why does a free market create more national wealth than a government regulated economy? Why did Rome collapse? How did the spread of Christianity change pagan culture? Why were the Nazis anti-Semitic? What is the source of depression? What is the impact of social media on the cognitive development of youth?

Our lives are governed by cause-and-effect relationships. This is why we use the word "because" so often—it's the modernized version of the old English expression "by-cause." The standard form statement "y happened *because* of x" literally means "y happened *by the cause* of x."

Definition of "cause": We all assume that whatever happens has a *cause* of its happening. We will define "cause" as *that which brings about an effect*. If this seems like a circular definition, that's because the terms "cause" and "effect" are interdependent, somewhat like "right" and "left," "up and down," "life" and "death." To say that two things, *x* and *y*, are related as "cause" and "effect," is to say that they are *connected* in such a way that one *cannot exist without the other*. To say that

x is the "cause" of y implies (at least) that if x is present, y will also be present, and that if x is absent, y will also be absent.

Suppose you are trying to identify the cause of a skin rash. You suspect it might be the new laundry detergent, "Chemo-Clean." To test this hypothesis, you revert to your old detergent for a few weeks. The rash goes away. You then try out the Chemo-Clean again. The rash returns. You then infer that the new detergent is causing the rash. This test is based on an understanding of what it means for one thing to cause another. If the new detergent is in fact the cause of the skin rash, the following two propositions are true:

[1] If you wash with Chemo-Clean, the rash will return.

[2] If you do not wash with Chemo-Clean, the rash will go away.

Notice, moreover, that this gives you two different ways of falsifying your hypothesis.

[3] If you wash with Chemo-Clean, and the rash does *not* result, you can infer that Chemo-Clean is not the cause.

[4] Or, if you do not wash with Chemo-Clean, and you *still* get the rash, you can infer that Chemo-Clean is not the cause.

To summarize, suppose that x really is the cause of y. We can then assign corresponding truth-values:

If [x is the cause of y] then:
- It will be *true* that "If x, then y."
- It will be *false* that "If x, then not y."
- It will be *true* that "If not x, then not y."

Personal causes (mental) and impersonal causes (material): In an earlier lesson on induction and the uniformity of Nature, we distinguished the hard sciences and the soft sciences. The hard sciences (physics, chemistry, and biology) study material causes, such as atomic forces, chemical reactions, and the development of cancer. But much of our causal reasoning relates to people as free agents. This gives rise to the soft sciences, which study the causes and effects of human behavior.

Beliefs and desires are among the *causes* of our behavior. The Nazis' *beliefs* caused them to persecute Jews. The Jews' *desire* for self-preservation caused them to hide. Likewise, beliefs and desires can also be effects. Debaters try causing others to believe their position; they are trying to bring about beliefs. Coaches try causing their team to practice harder; they are trying to bring about desires.

Potential fallacies of causal reasoning: When it comes to causal reasoning, we are all prone to a variety of fallacies. We will now overview some of the more common ones.

***Cum hoc ergo propter hoc* ("with this, therefore, because of this")**: The mere fact that two events *occur together* does not necessarily imply that they are causally connected. It's rumored that in a nineteenth European town an unusually high number of babies were born during an upsurge in the local stork population. Did this mean that the storks caused the births? Or did the births cause the storks? Or was it simply a bizarre but unrelated coincidence? I'm opting with the latter.

One of the basic principles of causal reasoning is that *correlation does not imply causation*. Suppose that my favorite team wins whenever I wear a red cap, and that they lose whenever I do not. This is a "coincidence," i.e., a mere correlation without causation. Consider the laundry example again. Even if a correlation exists between Chemo-Clean and the skin rash (one is present when the other is present, and the other is absent when the other is absent), this might be a mere coincidence. There might be another cause of the rash. Maybe the rash is caused by new clothing instead. Suppose the true culprit is a new shirt, which (coincidentally) you wash with Chemo-Clean, and which you forget to wash whenever you try out other detergents. This coincidence blinds you to the true cause.

***Post hoc ergo propter hoc* ("after that, therefore, because of it")**: If we find one event coming after another event, we tend to suppose that the first event caused the second. If we hear a loud noise prior to a light bulb burning out, it is almost irresistible to infer that whatever caused the noise somehow caused the light to go off; the light went off *after* the noise occurred. Such reasoning looks like this:

Y occurred after x; therefore, *y* was *caused by x*.

Nevertheless, the mere fact that event *y* happens after event *x* is not always a reliable indication that *y* was caused by *x*. It is a fallacy to assume that temporal succession *necessarily* indicates causal connection; or (better put) it is a mistake to assume that temporal succession *alone* indicates causal connection.

Confusing causes with their effects: Consider this reasoning: "Since well-paid teachers tend to be high quality teachers, perhaps we should raise Mr. Jones' salary next year." It's true that a higher salary motivates some people to become better employees. To that extent the pay is the *cause* and the quality of work is the *effect*. But usually the reverse is true: better quality work is the cause of employees receiving better pay. It's probably a mistake, then, to try making a person a better teacher by paying him more.

What causes depression? Some say that chemical imbalance in the brain causes depression. They reason, "Joe is feeling depressed because Joe has a chemical imbalance." Others think that the chemical imbalance is the effect of one's attitude and behavior. They reason, "Joe has a chemical imbalance because Joe is thinking and acting in a depressing manner." Both sides agree that there is some sort of *correlation* of (1) Joe's feeling depressed, (2) Joe's chemical imbalance, and (3) Joe's attitude and behavior. The debate hinges on which of these things is the cause and which the effect. Does the chemical imbalance cause the depressed feelings, or do the depressed feelings cause the chemical imbalance, or does the attitude and behavior cause the chemical imbalance which, in turn, causes the depressed feelings, or is there some fourth or fifth option?

This example shows that even where correlation is strong enough to indicate causation, it still does not tell us the *direction* of causation; causal correlation does not, by itself, tell us what is the cause and what is the effect.

Oversimplification: The previous example points us to another crucial fact about causal reasoning. An effect can have more than one cause. It's a fallacy to argue, for example, that someone becomes a criminal *solely* because he played violent video games as a youth. That explanation would leave out the role of personal temperament, parenting, schooling, peer-pressure, and a host of other causes. Or consider this inference: "Jones is an excellent debater because he took a logic course." This too is an instance of oversimplification. Merely taking a logic course will not make one a good debater.

The fallacy consists in attributing an effect with multiple causes to a singular cause. Moreover, there can also be a causal "feedback loop." Take the example of depression. Perhaps attitude and behavior cause a chemical imbalance, which then causes depressed feelings, which then causes a worsening of one's attitude and behavior, which then further increases the chemical imbalance and depressed feelings. Do heavy-set people gain weight because they eat more or do they eat more because they gain weight? The answer is both. There's a type of cause-and-effect cycle occurring here.

Hypothesis contrary to fact (i.e., counterfactual fallacy): This form of reasoning is especially prevalent in the study of history. A historian tries to identify the cause-and-effect relationships responsible for making History. They can estimate the causal importance of an event by imagining what might have occurred in its absence. John Locke wrote a book (the *Second Treatise*) that influenced the American Revolution. Suppose one argued: "If the *Second Treatise* had never been published, Americans would not have sought independence from England." The *fact* is that John Locke's book was very influential among the revolutionaries, and the *fact* is that Americans did seek independence; but what is asserted by the hypothesis (i.e., the *Second Treatise* not being published) is *contrary to fact*, because the *Second Treatise* was in fact published.

This inference involves the use of a statement known as a "counterfactual." A counterfactual is an assertion about what *might have been* the case. The statement "Hitler might have won World War II had he taken Stalingrad" is a counterfactual statement, since Hitler did not in fact take Stalingrad. A counterfactual is not an assertion of fact; it asserts something *contrary to fact*.

The hypothesis contrary to fact fallacy may be defined as *any dubious inference from a counterfactual premise*.

Not all counterfactual inferences are fallacious. It is virtually certain that had Japan not bombed Pearl Harbor, the United States would not have declared war on Japan on December 8th, 1941. Or again, had electricity never been discovered, the light bulb would not have been invented in the 19th century.

Counterfactual inferences are hard to prove in the case of human actions. Suppose someone argues: "Had William the Conqueror lost the Battle of Hastings, he would have tried invading England a second time." Because human choices are not causally determined in the manner of a ball in motion, we cannot predict what someone will do in a scientific way. Based on what we know of them, we can *guess* that they will probably act in manner x if in circumstance c at time y. But if we cannot determine what a man *will* do, we certainly cannot determine what he *would have* done. Historians can make "reasonable conjectures" about what people would have done *if* those people had revealed their intentions. For example: "If Caesar had not been assassinated, Rome would have conquered Parthia." We know that Caesar planned to invade Parthia. Caesar was a magnificent general with a powerful army. Because we know of his actual intentions, and that the likelihood of success was strong, this inference is not fallacious. Even so, it cannot be proven with certainty. Perhaps Caesar's fleet would have been wrecked by a storm (as happened in the Adriatic during his pursuit of Pompey), and perhaps Caesar himself might have drowned.

Slippery slope: Picture yourself placing one foot on the edge of a steep icy mountain ridge, where one false step could send you sliding down the mountain. Some arguments, known as "slippery slope" arguments, have the same effect. For example: "If we legalize marijuana, we will find ourselves forced to legalize opium and cocaine. If we legalize those, we will create a culture of drug addicts. If we create a culture of drug addicts, society will implode with crime, unemployment, broken families, and drug-rehabilitation taxes. Therefore, we should not legalize marijuana." The idea here is that we should stay away from the ledge of the slippery slope by not legalizing marijuana. A slippery slope fallacy asserts that an action/event will bring about a *logically suspect* sequence of other actions/events.

Why treat these arguments under the category of probable inference rather than necessary inference, since they appear to have a formally valid structure?

1) If we legalize marijuana, we will legalize harder drugs.
2) If we legalize harder drugs, we will create a society of addicts.
3) We should not create a society of addicts.
4) Therefore, we should not legalize marijuana.

This appearance is deceiving. When we translate these antecedent and consequent propositions accurately, we get:

1) If p, then q
2) If q, then r
3) <u>Not s</u>
4) Therefore, not t

In the original argument, premise 3 is not a denial of the consequent of 2: that is, premise 3 is not saying, "We *will not* create a society of addicts," but rather "We *should not*..." Likewise, the conclusion is not saying "We *will* not legalize marijuana" but "We *should* not..."

Moreover, the connection between the antecedent (e.g., legalizing marijuana) and the consequents (legalizing harder drugs and widespread addiction) are not *necessary* connections. It is possible for these consequents not to follow. Slippery slope arguments involve causal connections, which are more or less probable. We should therefore treat these as probable inferences.

Some logic texts teach that slippery slope reasoning is a "fallacy." This is misleading, in that some of these arguments are reasonable. A pastor might reason with a married Christian: "If you keep spending time with the female co-worker to whom you're attracted, you may become romantically involved with her. If you become romantically involved with her, you'll compromise your marriage. You do not want (and should not be willing) to compromise your marriage. Therefore, stop spending time alone with this woman." Far from being a "fallacy," this is solid counsel.

Slippery slope arguments become fallacious *when the slope is not in fact slippery.* I once heard a debate in which one team argued that "shark finning" (cutting off the dorsal fins of sharks to make a popular Asian soup) would lead to World War III. The argument was more or less as follows: "Americans should not oppose shark finning. For the Chinese economy depends on this industry. If we oppose it, we will become embroiled in a war with China. If we go to war against China, Russia will back China. This would result in WWIII. Therefore, we should allow shark finning." This is a bad argument, not because it is a "slippery slope" style argument, but because the slope is not in fact slippery.

Made in the USA
Columbia, SC
21 April 2022